Wales's Best
One Hundred
Churches

"An excellent volume" – *The Times*

"A really wonderful book" – Simon Jenkins

"It is a splendid guide… With the help of well-chosen colour
photographs, it is strong on the atmosphere of the churches
and chapels of Wales." – Christopher Howse, *The Telegraph*

for Vanessa, Esther, Owain, David and Morgan
with great love and gratitude

Wales's Best
One Hundred
Churches

T.J. Hughes

SEREN

Seren is the book imprint of
Poetry Wales Press Ltd
Nolton Street, Bridgend, CF31 3AE
www.seren-books.com

Text © T.J. Hughes, 2006
Photographs © the photographers, see the acknowledgements
First published in 2006
Paperback reprinted in 2007, 2009

Cover image: Valle Crucis Abbey, Denbighshire, courtesy of CADW

The right of T.J. Hughes to be identified
as the author of this work has been asserted
in accordance with the Copyright, Designs
and Patents Act, 1988

ISBN 978-1-85411-426-6 hbk
ISBN 978-1-85411-427-3 pbk

The publisher works with the support of the Welsh Books Council

Printed in Perpetua by Akcent Media Ltd

Contents

Here, where the earth is green, where heaven is true….
Who in his heart could murmur or complain:
'The light we look for is not in this land'?
That light is present, and that distant time
Is always here, continually redeemed.

Vernon Watkins
from 'Peace in the Welsh Hills'

Llangelynin, Meirionnydd

INTRODUCTION

Churches in a Landscape

The churches of Wales constitute one of Britain's great unheralded treasures. For some time there has been no current book devoted to them, and they still await the kind of complete coverage given to churches elsewhere in Britain. Astonishingly, this is the first opportunity for a book on the subject to show them at their best in colour as well as words.

England has had for decades its Pevsner, its Betjeman, its Alec Clifton Taylor. Each of them brought his own distinct perspectives, but all of them in common were excited by architecture, and by the quality of materials and design. All three reached a halt at the border. Perhaps they understood only too well that across the border, something in the balance changes. Classifications into styles – Early English, Decorated, Perpendicular – get sidestepped, lost in the landscape. The whole narrative by architecture misses something at the heart of what the churches of Wales convey.

In Wales, something altogether different is going on. Every journey to Wales's ancient places leads to the same sense that setting and atmosphere make more impact than architecture. Buildings that elsewhere could be convincingly separated into major and minor by design alone do not impress on that neat scale in a land where landscape has such dominating presence.

The glories of Wales lie in other places, from other times, and quite another culture. The archetypal church of Wales is not the town or village church, architecturally enhanced by generations of rich and demonstrative local patronage: it is the isolated, simple, evocative walls-with-roof, in a landscape often spiritually charged. The trace of earlier times was not erased by the growing wealth that came to other places in the later middle ages. The Welsh churches, as a group, have much to tell us about those times, and the Age of Saints that came before, and amazingly, of the pagan Celtic times before that, which they had been raised expressly to shatter.

In Wales the church may be halfway down a cleft in a cliff, half-sunk in a dune, remote up mountain lanes, out alone on a tidal island, in a field encircled by pagan stones. The nave may be raised on sculpted shafts above a holy well, the chancel wall have a gash to help the anchorite above to hear, the walls may be full of bones, the name of the place Llanfihangel-yng-ngwynfa, St Michael in the Winds; Llanrhaeadr, the Church of the waterfall; Betws-y-coed, the chapel in the wood; Llanaber, the Church by the rivermouth. The place names of Wales are, more than anywhere, religion and landscape conjoined.

More than perhaps anywhere else in Europe, the environment that produced these churches was not an urban one. It was barely even a village one. The idea of the village – like the idea of the parish church – so central in England, is here displaced, as it could only be in the nomadic rural life of medieval Wales, shifting from *hendref* to *hafod*, lowland to upland, with the changing seasons. Like an iron age land, medieval Wales was a country of isolated farmsteads, spread out among the hills and valleys which themselves were separated by vast tracts of uninhabitable moor and mountain.

The church was at a place which folk from far-flung farmsteads had to reach, and come together, perhaps for the only time in a week or a month. It provided one of the few expressions of a larger sense of community. For almost every one there was a journey, not along a few short streets, but often right over the hills. In the old counties of Anglesey, Brecon, Caernarvon and Pembroke, half or more of the old churches are still, even now, solitary buildings in isolated places. The landscape, the setting, the travelling through in all weathers, were part of the experience of churchgoing. Churchyards can still be found, as at Tal-y-llyn or Pennant Melangell, with two gates, one on either side – one for the people who came over the moor, one for the people from the valley below.

There are places encircled by mountains, a circular hoop of a valley, at its centre a smaller hill, with a circular summit, a circular graveyard, a circle of trees. Bryn Eglwys, Llansantffraid-ym-Mechain, Cascob in the Radnorshire forest, the old church up from Llanbrynmair, there are many which show something of this, wheels within wheels within wheels, the site so telling that the building, the church, its interior, almost cease to matter. They are only the latest versions, the latest marker, of the sacred space – a truer translation of 'llan', the name associated now with so many hundreds of churches and villages. The visitor to ancient Welsh churches needs eyes wide to his surroundings: the religion of pre-modern Wales is inseparable from its elemental landscape.

Villages at sacred spaces: something extraordinary happened to create the map of community in Wales. Unlike elsewhere, the people did not build their churches at the places where they lived, chosen for safety or comfort or farmable land. Frequently instead, they built them at places chosen for reclusive prayer or for their sacred power, often wild, remote, uncompromising. And then, over time, they came to live there. It is an upturning of the order of things – a pattern of settlement in reverse, where the sacred has a generative role. The mark on the culture, and its essential *difference*, remains unmistakable.

Again and again the traveller to ancient Welsh churches has a shock of wonder at the majesty and beauty of the chosen locations. They can be only fully understood as the exacting choices of Celtic holy men and women, seeking out sites to praise and reflect the God of Creation. They belonged to a culture which through the long pre-Christian centuries had felt the sacred in the rocks, the trees, the water; which knew that at particular locations the world of the spirit intensified; which recognised holiness at points in the landscape with a powerful sense of place.

Their capacity for awe and wild solitude was frequently balanced by a practical eye for fresh water, and the lee of the prevailing wind. They wanted to praise, but also to live, and sometimes to run a mission. In a largely unpeopled land, they were able to search out the places which met their requirements with remarkable precision. They worked in the inherited tradition which had placed the holy stone circles with the same precision, echoing the alignment to the sun with eastward altars, preserving sometimes the same locations.

From the circular churchyard on the strange and perfect dome of Mynydd Carnguwch, the mountains of western Llyn appear as an uninterrupted line to the west, the mountains of western Snowdonia as a line to the east. If the churchyard were a few yards further east, it would lose the view of Yr Eifl and Tre'r Ceiri. If it were just a few yards lower, it would lose the view of the sea, and of the sacred islands of St Tudwal. If it were a few yards higher, it would have no shelter from the neighbouring brow – and be further from the water of the river.

The church at Llangynydd at the west end of the Gower, invisible from the great four-mile beach away below it, comes into view only and precisely from Burry Holms, the beach's northern tidal island, on climbing to the level of St Cenydd's hermit outpost. The church, now ruined, at Llanddwyn Island, is just exactly far enough out on the promontory for Holy Island to come into view beyond the headlands of Aberffraw – but no further. It dared the sea and its gales, but no more than it needed. As those at Llanddwyn could see Holy Island and Clynnog Fawr, so those at Llanfaglan could exactly see Llanddwyn. Further south, the churches of the curving Meirionydd shoreline looked out at Ynys Enlli in marine haze, and high above, St Tecwyn at Llandecwyn watched over those along the southern line of Eifionydd, in a view that must have made him feel a Lord of Creation.

This was a watching mission community, mutually protective and aware. Missionaries and mariners in passing ships, like those in the carvings at St David's and Llanfaglan, would have looked out in the night at the outlines of belfries, and the red flare of fires on the hillsides. The spirit of God was moving on the face of the waters. Inland, something similar was happening. The mountain churches up above the industrial valleys of the south seem linked in a web of sightlines and the high llan at Bedwellte is also placed to gaze out at the peaks of the Brecon Beacons, a purpose shared by a church more than twenty-five miles north at Llandeilo Graban (St Teilo of the corn marigold), from which the land falls steeply away for several hundred feet to the gorge of the Wye below.

In a country where cathedrals can be in villages, and village churches out in fields and farmyards, and where remotest places yield an abbey or a simple cell, the often made dividing lines between parish church, chapel, abbey, meeting house, cathedral, seem to intertwine like Celtic knots. There is a constant upturning of expectation as to what lies behind the next corner, at the next holy site, which evidences Wales's levelling, angular and independent spirit.

There is a multi-culturalness to this heritage too little emphasised: early British, Roman, Irish, Gallic, Norman, Viking, French and English cultures jostle in with Welsh – and occasional infusions of Italian or Byzantine. There are unique sights too little trumpeted: the last remaining Romanesque saint's shrine in northern Europe; the only holy well continuously used for fifteen hundred years; the last remaining of the giant wooden saints and patriarchs that stood at medieval altars; an astonishing collection of pre-Reformation masterpieces – screens and carvings and monuments; and curiosities – a cresset stone, a portable sepulchre, a seventh century handbell.

There are interiors near-perfectly preserved from several centuries past, and exteriors of every style constructed in the past millennium. While the headline contrast of English wealth to the mountain simplicity of Wales is telling, it is not the whole story. There is a richness to the settings, details, contents, craftsmanship and sheer evocative power of the ancient churches of western Britain which demands to be better known and recognised.

For all the justifiable fame of the tall glass churches of East Anglia, and the beautiful profusion of decorated stone from Devon to the Cotswolds, nowhere in Britain can compete for variety and quality – and in such quantity – with the southern border country, whose claims have been underestimated simply because writers have concentrated either one side or the other of the border. A journey through, for example, the regions of the Wye – say southern Radnorshire, Breconshire, western Herefordshire (itself still so Welsh in settlement pattern and the names of villages) – brings Gothic abbeys, hidden hermit churches, mother church foundations of the Welsh dark ages, Benedictines, Cistercians and Knights Templar, Viking carving, very early chapels and hill country churches of irresistible vernacular. Every few miles there is more, and in natural surroundings of exceptional beauty, endlessly curving, concealing, unfolding.

The westward roads lead on into the haunting sites of the central and northern mountains, through broad green vales of Clwyd or Teifi, llans with churches built of river stone and rubble, defensive on hill-tops, hidden in forests, huddled back from cliff-edges, culminating in the strange and sacred landscapes of Bardsey, and of St David's beyond the Land's End of Wales.

Every region has its local flavour – island churches off Anglesey, timber belfries in Montgomery, pilgrim naves in Llyn, tall watchtowers in southern Pembroke, fine glass in Denbighshire, Norman in the vale of Glamorgan, but everywhere a pattern that is both multi-cultural and inescapably Celtic. How and why the map of Wales came to hold this range of signposts in religious landscape is at the heart of the country's history, and one of its most remarkable stories.

There are no better doorways to the culture of the country, still so unknown and elusive to the visitor, than these old churches and chapels. The fifteenth century bards at Valle Crucis, R.S. Thomas at his lychgate in Eglwysfach, Dylan in his grave at Laugharne, the painter Thomas Jones restored to gentry life at Capel Caebach, the passionate preaching men like Evan Roberts, catching the fire in his pew at Blaenannerch, the fighters for an independent Wales, Llywelyn Fawr at prayer in the hill church of Llanrhychwyn, Glyndwr at war on the slopes by Pilleth steeple: the churches are integral to the genius loci that inspired them. They bring us in to their world.

And there is something more than this. What is going on when we visit old churches? – visit, that is, as day tripper, not as worshipper. What draws us to them, rewards us about them? Is it as Philip Larkin famously proposed, that we are forever surprising in ourselves a hunger to be more serious, that we see there all our compulsions robed as destinies?

It must be more than this, or different from this, because some churches leave us cold while others grab at the heart. More strangely, they do so not after careful study of fittings or architectural finery, but in the first moment of pushing open the door, sometimes even of walking up the path, or in the first glimpse on the horizon. What is going on in us?

It cannot be age alone, or design alone, or surroundings alone, because good and bad can share these things. It cannot be a feeling of prayer alone, because in all of them, prayer has been valid. It has something to do with a sense of harmony, of all the elements in the setting and the fabric of it, that there is nothing which jars or diminishes it. Responses of peace, of delight, of aesthetic or spiritual recognition, are all scrawled in the visitors' books that lie on tables near the font – it is a common but uncommon currency. And some churches have a power of generating this, far over others.

How do we know, in the moment of first walking into a home in which we feel we could live, or first meeting someone with whom we know we will connect ? These are not simple things, but things we all recognise, beyond logic. Visiting the old churches can be something like these things, and at its best it is infused by the vivid presence of the past, of otherness, and an unmistakable sense of place. That this should be especially, compellingly so in Wales can be seen as not merely by time and chance, but by the deliberate design and choice of the early Celtic and Welsh people who recognised the power of these locations, and who placed in them these buildings of a human scale, which honoured the land and also the people, body and soul. It is a message they still have for us now.

To see them all would along the way be also a tour of magnificent landscape, so concentrated in a small country, and often so oddly and unexpectedly juxtaposed. It may be truer still to say it the other way around, that it is a tour of magnificent landscape in which fine churches have been built – and that setting foot in this sacred landscape, sensing and responding to it, is a defining part of the experience.

These are the steep paths of the saints, the places, as R.S. Thomas recognised, where the landscape itself feels like a church, where the air crumbled and broke on him as generously as bread, where Dafydd ap Gwilym heard the wild birds singing mass, where Dylan sensed the holy of holies in the wood, and a hill reach up to touch an angel. Angels would be walking here, wrote Gwenallt, their footprints on the roadways. On a visit to Tintern Wordsworth, Cumbrian like Taliesin, was inspired to feel that being in such a place could be restorative to blood and heart and mind, could make kindness come more easily, "while with an eye made quiet by the power/Of harmony, and the deep power of joy,/We see into the life of things." And gazing down at St David's from high upon Carn Llidi, the poet Waldo seemed to move outside time, and heard the song which has not been sung.

There is, for the traveller on these roads, a consistent, recognisable response: the long literature of Wales has ravelled round this mystical core. For the poet-artist David Jones, the land was nothing less than "the Sleeping Lord". The country, wrote Alice Thomas Ellis, has a unique and magical quality, "and in some aspects is not to be easily distinguished from heaven". The old churches hug the land as if they know this: there was no need here for tall spires or vaulting arches to lead the eye to some other heaven up above.

One Hundred Best

A selection of 'best' must reflect all this difference, weighing along with design and architecture the atmosphere, the place in the landscape, and the power to evoke the past. It should go without saying that the idea of a definitive one hundred best – of anything – is like frost in the summer, and for each of us the list will differ. This selection is intended to display the full range and variety of expression of the Welsh church, from the smallest to the grandest of its structures, and to draw on those residues of the Age of Saints which remain to us to be touched. It may also make the point that for pleasure, and for the impression they can make on the visit and the memory, small rural churches can rate as high as cathedrals. To include as many as possible of them in a selection this short has meant leaving some major churches out: a hundred churches and chapels is, after all, not even one and a half per cent of our heritage of such buildings – more than seven thousand of them in total, and almost two thousand of them thought important enough to be listed Grade I or II. Every one of them has its own unique story, worth taking time to hear.

So this list is offered as a celebration of Welsh churches and chapels – of all of them – above all in the hope of encouraging more people to see and to help preserve more of them. If there are more visits, and more conversations about churches which have been included – or omitted – then something of the aim of this book will have been accomplished.

The maintenance of this national treasure is and needs to be more recognised as a national issue. Not a church selected here is not vulnerable to under-resource or neglect: the most remote, whose preservation is dependent on sometimes less than a dozen people, perhaps most of all. The dark and narrow church at Llandeloi, often admired, has lately closed: it did not seem practical to carry on for the Sunday congregation of two. There was talk of demolition before the rescuing and admirable Friends of Friendless Churches stepped in. A number of churches in this book, active when the writing of it began, are inactive now. A chapel is demolished every week. In the past twenty years many more have become warehouses, galleries, barns, even piggeries. We seem to be at a watershed. What will become of the old sacred spaces, where for so many centuries people have felt, even especially and restoratively, the presence of God?

Any visitor to the dripping cave that is Gumfreston, or the old church at, say, Llangelynin, which stands exposed to the Atlantic wind, roosted in by martins, without any congregation to attend it, can see the cracks and the challenge, but must inescapably feel the presence of the place, and recognise its value to the heritage – both spiritual and cultural – of the dogged, enduring, inspiring spirit which is Wales.

> Chwilio amdanat, addfwyn Arglwydd,
> Mae fy enaid yma a thraw
> Teimlo 'mod i'n berffaith ddedwydd
> Pan y byddost Ti gerllaw

W. Williams Pantycelyn

Rhulen, Powys

THE PAST AND WHERE TO FIND IT

Pre-Christian

Two thousand years ago in Wales, the sacred emanations of nature inspired pre-Christian worship: sources of streams and rivers, groves of apple, hazel, oak or yew, lakes and offshore islands, huge mysterious stones, places of commanding views and wild weather. To see Pentre Ifan, one of the great cromlechs of Dyfed, in its high place in the Preseli hills, with the land surging down below into a great sweep of the sea, is to realise the power imbued by such locations.

Gods were in these places, gods of water, wood and stone, each in their own specific local setting which was charged with their spirit and power. Even in water, the traces of Celtic culture remain to us – in discoveries of offerings cast into lakes, the memory of the holiness of islands and springs, and the names of rivers such as Aeron, goddess of battle, and Daron, goddess of oak.

The oak and the yew were revered perhaps above all woods. There are spectacular gatherings of ancient yews in many churchyards, among them Pennant Melangell, Llanfeugan, Llanspyddid, Llanfihangel nant Melan, and Nevern where the red sap famously bleeds. Their evergreen leaves and longevity symbolised immortality. Some are certainly pre-Christian, others marked the burial place of Celtic saints: there are reasons to believe that the sacred Celtic heritage across the border in England, as well as in Wales, is mapped out by such surviving trees. But the greatest concentration of them is in Wales, where the twisted and encircling yew at Llangernyw is said to be among the oldest living things on earth. Circles of yews (which are unique to Wales) within the circular churchyards, like the small holy islands encircled by the sea, seem to echo the map of the Celtic cosmos, a concentricity of circles for the upper and lower worlds. The druids, the priestly lords of the Celtic age, had their greatest sanctuary on the holy island Anglesey, in a sacred grove. The Welsh words druid – *derwydd* – and oak – *derw* – are inextricably linked.

The power of stone – and circles of stone – is rooted even deeper, and may long predate the rise of druid culture. Massive stones were the watchers at the ceremonies, the waymarks on the ridges, mantels for the burial chambers, and stands for the severed heads of enemies.

The ancient Celts, a name or race still not yet quite defined, are blurring as we try to get to know them. They remain little understood, their system of beliefs evidently complex and never written down, their story written by those who destroyed them. The Romans came, to cut them down most famously in Anglesey, but centuries later, after the last legions departed, their culture still seems to be there. For more than another thousand years, water, wood and stone, circles and places and lordly priests were to be defining elements of Christian Wales as surely as of pre-Christian.

Roman

Once the Romans had smashed the Celtic princes and their druids, they found much to share in the local culture of religion. The idea of sacred space, the recognition of each local deity, was part of Roman as well as Celtic thought. As the British took on Roman culture, they matched their gods to Roman gods, Lugos to Mercury, Camalos to Mars, Sulis to Minerva, and their greatest shrines and temples turned imperial.

Romano-Celtic temples, sometimes circular, were built to the deities of both traditions. Bath, in the Romano-Celtic heartland until the late sixth century under its Roman name of Aquae Sulis, has many altars inscribed to Sulis-Minerva, a fusion goddess of health, worshipped in this place where hot springs bubbled from the earth.

The new religion of Christ was settled in Britain, patchily, by the fourth century. What may have been Wales's first churches can be picked out in the ruins as at Roman Caerwent. They seem to be rectangular, perhaps related to the type of a basilica, like the temple at Segontium (Caernarfon). This new religion was urban, not reaching the mass of people in the countryside beyond, although there would have been worship in villas, in the rural privacy which was to recur as a defining element of Christian Wales, from the Age of Saints to the early chapel movement.

By the following century, the British church was expansive enough to look beyond its boundaries, sending Patrick to Ireland, perhaps from a port in western Wales. The ideas of Pelagius spread out across Europe. But Rome had fallen, and Roman Christian culture was coming under threat. The flow of English – pagan – immigration into Britain had begun to swell. In parts of the east of the island, Christianity was driven out.

The Ruin of Britain

The years around 500 are the years of Arthur. His power, if nothing else about him, is evident in the manuscripts. But after his death, things fell apart. Gildas, a monk educated at the school of Illtud in the vale of Glamorgan, wrote of the time as the Ruin of Britain. Local warlords destroyed the vestiges of civil government, and the best hopes for safety and for peaceful communities. War and civil collapse brought agricultural failure, and into that void came the plague.

Gildas is a voice of anguish, warning, and of turning to God. The secular world had failed. In one of the most long-reaching religious movements ever to affect these islands, a new generation set out into the western hills, and across the Channel into Brittany, many of them dedicated to a life of prayer.

The Age of Saints

This is the time when the map of Wales changed – when the web of modern place names became remarkably complete through much of the country. Several hundred holy settlements seem to date from this period, the origins of many of them concentrated into one generation from around the year 540. These are the llans of Wales and Herefordshire, the lans of Cornwall and Brittany. Only a few, like Llanilltud Fawr, are earlier. Given the background and culture of the men seeking out these refuges, it was natural that many of them came to places recognised for sacred power. From these alluring bases, they drew a rural people into their religion.

Over the next fifty years, the pagan English pushed forward to take over control of almost all of modern England. The old culture of Britain was concentrated forcibly much more within Wales, just at the time when its society was newly charged and shaped by passionate religion. Christianity, wiped from the English maps and under threat from invasion even in its Roman heartland, was putting down deep and clenching roots in the river runs and mountain fastnesses of Wales. Welshness was born in a war of race and faith.

Its cultural exchanges were with the west, not the newly cut-off east, by way of the Irish Sea, the Severn Sea, the Channel and the Bay of Biscay. The Irish Sea was a Celtic Mediterranean. The proximity of the successful early mission bases – Llanilltud Fawr, Llancarfan, St David's, Bangor, Tywyn and others – to the coastal reaches is a part of this pattern. Welsh saints took new religion to Cornwall and to Brittany as well as Wales: they were seafarers like St Paul.

The holy well of St Seiriol at Penmon

The arrival of Christianity in rural Wales was a curious, but ingenious, combination of rejection and adoption – rejection of the old gods and rites, but adoption of many of the sacred values, which must have greatly eased its acceptance. Adoption of sacred sites was certainly a part of this: one interesting example is the number of places dedicated to St Bride (St Ffraid). They seem conceivably to be inheritances of the cult of the Celtic fire goddess, whose name the saint conveniently shared.

This Age of Saints came to a deeply Celtic world, the lordly saints almost a new kind of druid, even a new local deity. Many have been traced to royal lineage: St Tysilio son of Brochwel Ysgythrog, a prince of Powys; St Cadog son of Gwynllyw, a prince of Gwent; St Cadwaladr, 'king of Britain'. The sons and daughters of Brychan, the local king remembered in the name of Brecon, became the saints of the surrounding llans.

The dedication of Welsh churches to local holy men is typical, and common. Cynyw, Gwynnog, Idloes, Illog, are saints unknown even to the valley beyond. Or Beuno, Cadog, David, Illtud, whose fame went countrywide and further: from North Wales the range of Beuno's reach is marked in Llanveynoe, Herefordshire and Culbone (*Cilbeuno*), Somerset, and from the south, Illtud spread out to Llanelltud near Dolgellau and Lanildut in northwestern France.

Dedications to particular saints can frequently be tracked along old Roman roads, sea-routes or river valleys. Patterns like these reflect the successful extent of their missions. Like Celtic gods they have their *patria*, their territory, within which one location above others functions as a sacred centre. Teilo's is in the south, Padarn's in the central belt, Tysilio's in Powys.

Most must have been native British, but there were others. Especially on the west where Irish immigration was substantial, Irish holy men are remembered at Dolwyddelan, Llanengan, Solva (the intriguing St Elvis) and numerous other places. There was also, as there was to be again in the eleventh and twelfth centuries, an influence from France, where monastic culture had recently renewed through men like Martin of Tours. The trail of surviving stone inscriptions, like one at Penmachno from around the year 540, links this Christian community with the district around Lyon (a place name, incidentally, which shares the same holy Celtic derivation as London). In some places these influences combined and there are stones, as at Nevern, with messages in both Latin and the Ogham script of southern Ireland.

Not infrequently there are holy women, such as Gwenfrewi, Tegfedd and Melangell, whose status could also draw people to the place where they had lived. The sense is always of place, of locality, of something quite different from the mainstream European tradition of dedications to the great international saints and apostles, and above all to the Virgin Mary. Perhaps a majority of the oldest medieval English churches are dedicated to Mary, but the churches of St Mary within Wales are strikingly grouped in the areas of the country where later the Norman French – and through them the world of international Christendom – made their greatest impact.

Thirteen feet high sentinel of the past one thousand years, at Nevern

The Age of Saints drew on druid magic: it left its trail in the myth of Merlin, and the magic attributed to holy men like Beuno, with his fearsome curses, and power of healing, and the murderous oak he planted on his father's grave. The Welsh lives of the saints are threaded through with demonstrations of their power of command over wells and water, their miraculous gift to inspire water to break out through the rock and run in profusion, their power to draw out from a stream the evil, poisonous spirit (the old paganism), and make it run pure.

The theme and presence of holy wells – now dedicated to Christian saints in place of pagan spirits – is a central one to the location of churches, in sites where the heritage of worship clearly goes back much further. A new church might be put up close by a well, even over a well, and the well itself was often covered, with its own adjoining chapel. At Llanfair Caereinion and Gumfreston and many other places, there are wells and springs in the churchyard. Well chapels are themselves one of the country's great lost heritages, though there are eloquent remains in isolated fields at places like Llangybi. At Holywell in Flintshire, church and well chapel are fused as one. The water source at Holywell (before the modern damage caused by mining) was a marvel, a great profusion of endlessly gushing springs, the natural world at its purest and most fertile. Here above all was not so much a base for local worship as a *destination* of sacred value.

There are countless riverside llans, with the church down by the water as at Llanidloes, Llananno, Llangwnnadl, Llanrwst, and some at the lakeside: Llangasty, Llanycil, Llangower. The sea had a special resonance. Western coastal churches were built in the teeth of the wind at places like Mwnt, Llanaber, Llansantffraid, and Cwm-yr-Eglwys which, a hundred years ago, was swept out to sea in a storm. There is a small and ancient chapel still standing on a northern beach at Llandrillo-yn-Rhos. The church at Oxwich, its site evidently long predating the nearby castle, stands on a sheltered woodland promontory above the blue and curving bay, and the stately hulk at Llanfrothen, now stranded someway inland by the nineteenth century drain-ing of Porthmadog, must be regained in the mind as a sea-girt sanctuary for praise and thanksgiving, the view from its green slopes trumpeting the snow-capped mountains of Eryri. Communities of hermits gathered on islands: Bardsey, Caldey, Priestholm, Burry Holms, Flatholm, to be away from man and elementally closer to God. The holiness of places such as Bardsey only intensified over generations as so many holy men were ferried there in death for burial. The same spirit pervaded neighbouring domains of Celtic Britain, and can still be sensed in the air at Lindisfarne, Iona, Skellig Michael. Evil spirits, it was thought, would not cross water.

Ancient stones were linked to saints and their secular protectors, like the tall memorial stones at Llanilltud Fawr and the cross of Meiliog at Llowes. At Ysbyty Cynfyn near the river Rheidol the church still stands within a circle of old stones, making the sacred succession explicit. Great stones could be turned into preaching crosses, over a dozen feet high and intricately carved. Some, as at Carew and Nevern, are Christian crosses so designed, with round head, and tall base with taper-ing shoulders, to show their ancient anthropomorphic origin. These two, with Maen Achwyfan near the estuary of the Dee in Flintshire, are the best of the surviving high crosses and are placed close to the sea or its inlets, part of the seascape map of great crosses which stretches out around the Irish Sea to Monasterboice in County Louth, Ruthwell in Dumfrieshire, Bewcastle in Cumbria and Kirk Michael on the Isle of Man. Crucifixions are carved in stone at Meifod, Margam and Llangan, and stones too record the first traces of the new language: at Tywyn the first known Welsh inscription, at Llanaber a kind of proto-Welsh inscription. Locations and stones are the legacy of the early Welsh church. No buildings, but a few small ruins like Penmon, St Non's and Ffynnon Gybi, survive from the Age of Saints.

Catholic

Wales was a Roman Catholic country for close on a thousand years, and it is to this time – really the second half of this time – that almost all the old church buildings belong. This was when the network of parishes was completed, and the churches rebuilt in stone. The earlier survivals, mostly thirteenth century, are protective shells, from evil spirits and from local war, but in the later years, with the country conquered but peaceful, the walls were opened up and light let in.

Many of these churches can be difficult to date because they are so simple in style, but they lodge in the memory by extraordinary settings, contents, or the atmosphere they hold. They sit frequently on rising ground, views from the south door over the slanting churchyard, through a ring of yews, and out to the wide green landscape spreading round. Their walls are piled stones and the roofs are wooden beams, covered over with layers of tile and moss. There are no vaults or bosses or complexities. If they have towers, they are rough and squat. More often there is just a belfry.

These buildings are the essence of the church of Wales. Every region has its local variations, but a country road like the one that leaves the Wye by Llandeilo hill and winds across to Radnor, by Aberedw, Llanbadarn-y-Garreg, Rhulen, Cregrina, Glascwm and Colva has a trail of churches as typical as any.

Here their communities sought out God, prepared themselves for death and judgment, took shelter in times of danger, danced and sang and tried for healing cures for illness and disease. Many accounts testify to the persistence of old traditions in the Welsh church – and just as the pagan was not entirely expunged by the Christian, the Catholic was to last long into the age of determined official Protestantism. Something must be said of these centuries of pilgrimage, holy relics, saints' days, festival and ritual, the traces of the living Christian year of medieval Wales and of all the varieties of religious building undertaken in these years. Every holy site had its place in an annual cycle of celebration and the binding of communities: dancing and procession at the shrine of St Eluned on the first of August, her name day; bringing calves and lambs to St Beuno for slaughter on Holy Trinity at Clynnog Fawr, in an echo of pre-Christian bull sacrifice; all the village saint day fairs in churchyards across the country in an atmosphere of drunken abandon, an echo too of the marking of the pagan Celtic quarter days.

The glorious thirteenth century poem, the 'Loves of Taliesin', written perhaps at Strata Florida, speaks of the beauties of the year, of berries at harvest time, summer days long and slow, the fish in his bright lake, of visiting the ones we love, of a faithful priest in his church, a strong parish led by God. God and community, in the natural world of Creation, were the three defining elements of Welsh religious life and the aspirations of the Welsh aesthetic. As with the poetry, so with these churches, which were located and built to represent these things in the physical world. They are where the three unite: God in the eucharistic moment physically present with His people, in their beautiful land.

Pilgrimage and *clasau*

The holiest sites of Wales attracted pilgrims, land and money, and these in turn enabled numbers of holy men to be sustained there and act as guardians to them. Sometimes hermitic and celibate in origin, they turned over time into family communities, with wives and children, and the sons inherited and carried on this life and role from their fathers. These were the *clasau*, or *clas* churches – shrines, schools and mission bases all in one – a most distinctive feature of the pre-conquest church in Wales.

Among the greatest of these were Meifod, Llanddewibrefi, Llanbadarn Fawr, Glasbury (Y Clas-ar-Wy), Tywyn, Holyhead, Clynnog Fawr and above all St David's. St David's stands as the definitive church of Wales in many ways – the saint, the shrine, the springs, the pilgrimage, the legends, the mission. All the elements come together here as a concentrate of medieval Welsh Christianity. The building and its environment, together with the stories contained in the *Life of St David* written down by Rhigyfarch – himself from a famous clas dynasty – at the end of the eleventh century, are of the essence. The pilgrim grave in a lonely churchyard on the muddy estuary banks of the Taf at Llanfihangel Abercywyn and the pilgrim effigy at Haverfordwest were both perhaps for people bound for St David's.

Llyn peninsula, with Beuno's shrine at its eastern gate and Bardsey Island –Ynys Enlli – at its western tip, has a regional character shaped by pilgrimage. The roads along its north coast and its south were changed into pilgrim trails for many centuries, each church a station along the way. The huge size of the church at Clynnog Fawr conveys the numbers of people who had to be provided for, as do the

The lame walk: a scene from Tudor Holywell

21

double naves of Llanengan and Aberdaron, and the triple nave at Llangwnnadl. They were on their way to Bardsey, the island of ten thousand saints, three journeys to which were worth one to Rome in the privileges they bought on the road to heaven. For centuries thousands braved the whirling sound in vulnerable boats to rest in the pure parish in the sea, their nights alive with the crash of waves and the wailing of seals and shearwaters.

Holy relics mattered just as elsewhere in Christendom. The Holy Grail resided in Strata Florida, disintegrating through the years as over-eager pilgrims took to biting splinters off it, and a fragment of the True Cross was kept at the court of Gwynedd until despatched to London at the conquest. The bones of saints had healing power worth travelling distances to reach. Pilgrims set out for physical as much as spiritual healing and the gathering of so many sick, crippled or dying must have given an atmosphere to these places quite lost now in the western world. Where a place has Merthyr in its name, it marks the resting place of saints' bones, and many llans and churches kept them as part of their treasury of holy power. The Romanesque shrine for the bones of St Melangell survives at Pennant Melangell at the edge of the Berwyns. St Teilo, prophetically aware that three churches would fight for the keeping of his bones, obligingly, miraculously, provided them three bodies.

In the high middle ages, the Virgin Mary was to associate herself with sacred places as particular as those of local saints. She was visited at Cardigan and Haverfordwest and all the places with the name Llanfair, but her most famous shrine was at Penrhys. Here an image of Mary had fallen from heaven into an oak tree, from which it could not be dislodged: the Christendoms of Wales and wider Europe in symbolic locked embrace. A church was built around them, to house both oak and image. Its surroundings long ago industrialised, the Penrhys shrine has to be seen now in the mind's eye through the lines of medieval poets, sunlit in its heath of trees, lit at night by flaming torches. Lewys Morgannwg went there in penitence, stripped to his shirt "my intention and all my prayer/to cry aloud to Mary with my voice." At the Reformation, Our Lady of Penrhys was taken secretly away to London, and burned.

Benedictine

In the years after 1066, as the Norman conquest spread west, small outposts of French culture and language set up home at strategic sites in the borders and the southern valleys, just as they had done all across England, fortifying themselves behind high stone walls and castles. Sometimes, as at Monmouth, these men were Bretons, descendants of the Welsh emigrations of five hundred years before. At Abergavenny, the leader seems to have come from Boulogne.

The pattern was always to build the castle, then a small walled settlement, and then to bring over a cadre of Benedictine monks, to build a daughter house to the monastery from which they came. At Ewenni, they were right on the front line: the massive protective curtain wall remains beside the church. But the monks who came to Abergavenny from Le Mans in 1087 came evidently to an already dominated neighbourhood, and their priory took shape outside the walls. The founder's grant gave them orchards, vineyards, farmland and fishing rights, "and an oven of their own".

The richest of the priories was Goldcliff, long lost from the Wentlooge levels east of Cardiff. There are great damaged torsos at Chepstow and Kidwelly which still convey the grandeur of their original interiors, but the best of the survivals is Brecon where, although the cloister and chapter house are gone, some of the monastic complex – tithe barn, almonry, priory house – remains beside the church. Some locations were simple cells of just two or three monks, like Llangynydd and Cardigan.

The Norman conquest was also a Benedictine conquest: together they seized the seats of Welsh church power as well as landed power. William I's Archbishops of Canterbury, Lanfranc and Anselm, were Benedictine priors, committed to the wind of reform blowing through Europe from Rome. By the turn of the eleventh century, Norman lords and their archbishops had won control of numbers of appointments in Wales. The *clasau* were dispersed, their revenues and those of other church lands diverted to Normandy or England, or simply to the local castle.

Cistercian

At the end of the eleventh century, there was a movement of men into rural wildernesses reminiscent of the age of saints. This time it seems to have begun in northern and central France, perhaps in direct reaction to the politicisation of the monasteries. Those in search of the reclusive, the ascetic, religious life, looked elsewhere for fulfilment.

They headed out into the forests, communities of monks and hermits not unlike those of the old Welsh settlements in Beddgelert and Priestholm. In Wales there were men like Caradoc, who went to live alone on Burry Holms off the coast of Gower, and the handful of men who tried to settle in a lonely strait of the Honddu valley at Llanthony. But the place where it turned into a movement was Citeaux.

The Cistercian abbey churches fit the pattern of alien grandeur set by their Benedictine forerunners, but take it out into the landscape. Vast cathedral spaces were built in lonely valleys. In Wales they came first to Tintern, and then directly from St Bernard's Clairvaux to Whitland, from where daughterhouses spread out through the country.

The losses are great, but Tintern, the most famous and the best, has kept more of its church perhaps than even Fountains and Rievaulx. The monks that came to found Tintern came intact as a group from France, and it was French design they brought, and in which they rebuilt in the late thirteenth century. But given the culture into which the Cistercians were tapping, it is hardly surprising their appeal was so great to the Welsh. The ruin of Abbey Cwmhir, deep in the long valley of Clywedog brook, its endless once-high nave aligned with the steep walls of the hills,

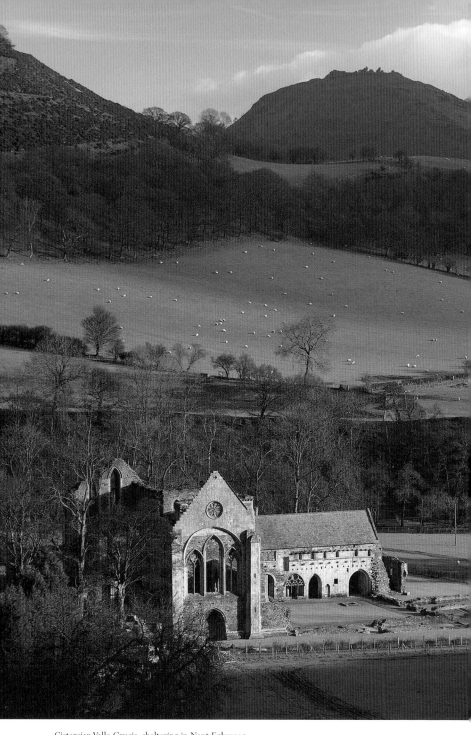

Cistercian Valle Crucis, sheltering in Nant Eglwyseg

feels much like the ancient holy sites of the Welsh, another St David's or Llandaff crouched in their hollows, the tops of their towers barely reaching the level of the road. While other monastic orders stayed culturally foreign, Welsh princes turned their money and land to this new order.

When Rhys ap Gruffydd gained the patronage of Strata Florida, the doors were opened to native people and their language. *Brut y Tywysogion*, the Chronicle of the Princes, was probably written there – and *Llawysgrif Hendregadredd*, the fullest collection of Welsh court poetry. Native princes were buried beneath its arcades, and its national and literary laurels seem complete in the belief that Dafydd ap Gwilym, the greatest of the native poets, lies beneath one of its yews. Other Welsh Cistercian houses were to follow, at Valle Crucis, Aberconwy, Cymer, Strata Marcella, Llantarnam and elsewhere.

Urban

Towns as an idea arrived in the wake of foreign settlement. Conwy, like Tenby, still preserves the imprint, a chequerboard of streets surrounded by fortified walls, with a centrally placed church – tellingly devoted to St Mary – dominating the interior townscape. Built for English colonists, the local Welsh were allowed in only by day. Its utter alienness to Wales at the time requires a leap of imagination now – although one which a winding descent to it from the ancient mountain churches up above can still impel.

Most of the larger thirteenth and fourteenth century churches in the country owe their origins to settlements established by the Anglo-French lords or the king. They have aisles or transepts as well as chancel and nave, and are the visible products of wealth and ambition. They can be found at most of the Anglo-French castle towns: Montgomery, Caernarvon, Usk and Beaumaris are all examples, and are perhaps epitomised at Haverfordwest, which is the church as political badge, where royal allegiance, imposed nobility, and mockery of the local Welsh, are incised across its fabric. Where Welsh towns grew in later times, there are fine urban churches, often richly set out in late fifteenth or early sixteenth century style. In market towns such as Wrexham and Llanrwst, growing rich from trade and agriculture, new wealth and patronage were reflected in churches on a model more recognisable across the English border. Architectural design on familiar international lines thus plays much more part in the shaping of individual urban churches, but even here it is often the local, the unusual, among the interiors, that make a church stay in the memory.

The character of Welsh life has determined that the contribution of the towns to our heritage of churches is lower than in other countries. The great urban cathedrals of France or England or Italy have no equivalent in Wales. St David's, like St Asaph, remains resolutely in a village, however claimed for city status, and Llandaff finds itself within a city only now by accident, having been encircled within the century by Cardiff.

Interior

Few churches were added to the Welsh landscape after 1500, until some three more centuries had elapsed. Until the time the chapels came, communities had the buildings they needed. Their resources turned from building to maintenance, and to refitting the interiors as needs and fashions changed.

More than exteriors, interiors shape the experience of visiting these buildings. In a country of limited resources, and weather so determinedly weathering, exteriors inevitably tend to plainness, roughness, a lack of inclination to awe or even to engage. The best interiors are contrastingly personal, home-made, the lived-in space of a community, and this order of priorities runs deep in the character of the culture.

Survivals of old fittings are often remarkable. Complete interiors of the seventeenth century remain at Rug and Gwydir Uchaf, of the eighteenth at Worthenbury, Llanfaglan and Llangar, and among those of the early nineteenth century, one of beautiful simplicity at Penllech on Llyn. At Manordeifi, the boxed and flagstoned spaces come with family fireplaces, and a coracle to float away in. Dolwyddelan is a museum of vernacular, from the Age of Saints to Georgian Wales: its ancient bell of St Gwyddelan, rediscovered in buried ground a hundred years or more ago, may be the most remarkable survival of them all.

Many of the richest interior survivals from the Catholic era date from its final years. To judge by what remains, there must have been towards the end of the fifteenth century finally the money, the peace, and the quickening of piety to

Eighteenth century furnishings at Llangar

26

produce a real flowering of new artistic achievement in the churches. This was the era of the great rood screens, spectacular new wooden roofs, carved holy figures and new arrays of stained glass filled with the teachings and contemplative images of the faith. The urge to deck out naves and chancels with all this new finery seems to have welled up from the people of the parish as well as from the churchmen and local lords whose patronage had shaped the work of earlier centuries, a creative community enterprise at its most vibrant right up until the point when Henry VIII, responding to new winds of spiritual change and a huge opportunity for personal aggrandisement, decreed the effective end of the honouring of saints and the screening of the chancels, and the abolition of the abbeys and of pilgrimage. The sheer profusion of this enterprise is witnessed now only by the worn survivors of a Tudor government policy of complete destruction – and more of the same a century later in the time of Cromwell.

The rood lofts and screens with their vibrant, highly skilled design and carving, many locally made, rank among the finest things in the artistic traditions of Wales. They have survived in surprising numbers, escaping the reformers through local determination, as at Llanengan where they were buried on the beach, or Llanegryn where they were said to have been carried over the mountains, or through sheer remoteness, as at Patrisio. Among the other most celebrated Welsh screens are those at Llananno, Llangwm Uchaf, Llanwnog, Llanfilo, Betws Newydd and St Margaret's, the last across the border in the old Welsh land of Herefordshire.

They clearly inherit the Celtic traditions of asymmetry and intricate and interweaving strands, and they are also, of course, the oak, brought in to enclose the church and screen the altar. They can be readily distinguished from those of English influence or origin, such as survive at Gresford, Cardiff, Conwy, Usk, Old Radnor and unexpectedly Clynnog Fawr, and which are characterised by their architectural vaulting, their repetition and their greater order – a contrast of qualities which seems to epitomise the difference in artistic impulse between the two neighbouring traditions, and which can be seen on a larger scale shaping not just the screens but the buildings which contain them.

There is a further difference too, in the English tendency to separate and organise the functional spaces of a church, with a preference for aisles and transepts and for chancels made architecturally distinct by entrance arches and a narrowing from the breadth of the nave, while the Welsh prefer integrated, communal spaces. Simple rectangular plans predominate all the way from the earliest shrine churches to the last of the grand chapels, and what is more they are generally *squarer* rectangles, epitomised by the short double-nave churches of the Vale of Clwyd or the wide naves of Monmouthshire, a contrast from the long narrow naves of Anglo-French style, as at Coity, Coychurch, Manorbier and Monkton, which mark the early conquest territories of southern Pembrokeshire and Glamorgan, and which seem more to direct the gaze forward rather than *around*. The screens reflect something of this too, in

England often painted with saints and angels which mark them as an end-line and focal point, while in Wales they are simply decorated frames around an open view, an idea pushed furthest at Llanengan where the lower panels as well as the higher are cut through with openwork and piercing.

The carved wooden figures which stood on these lofts or nearby altars have been very largely lost – the greatest victims of iconoclasm. The image of Christ at the foot of the Cross now in the nave at Bangor is a most poignant survival. It may have come from a forgotten Dominican abbey outside Rhuddlan. There are a Mary and a tortured Christ from Mochdre in the National Museum, and the unique, colossal figure of recumbent Jesse at Abergavenny.

In this same period roofs became not just canopies but canvases for the imaginations and spiritual longings of the congregation standing underneath them. Earlier roofs such as those at Grosmont and Cwmyoy are just plain and sturdy by contrast to the delicate decorative surfaces deployed around 1500 at Guilsfield and above all at St David's. Wrexham and Llaneilian have joyous heavenly hosts of angel musicians, but the darker, large-winged angels at Llanidloes, Tenby and Cilcain mark out a message of the pain of the Cross and bear its imagery of hammers, nails and wounds. The Tenby roof resolves this with an image of the crowned and resurrected Christ, and its endlessly imaginative images of beasts and mermaids, saints and stigmata and Celtic knots are exceeded only by the extraordinary canopy at Llangollen, a melée of the secular and spiritual, animal and vegetable worlds, in which angels mix with drunkards, lions with dragons, knights with matrons and choir boys, and pagan green men with the Virgin Mary in the messy, intertwined and boundary-less world of the medieval Welsh mind.

"Ar adenydd cân ar i Dduw": angel musician above the nave at Wrexham

In ways like these, in shape and screen and roof, interiors carry the heart and soul of the Welsh aesthetic, always communal and inclusive – with each man and woman close up and known and not placed at a distance – and where the lines are blurred between the secular and spiritual, the holy east and earthy west ends of the church, elevating the ordinary and seeing the heavenly within reach, just exactly as can happen in working or travelling in Wales's mystical landscape, which yields its harvests most to those year-round earthed in it and wholly devoted, and is all at once rough, rainsodden and filled with rainbows, a humbler of self-aggrandisements and maker of visionary dreams. The double naves, the screen at Llanengan and the roof at Llangollen take their place among its signatures, and they are joined by such others as the memorial stones of Carnguwch, the downward-reaching deities of Gwydir Uchaf, the close-packed all-angles benches of Capel Penrhiw, expressions in architecture to match the transcendent recognition of ordinary life in the novels of Daniel Owen, or of landscape in the art of Richard Wilson and his successors, from Thomas Jones all the way to Kyffin Williams.

There are also dragons – their manifestations in wood and stone must have studded medieval Wales like the winged lions in Venice or the she-wolf of Rome. The churches guide us to some of the oldest and most mysterious, with their turned heads, fierce teeth and twisted tails, at places like Penmon and Dolwyddelan, and to the dragons of the imagination at Cascob and the other mountain churches of St Michael.

The greatest single glass image in Wales was given by the local priest to his church at Llanrhaeadr-yng-Nghinmeirch, and almost certainly resourced by the offerings of pilgrims – a vast Jesse tree of 1533 by an artist whose dazzling skills in the latest style and techniques of his craft are matched only by his joyous desire to display them. No surviving array of pre-Reformation glass matches that of the tall east windows of Gresford, where the panoply of saints hover over the faithful, among images of stories from the Bible and the childhood tales of Mary. At Llandyrnog there is an intimate Annunciation and a huge damaged window of the Seven Sacraments, fed by the blood which pours in red lines of glass from the crucified body of Christ to scenes of ordinary folk gathered closely round their priest. A group of early sixteenth century glass remains in the Flintshire churches of Diserth, Llanasa and Cilcain. The depiction of the crucifixion at Cilcain, reduced to stark simplicity and made immediate by being set in hills like those outside, is among the country's most restrained yet moving images. All of this glass is in the land between the Conwy and the Dee, which has the richest finds, and perhaps the earliest too at Treuddyn.

Medieval painting was more profuse on walls than on the glass, but in Wales as throughout Europe what remains is a poor suggestion of what once filled all these interiors. Its role, as with the glass, was to instruct, warn and reassure the faithful with images of saints and of their lives, and of the essential moments in the Christian story. Large St Christophers survive at Llanynys and Llanilltud Fawr, a Doom at Wrexham, and looming figures of Death at Llangar and Patrisio. At the church of

Llandeilo Talybont, now being reconstructed at St Fagan's, there are incisive images of Christ being mocked, and as the Man of Sorrows. Gyffin has the best-preserved of the painted 'canopies of honour' which were placed above the altars, this one with images of the twelve apostles. The larger-than-life figure of Mary Magdalen at Llanilltud, dating from the thirteenth century, may be the oldest survival of them all. The painting tradition was to continue even after the Reformation in places where it could find gentry protection. At Gwydir Uchaf, an astonishing painted cycle of Creation, Trinity and Last Judgement spreads across the entire ceiling, and at Rug, the prayers, the poetry, even the monuments were painted on the walls beneath the patterned ceiling.

While the surviving heritage of painting and wood carving is largely late medieval, the interior images of the eleventh, twelfth and thirteenth centuries are memorialised in stone. There are remarkable early fonts at Llanrhychwyn, Patrisio, Llanfilo, Llanwenog and a whole trail of Anglesey churches such as Llanbeulan and Cerrigceinwen, where Celtic influences interact with Romanesque – something which also seems to be happening, but in a very different style, on the font at Brecon. The great Christ in Majesty at Llandaff and a small image of the Ascension at Abbey Cwmhir, both of them severely weathered, survive from the end of this period, and may be slightly pre-dated by a Jesse niche at Llanilltud Fawr. They were followed soon after by a carving of the Resurrection at the atmospheric church of Rhoscrowther and a tender Virgin and Child at Llanilltud, which perhaps had a place in the church's near-contemporary reredos.

Early gravestones such as those for the monks at Strata Florida or the small evocative community at Llanfihangel Abercywyn were in the open air, but sometime in the twelfth century burials began to be made inside the church. Most early tombs are carved with undulating floriate patterns, and sometimes also with beasts or shields and spears. The grandest surviving group is at Valle Crucis, among them the earliest Welsh tomb to bear a date (1290). In a few, the patterning flows into images of a head, or head and hands, as at Beaumaris and Llanilltud Fawr, which are among the earliest effigies. The first full length, life size effigies come in the second half of the thirteenth century, at major churches such as St David's, Tywyn and St Asaph, and are all of priests. At Abergavenny the extraordinary image of Eva de Braose may predate all these: it is full length but small by comparison. A damaged torso at the royal church of Grosmont, suggested (although on no real evidence) to be that of the Anglo-French war hero Hubert de Burgh, may also perhaps be from this time.

In the first half of the fourteenth century begins the long parade of effigies of armoured knights, among them Gruffudd ap Llywelyn ab Ynyr at Llanarmon-yn-Ial, the Berkerolles at St Athan and the Hastings dynasty at Abergavenny, for whom the earliest – and finest – effigy was made of wood. The sudden arrival of this fashion for military demeanour coincides oddly with the end of the fighting in Wales, after the completion of the conquest. A beautiful exception in these early years is the

The early fourteenth century Valle Crucis effigy of
Gruffudd ap Llywelyn ab Ynyr, now at Llanarmon-yn-Ial

Awbrey tomb at Brecon, where a pious husband chose to be depicted in a long
ascetic gown, and in the company of his wife. From the grander families through
subsequent centuries came extraordinary gatherings in stone at churches such as
Stackpole Elidor, Rudbaxton, Montgomery and Tenby, reaching a late medieval peak
in the Herbert tombs of Abergavenny and bridging into the Renaissance with the
Mansel monuments at Margam.

The interiors of Welsh churches thus reflect their place in the mainstream of
European Christendom, while drawing on regional styles and sometimes local
workshops for their craftsmanship. The evidence suggests that there were influential
groups of stonemasons in the environs of the Dee, at work across the Berwyns from
Pennant Melangell to Llanaber, and on the Herefordshire-Monmouth borders, all of
them drawing on a local heritage and influences from wider Europe – and there
were grander workshops at Bristol and further afield which produced tomb
monuments for the conquest aristocracy and their successors. North Wales glass is
part of a wider production spreading into Shropshire and Cheshire – and some of it,
at Tremeirchion and in the Wynn churches of the Conwy valley, has strong affinities
with York. The cultural orientation of the country had followed the drift of power to
the east, and the Celtic sea-world of earlier centuries was just a distant memory.

Protestant

In a book about church buildings, the mark of the Reformation is absences rather than presences. It caused the stripping out from churches of the shrines, the screens and the carved and sculpted effigies, the whitewashing over of painted walls, and the demolition of the abbeys and the priories. It meant that the churches were bare for perhaps the next two centuries, and their role and revenues reduced. Only later, in a more literate society, would its ideas fully reach home: extracts of the Bible being written on the walls, as at Llanwenog and Eglwys Gymyn, and the Word championed in the pulpits and the chapels.

But the foundations on which this later world was built were effectively laid. William Morgan turned the Bible into Welsh: an original edition can be seen at his last church in St Asaph. It was printed in 1588, helping to solve the Reformation problem of Sunday services in English, which had been to most congregations as mystifying, but not as mystical, as Latin.

Where the message of the Bible was made accessible over the years ahead, there are characteristic signs of deep response. Vicar Prichard viewed his parish of Llandovery – a ferment of 500 souls – as nothing less than Sodom and Gomorrah, but his godly verses were hugely loved and remembered. Walter Cradock, in the excitement of the puritan interregnum, recorded that "the gospel is run over the mountains between Brecknockshire and Monmouthshire as fire in the thatch". Itinerant preachers became a new attraction, most of all in the eighteenth century, when men like Howel Harris, Daniel Rowlands and William Williams Pantycelyn took their sermons, hymns and missions out of the churches to the farms and fields.

The history of hymn in Wales, surprisingly, still needs to be fully written, but no one underestimates its role in the sustenance of language and culture, and the remarkable absorption of the Bible into common knowledge. It is an inner strand of the history of poetry in Wales, unsurprising in a country where for centuries poems had been written to be sung. In finding words for religious experience, Pantycelyn found words for psychological and emotional experience too. The poets Robert ap Gwilym Ddu and Eben Fardd, from the long bardic line of Eifionydd, were hymnwriters too, choosing hymn for some of their most personal statements. "*O! fy Iesu bendigedig/Unig gwmni f'enaid gwan*," wrote Eben, battered by the deaths of his wife and three children: Jesus, lone companion of my soul. In her mountain farmhouse in the Berwyns, Ann Griffiths dreamed up verses of almost physical longing, drawing deeply on the Bible's strength and power, which after her early death became familiar as hymns. These and others gave a passionate dimension to everyday lives of gruelling and repetitive labour.

Alongside them, the traditions of *plygain* kept Bible stories familiar through song. Gerald of Wales speaks famously, from the 1190s, of noted Welsh skills at part-singing. Plygain has come through, it seems, from the middle ages, and can still be heard in the country round Lake Vyrnwy: three or four men, one to a part, Tenor,

Bass and Melody, plaintive and close. It is the singing of carols at Christmas, originally at Christmas dawn after a night of vigil, gatherings, torchlit procession. Plygain carols hail the Nativity, or tell a Bible narrative, like a wall painting in song. Their central theme is grace and mercy. They bind together Protestant exegesis with Catholic mystery, and sustain a still older undertow. What resonates in these old Meirionydd lines? "*I ti'r agorwyd ffynnon / A ylch dy glwyfau duon*.": For you a well is opened / To wash your dark wounds.

These things happened in a country where many, perhaps most people right up until the nineteenth century lived their lives in a state not far removed from ignorance and superstition, with the church arguably less a part of life in early modern times than had been so for the thousand years before. In every era, from Gerald of Wales to Evan Roberts, it is possible to find observers who record the immorality of ordinary life and yet the widespread honouring of the sacred; the troubling failures of the church, and yet the urge for driving through reform. Churchyards were places of meeting, of feasting and dancing – and sometimes drunken fighting – as well as of schooling and preaching. In each generation, they served the religious and the irreligious, and the dialogue between them:

> Who ever hear on Sunday
> Will practis playing at ball
> It may be before Monday
> The Devil will have you all

says a notice in the church porch at Llanfair Discoed.

In 1721, a man called Erasmus Saunders wrote a volume called *The State of Religion in the Diocese of St David's…with some Account of the Causes of its Decay*. A few parsons trekked from church to church, while sextons sold ale by the churchyard to make a living. Although churchmen would learn languages for missionary work, he wrote, they would not learn Welsh to preach in Wales. "The doctrines of the Reformation begun about two hundred years ago in England have not yet effectually reached us."

And yet: "there is no part of the nation more inclined to be religious, and to be delighted with it than the poor inhabitants of these mountains. They don't think it too much when neither ways nor weather are inviting, over cold and bleak hills to travel three or four miles or more on foot to attend the public prayers, and sometimes as many more to hear a sermon, and they seldom grudge many times for several hours together in their cold and damp churches to wait the coming of their minister".

Modern times

For all that we are seeing medieval churches, we are of course seeing them somewhat modernised. Eighteenth century tourists' accounts of their visits leave no doubt of the state that most were then in, and the shock that the neglect and poverty in which they stood gave to perceptions formed in richer counties. Frequently in those days what funds there were were drawn away by the local squire, or some more distant landowner, reverend or institution.

As few churches had paved floors, most stood on bare earth. In this earth the graves were still dug, the feet of the congregation wearing away the topsoil above them. At Nevern the result of so many centuries of burial was that the interior floor had risen several feet above the level of the ground outside. Dr Johnson on his tour remarked on a church with a hole in the roof – there are some like this today – just as he remarked that the conversation at dinner one evening in the Vale of Clwyd was of preserving the Welsh language. *Plus ça change*, as we say in Wales.

More so than in England, the Welsh churches have not had the full support of communities. When 'Chapel' arrived, 'Church' became in many places marginalised. Some of the old locations by the churches suffered huge depopulation: many thousands emigrated to the coal and iron of the south, or to such open lands as Patagonia and Pennsylvania where Welsh place names still cluster on the map. Where big population growth came in the past two centuries, it did so often in new locations where few people lived before, and where there were few old churches – and these new generations became tied more to chapel than to church. This partly explains the escape from transformation of some old churches in the last two hundred years. Paving, new seating and new stained glass are often the extent of it. Lack of people and money saved many churches from too radical a Victorianisation.

In making changes to the fabric the Victorians were primarily engaged in bring-ing people back into church against the competition of the chapels, and in more comfort. Without their work in restoration many churches would not have survived to us at all. An account of St Asaph before Scott was engaged there makes the contri-bution to posterity only too plain, and isolated churches like Llandanwg and Cascob had been abandoned to the wind and rain before being reclaimed in the late 1800s.

There was also, as in England, a vigorous campaign of new church building, with wealthier patrons reaching out to the best of English architects – Scott, Street, Pearson, Butterfield and Bodley – who built grandly and in their own tradition. They were bringing in a High Anglican vision, elevating altars and pushing roofs skyward, and they were joined by Glamorgan-born John Prichard, who worked on major Cardiff commissions including Llandaff but whose masterpiece may be the compressed jewel-box church at Baglan. These churches tend to cluster in more affluent or more Anglicised areas – often the same. They seem to make more sense in the streets of Roath or the seascape of Penarth than in the village fields, but even there some lingering can be rewarded: Street at Llandysilio or Rhydymwyn, Scott at Trefnant, Pearson by the waterside at Llangasty Tal-y-llyn.

Different in kind and still under-appreciated was the work of English architects practising more locally, such as Bucknall in Swansea and Douglas in Chester, which looked closer to home traditions. This did not make them any less innovative: Bucknall's Pontargothi was Arts and Crafts before the phrase had arrived, and while Bodley's graceful St German's, Cardiff opened up sightlines and access to the chancel as part of a breakthrough in Victorian style, Douglas did so at Halkyn in renewal of a borders tradition: the difference of feeling, with Halkyn more grounded in the congregation while St German's aspires and lifts the eyes, is telling.

The rise of Arts and Crafts was part of the wider growth in appreciation of vernacular tradition and materials, and the great late Victorian campaign to save rather than replace the old fabric of churches is associated above all with William Morris, the originality of whose mind appears suffused by his Montgomeryshire roots, from his deep sense of social community to the shaping role of landscape in lives and buildings, and even to the lifelong imaginative spur of the myths of King Arthur: Wales for him was always the 'fatherland'. Morris and his friends made contributions of stained glass to churches such as Wrexham, Holyhead, Cardiff, Hawarden (where the glowing west window is Burne Jones's last work in the medium) and Llandaff, where they also provided terracotta panels of the Creation and a large painted altarpiece stuffed with their own self-portraits. J.D. Sedding, another craftsman architect whose business was next door to Morris's in London, built numerous churches in Wales, and he rebuilt at Llanfair Kilgeddin, bringing in the artist Heywood Sumner to fill the nave walls with huge sgraffito murals which responded to the local setting by depicting all the nearby hills. This was an idea matched by other artists further west: in the Good Samaritan window at Tal-y-llyn the certain man who fell among thieves is diverted from the biblical to the local – literally: an inn with a Welsh dragon pub sign, and in a painting at Goodwick, the angel of the Annunciation arrives at Fishguard harbour. Also on the

Philip Webb Arts & Crafts at Eglwys Gymyn

west coast, Sedding's partner Henry Wilson, in a one-off original at Brithdir, brought Mayfair Arts and Crafts to rural Meirionydd.

The work of Morris's Society for the Protection of Ancient Buildings can be seen at churches such as Eglwys Gymyn in Carmarthenshire, and his influence dominates the twentieth century treatment of old churches. Caroe's restorations, as at Llanbister, Patrisio and Brecon, are fine and sensitive early models of their kind. Crickadarn gained from Clough Williams-Ellis's peculiar charm, and in the 1920s John Coates Carter made a transforming reinterpretation of Llandeloi. After this frenetic century of work, the pace of church building slowed almost to a halt. The most talked-about work in the decades since must be the modernist rethinking of Llandaff. The most moving are perhaps the stark memorial chapel at Llyn Celyn, after the flooding of the valley and its farms, and the small shack turned by Italian prisoners of war into a Catholic church, which can still be found at what is now a caravan park at Llandyfriog in Ceredigion.

Chapel

A new reforming movement began to move outside the established church in the seventeenth century. People were meeting in rooms or barns or clearings in the woods to hear the message of the Bible expounded. Few of the first chapels remain: the walls are still there at Llanfaches, and the first Baptist chapel, built in Ilston Cwm on Gower in 1649, is marked now by a gathering of old stones beside a woodland footpath. In the 1650s there were Quaker missions into Wales: distinctive early Quaker houses survive at Llandegley and in a hidden fold on the Dolobran estate at Pontrobert, and there are two more, no longer used, attached to farms in Monmouthshire. Before too long the minister of Ilston and many of the Quakers had emigrated to America. More recently, the old interior of Dolobran, gallery and all, has followed them.

The early chapels, the most beautifully preserved of which is at Maesyronnen near Glasbury, echo the early churches, simple, communal, conveying the feeling of a small likeminded gathering pressed up close, and made in the wood and stone vernacular of the Welsh aesthetic which gives them their particular beauty. Some of them, like Capel Penrhiw and Capel Newydd at Nanhoron, started life as barns. Like so many of the churches, they were built in places sought out for rural seclusion, beside running streams which provided for the congregation and their ponies – another sign in another generation of how in Wales the urge for spiritual renewal seeks out the open landscape and an immersion in the natural world, as if from some deep ancestral memory.

Along a country road or footpath, the simple lines of a small Georgian chapel still sometimes appear, at Gwenddwr in the Nantoffeiriad valley, which looks more like a house; at Gwern-y-Pant near Deuddeur, one small exterior stone among the whitewashed brick incised with verses from the Bible; at Pentre Llifior on a green

A place of their own: the early Independent chapel at Nanhoron

valley brow west of Berriew. In plan they are simple rectangles, with one door in the short façade, or two doors on the long façade, and square or roundheaded windows sometimes placed in symmetry. In size they are not much more than cottages, and many share the same roof with an adjoining home for the minister, like the chapel at Pontrobert in the Berwyns – or with an adjoining stable, as at Capel Adfa west of Llanwyddelan. Many, like Soar-y-mynydd in the wilds of Pen Rhiw-clochdy, and farmyard Glaspwll below Pencarreg-gopa, are in settings so evocative of time and place that, plain as they are, they belong at the emotional centre of Wales's religious heritage.

Close to Llandrindod Wells, the gentry chapel at Caebach contrasts in its fittings with the country chapel a few miles north at Carmel, Nantmel, while the arrangement of space, the closeness of the pews and the central position of the pulpit – like a new kind of altar of the Word – have a shared sensibility. But with its elegant graveyard planted with yews Caebach also makes claims to the church tradition, while the nearby parish church at Llanfihangel Helygen, a simple barn with an undistanced pulpit, comes close to an early chapel. Rural scale and setting, vernacular construction and communal purpose thus bind the older chapels and churches of Wales in a common tradition which undermines the separating lines of category.

Except for their seclusion, these rural idylls do not convey that their congregations met at considerable personal risk. Those who broke from the church, or like the early Methodists wished to change its nature, met frequently with vitriol, violence and persecution. Tenant farmers might find themselves evicted from their homes. There were stonings, even murders. An inscription on a gravestone in

Ysceifiog is full of praise for a man whose life's achievement was to persecute the 'brainsick Methodists'. The arrival of Chapel drove a wedge down the middle of communities: people came to define themselves as either church or chapel.

Yet out of this atmosphere came the familiar tall and solid chapels of the nineteenth century, with a galleried second storey, proclaiming their names and dates on the façade. This change of type of building, from a chapel-barn or cottage to something unmistakably distinct, seems to have begun close to 1800 – although it took some decades to spread out, and in time to aggrandise itself. The cluster of survivals from the 1820s, all of them treasurable, illustrates the transition. Those from early in the decade are still single-storey, whitewashed, mostly square-windowed like an old house – Beili-du, Soar-y-mynydd, Glaspwll. By 1827/8 come the stately Jerusalem at Capel Gwynfe, Ramoth at Cowbridge and stonewalled Caerfarchell near St David's, still with the entrance on the long wall but taller and with a gallery, the windows now paired and distinctively roundheaded, raised up above the gaze of peering eyes. Before the later demolition and rebuilding which came with revivals and the growth of population, Wales must have been full of these buildings, all of which display a charm and sureness of vernacular touch their successors were never quite to emulate.

They are still, at first, in the discreet or undemonstrative locations where in many cases they simply replaced the congregation's earlier, smaller meeting house, like the memorable Gellionnen, in a dip on a deserted moor high above Clydach and Swansea Bay, and Maesberllan, another important early chapel on a turn in a rural road to Talachddu in Breconshire. But this begins to change: large chapels start appearing in the centre of communities – albeit at first set cautiously back behind the street as in Cowbridge. There were some expressions of regret about this – was it a true test of a worshipper's devotion to stroll down the street instead of trekking up the moor? It marks the end of reticence, the arrival of a new confidence for Dissent, which must have been both political and economic. Dissenters had weathered the French revolutionary storm, when churchmen and others had linked them (on the whole unsuccessfully) to free thinking and The Rights of Man. In the years from 1800 to 1850, a new chapel appeared in Wales with every eight days that passed.

The people who built them wanted to recreate Wales as a new kind of Israel – planting the place names of the Holy Land all through the country: Bethesda, Bethel, Peniel, Siloh, Salem, Saron, Soar – the second coming of religion to the map of Wales. Until this time, they had simply given chapels the names of the features of the land around them – like Maesyronnen, field of ash, and Caebach, little field. They had read something else in their bibles – the descriptions of the temple of Solomon. It was a rectangular box of a building, roughly eighty feet long by twenty five, and forty feet in height. It was built of stone, with tall narrow windows, and lots of panelled wood in the interior. It had a small entrance hall, and a main room for worship. It sounds familiar.

Discreet and undemonstrative: Pentre Llifior

As congregations grew and there was money, more of the detail could be afforded, like the pillars with floreate capitals mentioned in the first book of Kings. The first unmistakable temple planned complete with a portico of columns was begun in Tremadog in 1810, but it was not until mid-century that these were being built in any numbers. Other fine early survivals, from the 1830s, can be seen at Hermon, Fishguard and St James's Street, Monmouth.

Especially at industrial centres, with the clustering of congregations and competitive spirit – places like Newport, Newtown, Llanidloes and all the valleys of Glamorgan – there are chapels of outlandish grandeur – perhaps above all at Morriston, with porticoes on porticoes and a steeple for good measure. In such places, where street frontages cost more, the entrance was turned to the short wall, and more show was made of the façade. These chapels staked a claim for all the styles of design the church was simultaneously reviving, more often as surface pattern than as structure, and with Gothic rising over the years to compete with Classical style. They signalled the arrival of a new kind of chapel architect, often locally-born and linked to the congregation, but sometimes sought out well beyond the locality, like Owen Morris Roberts of Porthmadog, John Humphrey of Morriston (both originally carpenters – *pensaer*, meaning head carpenter, is still the Welsh word for architect), Rev. Thomas Thomas of Landore and George Morgan of Carmarthen, the last of whom, alongside adventures in Romanesque, produced the most grandly – and quite untypically – three-dimensional of Welsh facades. Inside, such chapels are galleried on three sides, the seats boxed or gated in rows placed at several angles, packed and close without a central aisle, or facing inward to others in the congregation. By holding to

39

this wrapped pattern of enclosure, not even the grandest expansion in size could disperse the sense of people enfolded, the deeply rooted feeling of community.

When they were built, there was also something traditional, perhaps even nostalgic, about them, at a time when the churches were redesigning, stripping out the boxes and the galleries, responding to new imperatives of order, and of altar over pulpit. As well as to their own tradition, the interiors of nineteenth century chapels looked back as if with longing to those of the eighteenth century church.

These larger post-1820s buildings had a new sense of privacy for the congregation, setting the windows high or using frosted glass. For the visitor now, access to them other than at service times is frequently a challenge: they are all almost without exception locked, and the visitor can get no compensating view in through the window. Only because of this, very few have been included in this book: Bethesda in Mold, The Plough in Brecon and Tabernacl Morriston stand for the North and Mid and South of the country, each of them remarkable as buildings and associated too with the musical, educational or literary heritage of Wales. Among the many locked masterpieces in the grand style are Capel Jerusalem at Bethesda, Crane Street Pontypool, Seilo Newydd at Landore, Tabernacle Haverfordwest, Bethania Cardigan, Seion Llanrwst, Bethesda Pentre, Ebenezer Tonypandy and the early Penuel Rhymney where all the seats appear to lean towards the pulpit in anticipation. There are whole neighbourhoods and streetscapes where clusters of important chapels shape the atmosphere in places as diverse as Denbigh, Llanelli, Llangefni, Carmarthen, Maesteg, Caernarfon and Cwmamman: our chapel heritage is one of urban religious landscapes as well as ancient rural ones. Five thousand chapels were built in Wales, more than in the rest of Britain put together.

But most chapels are plain enough inside and out: it is these that are typical, and where the chapel life was, and still is, mostly lived. Chapels were never meant to be about the setting or the building: they were about the preaching. What medieval churches did with painting and images, the words of the great preachers achieved in the chapels, belying the stripped plain walls with pictures as real in the mind, as vivid and sometimes terrifying, that tapped deep into the same psychological territory: the hovering presence of death and Judgement, and the saving grace of Christ. The customary contrast of a cool northern Protestantism – so seemingly apparent to the eye here – to the raw emotionalism of a Spanish or Italian altar misses a secret of Welsh chapel life – the transformation of these banned visions into words: "*Mae'r gwaed a redodd ar y Groes*", goes one of our most famous hymns – The blood that ran down the Cross. What we see now, peering in through the doors, are empty theatres.

Rev. John Parker, walking in Snowdonia back in 1832, described a dissenting chapel service something like a modern American gospel service, the call and response between preacher and congregation rising in intensity, the singing and crying loud and rhythmic. Earlier still, in 1799 near Caernarfon, he went to a service of the Jumpers, a group reminiscent, visually if not theologically, of the

Shakers, who had left Cheshire for New York not long before. Worshippers were shouting, singing all at once to different tunes, jumping in the air in their excitement.

Across both church and chapel, revival came in waves, as in 1735, 1859 and 1871, and there is another heritage of chapels visited for their associations with great preachers, like Thomas Charles at Bala, Daniel Rowlands at Llangeitho, David Davis at Llwynrhydowen, Caledfryn at Groeswen, or with missions like the first to reach Korea, which came from Hanover Chapel in Llanover, its visitors' book filled with Korean *hangeul*, or with the last irresistible revival of 1904, spreading out from Carmarthenshire and Ceredigion, led by men like Evan Roberts and Joseph Jenkins, and women like Mary Jones of Llanegryn, who saw lights in the sky like pillars of fire, just like St Columba the millenium before. Something of the Age of Saints returned to Wales. "Evan Roberts was like a particle of radium in our midst", wrote the moderator Evan Phillips. "There was a sighing of the wind.... I felt the waters begin to cascade." Roberts's chapel in Loughor, and the pew at Blaenannerch where it all began for him, are among these destinations. The 1904 revival was also to produce the last wave of major new religious buildings, almost all of them chapels, the work of W. Beddoe Rees at Maesteg, Resolven and Llandudno being perhaps the most notable.

A walk through Pontypridd or Rhosllanerchrugog or any of these urban streetscapes still speaks with force of the fervour that came to revival Wales and the preaching, hymn-singing, Sunday-school Sundays that rang through the decades beyond. At Capel Mawr, Rhos, every Christmas the Messiah, every Easter the Creation, with a villagefull in the rows upstairs and down. The chapels, so many of which in the nineteenth century had been knocked down and remade to hold built-in schoolrooms, performing stages, and community gathering places, were the frontline of education, thought and creative expression for huge numbers of the population. They were democratic in conception and ambition long before many of their members were entitled to the vote, and they were central to preparing ground for such social and political change to follow. These buildings carried a shock value to those who wanted to preserve the hierarchical society, which has been quite forgotten, and the arrival of them in such multiplying numbers was a pressing and thoroughly modernist statement of how ordinary Welsh communities embraced the urge for change as an integral element of their spiritual hunger.

More than religion had come to be involved by the Victorian boom years: in popular description, church was establishment, it was Tory, it was tinged with England; chapel was working class, *y werin*, it was Liberal, it was Wales. There was always more to it than this: the Welshness of church congregations has had to be recovered from the persuasive sweep of that version of history. But a divide, multi-faceted and real, remained a part of the social scene through much of the twentieth century. It provides something of the explanation for why the old church heritage of Wales has been so little championed in publications, and also, some of the particular pleasure in bringing together church and chapel, in this one book.

UNMAPPED AND UNSIGNED

Finding Wales's Best Churches

Few countries can be more reticent about this heritage than Wales. Only a handful of these churches are signed even from the next road, and for many of the rural ones an ordinary road map will not get you that close. A surprising number are in places unnamed even on the Ordnance Survey's detailed Explorer maps, but these at least have small crosses (+) to indicate locations, in all cases except Burnett's Hill. The Ordnance Survey grid references to identify these crosses are given at the head of every entry. A helpful website is www.findachurch.co.uk, which lists the great majority of these churches, and rings their locations in red.

Without such maps you must navigate by the kindness of locals, a serendipitous and frequently memorable way of travelling, sometimes sufficiently addictive to leave the maps behind. Almost without exception these churches are unlocked in daylight hours or indicate in the porch or on the lychgate where to get the key. Some openings are seasonal however, and of course may vary through the lifetime of this book: Rug and Gwydir Uchaf, for example, are currently closed throughout the colder months, and Llangar can only be visited by tour from Rug. Others are subject to such things as tides (Llangwyfan), or getting across firing ranges at declared safe times (St Govan's). You can be just unlucky sometimes with the absence or unadvised change of a keyholder.

If you are travelling a long way to visit, it would be wise to telephone ahead, although discovering who to telephone can be as interesting as asking for directions. Local tourist offices are unfailingly helpful and if they do not have the information are often willing to telephone around to get it. Some churches and some diocese have websites which give access information. Like everything which takes a little more effort to achieve, the sense of accomplishment expands to match. The combination of locating, opening, and travelling on winding country roads means defeat for those trying to do this in a hurry: these places have their own pace, and only by moving to it can you truly unlock them.

Access for people with difficulty in walking is a challenge at a number of locations – although it is only fair to say a challenge which was part of their everyday business back in medieval times. Llangelynin (Conwy), Llanfaglan, Capel Beili-heulog and Llangar are several minutes from the nearest road and the walk to Carnguwch, Dolobran or Llangwyfan can take at least a quarter of an hour. There are steep steps at Llangwyfan, St Govan's and Llanbister, and stiles at Carnguwch and Llangelynin.

ONE HUNDRED CHURCHES AND CHAPELS

I
THE NORTH WEST

ANGLESEY/YNYS MON, CONWY, GWYNEDD

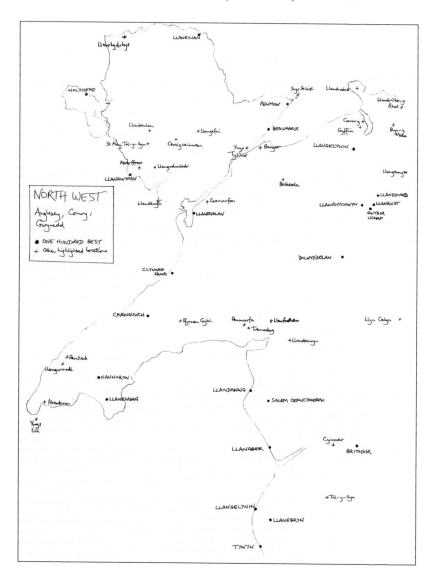

Beaumaris/Biwmares, St Mary and St Nicholas
SH 604 762

In 1282, the military French-speaking aristocracy which had dominated England for two hundred years finally completed their long conquest of Wales. Gwynedd was ringed with castles designed by their masterly Savoyard architect, the last and most refined of which faced out across the eastern entry to the Menai Strait. They gave it, and the town they built adjacent, the French name of Beaumaris.

Like the castles, the churches of the new conquest towns are varied in plan and role. Conwy church is at the centre of the grid, a sheltered meeting place for all the quarters of the town, its grassy churchyard a surprise approached from narrow streets. Caernarvon church is built right into the walls where they run along the shore, safe in the lee of the castle. At Beaumaris, with the castle at the south east tip, the new town colonists were less protected to the north and west – where the local Welsh had been ordered to resettle at a windy distance. They put the church at the northwest corner of the grid, on the long diagonal from the castle, and facing out to this uncertain land. They made it to be part of the defensive system, the west tower a watchtower, the long watches up there still signalled by the stone ledge seating at its windows. The north door has an inner drawbar to stop it getting beaten down.

Yet in true colonial manner Beaumaris mixes confidence with insecurity. It has the brand new style of Decorated Gothic, poised, airy, newly light with wide and frequent windows, its separate elements articulated by arcades and aisles and arches. It is, from this long perspective, the archetypal style of English parish church – but it never was to be in Wales, which has continually shown a preference for more

Seat of learning: Solomon and the Queen of Sheba on a Beaumaris misericord

45

shared and integrated spaces. The designer of Beaumaris used the new style well. Detail is sparing but original – like the window tracery in the aisles, playing on the Trinity with triangles and trefoils, and the portrait heads in the stops and corbels, some in contemporary dress. The arcade has lightly moulded arches rising to the clerestory, where circles and quatrefoils take over. Both aisles would have had altars: the piscinas remain. Around 1500 a new chancel was built, with a fine wooden roof above the later wood and plaster ceiling.

William Bulkeley's alabaster tomb is a Wars of the Roses classic: he wears the latest most flexible armour arrayed with buckles, straps and hinges. Unusually he is helmeted, though his visor is up. His wife Ellen Griffith lies beside him and around the tomb finely carved images of saints alternate with shields of family arms. The set of carved stalls for the new chancel have praying angels on the arm rests, and a fascinating gallery of faces in misericords beneath, where Solomon and the Queen of Sheba mingle with local people carrying flagons and sheaves of corn. Tudor flowers curl in the poppyhead bench ends. There is a rare brass triptych on the north wall showing the Trinity in the centre panel, the image of God the Father throned within a chapel-like interior, encompassing the crucified Son. Beside them is an image of St John holding a poisoned chalice, the poison hovering above it in the lithe form of a devil, and a crowned Virgin and Child, one of the last such images before the Reformation swept them out of fashion.

Much later, in the nearby grounds of Llanfaes friary, a huge stone coffin lid was found face down in a ditch. At its base is a carving of a wyvern, and a plant which ribbons out effusively towards a heart-shaped opening, from which grows the upper body of a woman. Her hands are held in prayer and she has a crown on her head. It is the tomb of Joan, wife of Llywelyn Fawr, daughter of King John, the adulterous Siwan of history and theatre, for whom the friary was founded – and its style is linked to the royal tombs at Fontevrault. For years it was propped up in a box pew, part of the congregation. Now it lies in the church porch, one of the most important thirteenth century sculptures in Wales, suffering every summer the attentions of swallows.

A Trinity in brass for the Bulkeley family

Brithdir, St Mark

SH 764 183

The impact of Art Nouveau on Wales would be a short book. At home in Paris, Brussels, Barcelona, it was a cosmopolitan effusion, and cities were in short supply in turn of the century Wales. The small triumph of Art Nouveau in Wales happened on a wooded hillside above the Wnion valley, deep in rural Meirionydd.

Henry Wilson has been given only a minor place in the history of arts and crafts. He designed and made flamboyant and expensive silverwork and jewellery, taking avant-garde commissions from Liberty's, and he worked for more famous architects. He had the chance to build his own campanile, still standing over the street cafés of Exmouth Market, a touch of Ravenna in Clerkenwell, as un-English as neighbouring Saint Paul's. He came nearer, wrote C.R. Ashbee, "to those Florentine jewellers who had their little shops on the Ponte Vecchio, and turned to necklaces, frescoes or cathedrals indiscriminately", explanation enough for his selection by the patron of Brithdir, the widow of the Rev. Charles Tooth who fifteen years earlier had created in Florence, in the ground floor stables of an old palazzo, the Anglo-Catholic and richly pre-Raphaelite interior of another church dedicated to St Mark, and who may not be unconnected with the art-hallowing chaplain parodied by E.M. Forster in *A Room With A View*.

Wilson's breakthrough had come with the commission for the firm of J.D. Sedding to build 'the cathedral of the Arts and Crafts', Holy Trinity in Chelsea. When Sedding died halfway through, Wilson took on the firm and the task, and many of the details are his. It is a vast space lit brightly by richly coloured stretches of glass – a nave wider than St Paul's, and the largest Morris and Burne Jones window in the world. But in 1895, when Wilson came to build his own church at Brithdir, he dreamed up something radically different.

On the B-road half a mile or so south of the village, there are steps up a steeply banked site through a gloriously planted churchyard. The path leads around the west end of the church, a fine plain design in local granite with steep roofs, small leaded windows curving upwards at the tops, and a stone cross in relief under a projecting gable arch.

The nave has a stark modernity that might still have shocked fifty years on. The only ornament is a slender inlay of ebony and abalone in the doors, and in the centre aisle a lead font shaped with shells, fronds, roses, and the dove of the Holy Ghost.

The chancel colours are honed down to just two bands of painted wall, blue above, earth red below, amazingly stark for the kaleidoscope years of late Victoriana. Uninterrupted light which flows in from the west is excluded almost entirely from the east, a Byzantine grouping of recesses and apses, compressed by six rising levels of stone steps through chancel and sanctuary. In these darker spaces, made for candleglow, Wilson placed great panels of beaten copper, a shimmering bridge to layered scenes of otherworldly contact. In the Annunciation on the altar, there are two tall figures watching over the angel's meeting with Mary: the Rev. Charles Tooth and a guardian angel of his own.

Reredos and pulpit have inscriptions from the Latin Bible, the former with vines and bluebells, the latter with a grape motif carried here from Holy Trinity. Wonderfully carved creatures enliven the choir stalls, kingfisher, dolphin, rabbits and squirrels among them.

Sedding and Wilson did build a church in Cardiff, but in the 1960s it was demolished. Wilson's reredos of the Adoration of the Magi was saved, and can be seen in St Samson, Pentre Gardens. His work turns up again, as unexpectedly, on the Upper West Side of Manhattan in the great bronze doors of St John the Divine, where his tall-winged angels and winding vineleaf recur.

A room without a view

Carnguwch, St Cuwch

SH 374 418

The ancient churches of Llyn are a special group, each one distinctive yet linked together by the chain of pilgrimage, more than the sum of their parts. Between the high church of Clynnog Fawr and the double- and triple-naves of the western end of the peninsula, there are only small grey single-chamber churches, most of them hidden down in the river-runs and valleys, away from the sea and the high rocky outcrops which disconcert the landscape at irregular intervals. Only two are up on the mountains, and one of those is in the smallest and least inhabited of the old parishes of Caernarfonshire. High above the roads and away from the world, it is nevertheless the most human and restoring of places, its long views beautiful and lonely, and its churchyard more filled with original poetry, and with the sense of the worth of the people who lie there, than any comparable other.

It has a darker past. Mynydd Carnguwch, long viewed as anthropomorphically soft and breast-like against the rugged profiles of Yr Eifl, and topped by a great bronze age cairn of giants' stones, was the site until modern times of raging Allhallows bonfires for Nos Galan Gaeaf, the beginning of pagan winter. An early saint staked a claim for all this by planting his church here, but who and when remains unclear. The first Ordnance Survey maps go for St Beuno, but older records have another name, the spelling ranging from St Ciwg (Welsh for friendship) to St Cuwch (Welsh for scowl) – the mischievous duality of an R.S. Thomas of the Age of Saints. Or perhaps it was only the mountain, the *carn*, which had the *cuwch*.

The church has something of the same ambivalence. Its heavy walls are massed and solid, on their guard against the weather or the stranger, and piled up to a rough western bellcote. Inside there are lines of old pews and a two-decker pulpit – and a wooden bier with which the funeral processions must have wound their way across the mountains. It has not been much used for services since the 1930s. The llan more than the building is Carnguwch's parlour, a natural llan on a rounded ledge in the green hillside, with an old stone circular wall and a hawthorn edging out among the taller trees. Above it the grey stone slopes are purple in summer with heather and down below, sheep graze and the river Erch glints and flows in the sun, winding like the stone walls of the fields. The way up from the south comes by Pen-fras-uchaf, farmed by the same family for four hundred years. On reaching the height of the llan, the view opens out again to take in the sea and the sacred islands of St Tudwal, while the line of mountains stretches out west, and east all the way to Eryri.

In this part of the country long renowned for poetry, poems of individual remembrance have been made for many of the people here, carved on their stones and signed only with bardic names like Madryn, Iseifion, Dewi Arfon and Alafon, the last a local labourer on the farms who became a chapel preacher at Clwt-y-bont, and whose words made the hymn '*Glan geriwbiaid a seraffiaid*'. They are deeply personal, honouring such as the genial and faithful family man Robert Roberts of Ty'n Lon, *Gwr hynaws oedd, graenus iawn – ei waith oll / Priod a thad ffyddlawn*, or Griffith Jones of Rhosfawr, *llanc llawn swyn*, a lad full of charm – and local, mentioning Carnguwch in the verse.

The inscriptions unusually record their work and their homes as well as their qualities, evoking a community extending over centuries, together here now as though time were nothing, waiting until heaven's morning breaks: Captain John Jones of Ceidio, son of Captain William Jones, lost at sea in the ship *Moel Eilian* off Sharpness Point at the age of 44 in 1896; Richard William, a young servant at Trallwyn until 1772; three generations of men called Ellis Roberts, one the police constable at Tregarth until 1901, outlived by both his parents; another Griffith Jones, who loved his religion and who worked for the quarry until 1864; and Kate, elder daughter of Plas Newydd at Llannor, who died aged 28 in 1885. And there is Evan Jones of Caernarfon, who died on 7th Jan 1784, aged 33, and left a message in a perfect englyn to his friends:

> Fy ngyfeullion Wuwlon Wedd na Wulwch
> Pan Weloch fy anedd
> Chwi yn fud or bud ir bedd
> Attaf dowch yn y diwedd

> [My friends, with your downcast faces,
> Don't cry when you see my home.
> Silently, from the world to the grave,
> You will come to join me in the end.]

Cefncymerau, Capel Salem

SH 603 274

If one building is the icon of old chapel culture, it is Capel Salem. In the search to understand how spirit of place can resonate so powerfully Salem is the most beguiling of subjects because, like so many old Welsh buildings, its claims can seem at first so modest. In a photograph, it could be just a row of cottages in a clearing. But to walk here by the mountain path which ends in steep steps at the chapel wall, or up through the deep wooded slopes from Pentre Gwynfryn, is to enter the world of green light and tumbling water in which Salem was made.

It is built of huge grey slabs of mountain rock on a steep site which is cleverly exploited inside. There are four high windows and three lower doorways, one now filled in. The right-hand door opens straight to a staircase to the top of the long raked rows of benches. The view steps down to the box pews at the front, with their separate access door – and beyond to the *set fawr* and central pulpit on the far wall, all in old schoolroom brown. The front box now belongs to the organist.

There are few details – a rail of hat pegs frames the whole interior, and there are candleholders and communion glass rings, but no ornament. Everything is functional. From the back windows green sunlight comes in through the ferns and leaves of the higher bank. Fifty feet below the graveyard there is a stone inscribed beneath its covering of moss *Bedydd Lyn* – baptismal pool – beside which baptisms were conducted in the river Artro. It is a building of mountain, wood and water, where setting, meaning and fabric seem to fuse together.

Built in 1850 mostly with free labour, it was altered to its present layout ten years later, and the small manse added on the end. It kept a strong resemblance to the local cottage where the Baptists had worshipped since 1826, which is still standing by the cattle grid lower down the road at Rhwng-y-Ddwy-Bont. Its congregation was rural but industrial – alongside the farmers and cottagers were workers from the tannery at Wern Gron, the nearby Manganese mines, the wool factory at Gwynfryn, and the timber men who cut oak for the Porthmadog shipyards. Their Sundays together here, with singing and picnics, made a sociable day.

When Sydney Curnow Vosper came riding by on his green bicycle one sunlit day in 1908, dressed in his characteristic knickerbockers and cravat, no one could have imagined that the painting he made would find such a place in the Welsh imagination. The women in their tall black hats and shawls and the men, two of them bearded and ageing, the other bowed in prayer beneath the clock, are furrowed, separate, far away in their thoughts. The clock says three minutes to ten. It is the quiet moment before the service begins.

All the people in the painting are known. Sian Owen is opening the door of a pew, dressed for the picture in borrowed hat and a now famous shawl. People have seen in its sumptuous folds and fringe the bearded image of the devil, but this was not the artist's intention. Sian lived nearby at Ty'n y Fawnog but was born up the mountain in the Maesygarnedd farmhouse of Col. John Jones, one of the fifty-nine who had signed the death warrant of Charles I. (In that high home throned by the walled peaks of the Rhinogs, a thousand feet above a glistening sea, kings must have seemed unimportant things). Behind Sian is Robert Williams, a carpenter at Cae'r Meddyg, now buried with his wife in the churchyard beneath an affectionate memorial "*Hunwch, mewn cyflawn henoed, / Wr a'i wraig, rhai gorau 'rioed*". Six year old Evan Lloyd grew up to be a quarryman at Dinorwig. Wiliam Sion was one of two brothers whose home was used by Vosper as the setting for another painting now in the National Museum.

The chapel interior remains unchanged as it was painted – only the clock has been renewed. The visitors' book is witness to its long-held role as destination of the chapel outing. It is resonant still of something valuable which it seems, by standing here for long enough, might be absorbed.

> Mor felys wedyn yw eich byd di-son
> Sian Owen Ty'n y Fawnog, Wiliam Sion.
>
> [So sweet then is your simple world,
> Sian Owen Ty'n y Fawnog, Wiliam Sion]
>
> T. Rowland Hughes

The most beguiling of subjects

Clynnog Fawr, St Beuno

SH 414 498

Clynnog Fawr, great holly grove, mother church in the Age of Saints, shrine and sacrificial altar of St Beuno, gathering point for pilgrimages down Llyn to Ynys Enlli, sometime abbey, sometime bishopric, is among the most historic and important churches in the country. Like the Spanish missions of California, close to the sea-routes and watching the inland passes through the mountains, St Beuno's must have dominated spiritual life for miles around and many centuries. The name of Beuno, greatest of the northern saints, spreads across a heartland in dedications on the westbound roads and down to Penmorfa at the mountain pass's southern end, breaking out again as far away as Herefordshire and Somerset.

The church's huge spaces, made for the crush of milling crowds about to set out on a journey, can seem now cavernous and empty as a railway terminus after the last train, and with as many entrances and exits in its walls – all but one now disused. On a thin day of *niwl*, the view from the great sheltering porch is of cloud dissolving into the sea. Here medieval travelling parties must have gathered at the time of departure, full of expectation, waiting for the rain to clear. There were not many years from completion of the building in its early Tudor guise of upscale pilgrim station to the day when pilgrimage was outlawed – yet it has unexpectedly survived for several centuries beyond the expiration of its primary role. For all the years since then, a small parish has wandered up the nave to take its place in the bareness and grandeur of its unsought surroundings.

The medieval spiritual powerhouse of western Arfon

Clynnog Fawr is a church where absences are powerful, evoking the past in half-given indications while also locking up its mysteries. Visitors are left to ponder on the remnant of the tomb of Beuno, the stripped shrine chapel, plaintive wooden dugout box, megalithic walls and the casually placed boulders by the thousand year old sundial and the path to the porch – all struggling to mouth the story of the medieval spiritual powerhouse of western Arfon, a gaunt old figure from whom the flesh has gone. Yet the church is, architecturally, one of the most ambitious in Gwynedd. 130 feet long and 70 feet wide, it has a cross-shape plan with transepts, great walls of glass and a western tower. Its projecting porch and vestry have upper rooms which housed its resident community of canons. The bell tower is among the sturdiest in Wales, and so are the bells, which could take the arm from a man not ready for their weight and force. The tower is screened from the nave by fine old panelling, and the nave from the chancel by a remnant rood screen without parapet or loft. Beyond it in the rising ground are battered choir stalls with double-headed eagles and some linen pattern, and sedilia with crocketed heads. Early nineteenth century iron dog tongs, for yanking unruly dogs out of services, hang on the south transept wall.

The shrine chapel is a separate place, approached down a barrel-vaulted passage from inside the tower. Bookended with heavy wooden doors, roofed by great blocks of granite and lit with vents too narrow to squeeze through, the passageway became the parish lock-up in the eighteenth century. In the chapel is a sacred stone associated with Beuno's tomb, incised with a long cross. Grey paving marks out the lines and position of Beuno's first church on the site, a small oratory just eighteen feet by ten. The early fabric must have suffered singularly from the pilgrim practice of scraping stone in powder from the columns, and mixing this with water from Beuno's well, a cure for damaged eyes. The well is still there, down the road a little to the west, a bare survival with seating stones and steps.

Right into the nineteenth century the crowds would return on Trinity Sunday, herding their calves and lambs through the great slabs of the lychgate, selling any newborns with the 'mark of Beuno' on them and stuffing the proceeds into the crumbling, triple-locked *Cuff*. Robert Roberts is buried in the churchyard, the minister who gave Christmas Evans his *hwyl* and preaching style, up the hill at Capel Uchaf. The land around here is charged with the signs and memorials of myth and religion. At Llwyn y Nef (Heavenly Grove) on the hillside above the village, a monk fell under a bird's enchantment. Down the lane to the sea, beyond the cupmarked capstone of Bachwen cromlech, is the coast of the old spirits Lleu, Arianrhod and Dylan, and, it is said, at low tide still, the surfacing remains of Gored Beuno, the monks' sea-harvesting fishing weir.

Dolwyddelan, St Gwyddelan

SH 736 523

The Wynn family which came out of Eifionydd in the late fifteenth century is indelibly associated with the art and architecture of the Conwy valley. Their extraordinary chapels at Llanrwst and Gwydir Uchaf and their houses at Gwydir and Conwy teem with aspirations and visual fantasies enchanting and sometimes faintly ridiculous to modern eyes. But there is an overture to these well known accomplishments higher upriver in the mountains, which is by comparison a well-kept secret – a first jumbled treasure-house of vernacular art and craft.

Dolwyddelan church, built around 1500 by Maredudd ab Ieuan, father of John Wynn of Gwydir, is the family's first grand gesture of gratitude to God, of their relish in images and pleasure in their wealth. Behind it the mountain climbs towards three thousand feet above the ruin of the castle, but the churchyard is on broad flat ground where the river curves. It was put there deliberately, to give Maredudd's men due sight and warning of any imminent attack by the gangs of bandits who preyed on them and on the great livestock ranch which they had thrown across the southern and eastern slopes of Snowdonia.

From the churchyard wall the lychgate frames the view to the porch. At the back a three thousand year old yew tree rubs up against the south wall among the slabs of slate on the graves. The old door still has its sanctuary knocker: pushing it open, the impression is of dark oak clustering in a small interior. First comes the screen, probably fifteenth century, taken from the predecessor church which was sited more vulnerably against the slopes. The balustrade from a lost music gallery has been propped on top of it, complete with candle sconces to light the scores at Christmas services. Over the opening at some uncertain time, a pattern of bent feathers has been carved.

A wonderful assembly of candle-lit pulpit, reading desk, altar rails and pews – which are in the sleigh style also seen at Rug – has been here for almost three hundred years. There is an offering tray still hooked to the altar rail. A front pew is inscribed '*Maingc i'r dyla i clyw*' – a bench for the hard of hearing. To the right is the south chapel, with a great stone pillar and a battered old poor box at the entry. To the left on the north wall are the Wynn family's memorials, Maredudd aptly at prayer in full armour.

Among the fine fragments of late medieval glass are the bearded face of Jesus with closed eyes, and a St Christopher. Between these two on a supporting beam for the canopy of honour is the doubleheaded Dolwyddelan dragon, winged, knotted, looking left, right, up and down all at once, and much older than the building. But it is a new-made thing compared to the small bell hanging overhead.

Gwyddelan, the name given to the holy man who founded the church, means 'little Irishman'. In the years around 600 when he came to this lonely spot in the high mountains, the interchange between Welsh and Irish Christian culture was considerable, and Ireland held in great affection here. Holy men used handbells of cast bronze to scare away the spirits of evil. Six hundred years later, Gerald of Wales wrote that both laity and clergy held these bells in great veneration, for their hidden and miraculous power. Could this small bell have been Gwyddelan's own?

A sanctuary in the mountains

Gwydir Uchaf, Holy Trinity

SH 795 608

Rome had Caravaggio, Venice Tiepolo, Paris and London Rubens – but it took the Conwy valley to give us the anonymous master of the Gwydir Uchaf ceiling. He is not usually mentioned in such company, and looking up at his cheerful endeavour in a one-room chapel on the edge of Snowdonia, it has to be admitted that any such connection seems a bit of a stretch. But that might also be wrong. There was a direct line to Gwydir Uchaf from the heart of Rome, and a triumphal new outburst of Italian baroque.

From the riverbank at Llanrwst, Gwydir Uchaf chapel can be picked out on the rising slope of the hills, standing among pines. It was built in 1673 as a private family chapel by Sir Richard Wynn, following the example of his uncle and namesake who raised the Gwydir chapel in the town. Originally the family home was right alongside, surrounded by a deer park and gardens in the latest style, which came complete with ziggurat: its sad remains survive behind the chapel. He marked his commission with a stone bearing his initials over the rounded, moulded doorway, and carved hearts both inside and out which sign it as a labour of love.

The Wynns were no strangers to Catholic tradition: in earlier years they had built churches filled with images of saints, had served Queen Henrietta Maria, and had travelled to Italy for generations. Sir Richard was a friend of Father Petre, the

Italian baroque – Conwy valley-style

Jesuit confessor at the English court, and they corresponded over fitting out the chapel. As it happened, the Jesuits were just refitting their own mother church in Rome: one year earlier they had decided on a painted ceiling – sparking the moment when painters of the high baroque came in from the palazzi to reclaim the church, after decades when ceilings had been architecturally clever, but just plain white. It was to be a new style of masterpiece from Bernini's Genoese protégé Gaulli, filled with celestial beings, dazzling light and a proclamation of the name of Jesus, all spilling over into the architecture – and this appears to be why, whether turning just off the Corso into Piazza del Gesù or climbing up the hill to Gwydir, there is a haloed image of the IHS surmounted by a cross, wrapped around by angels of both two and three dimensions, dissolving into cushion clouds.

But everything that comes to Wales becomes transmuted by it. In Rome the figures swirl endlessly upward in restless adoration and steep aerial perspective. At Gwydir too the heavenly host are up amongst the moon and stars, but their domain is accessibly low and the sky they occupy is a flat zone. They show their desire to reach down, to be earthed by the messages with which they are surrounded – the Son by angels pointing down as well as up, the red-robed Father proclaiming peace to men on earth 'Et in terra pax, in ho: ec.' and the Holy Spirit sending Pentecostal tongues of fire, concerned to fill the hearts of the faithful: 'Et Reple Corda Fidelium'.

Along with this human dimension is the equally characteristic Celtic love of the intricate and mystic power of the number three: the Roman focus on the Son has multiplied into a final outburst of the visionary Trinitarianism of the Welsh high middle ages, burning with light as witnessed centuries before by the Anchorite of Llanddewibrefi. The panels of the Trinity are framed east and west by medieval-style images of Doomsday, though the warning message in a long painted taper cuts straight out of Latin into English 'Watch for you know not ye day or howre'. The painted angels sounding the last trump are placed wittily with the real musicians in the gallery – a more than *trompe l'oeil* three-dimensional effect which would have made Bernini smile and tip his hat. The ideas behind the Gwydir Uchaf ceiling were thus something strikingly new yet achingly traditional, a combination oddly echoed by our innocent painter, who happened to catch the new baroque spirit of clustered shapes of dark and light, while appearing never to have heard of perspective.

All this hangs above an arrangement of furnishings equally contemporary, but this time completely classical and English – just the way Wren was then fitting out the Cambridge colleges of Pembroke and Emmanuel. There are plain flagstones and high panelling of poplar and spruce behind a single pew that runs along the line of the walls. The pulpit faces the door with a large, freely-painted arms of Charles II behind it. The proportions are similar to those at Rug, but despite the addition of colour on the gallery railings and a few well-carved cherubs, the effect here is plain and clean, more theologically focused on the messages from the pulpit, and from the heartfelt schema above.

Holyhead/Caergybi, St Cybi

SH 246 826

All the islands of Wales were holy, a history more obvious in the Welsh language, where almost all of them bear the names of saints. Islands like Seiriol, David, and Patrick have been secularised in English to Puffin, Ramsey and, most unlikely, Middle Mouse. But the special status of St Cybi's Island comes directly through to English, as Holy Island, with its Holy Head.

Holy long before Christian times, its key position between Wales and Ireland in the Age of Saints must have strengthened these associations. Cybi's mission work had more than local reach. It is said he would meet St Seiriol at a mid-point in Anglesey, walking east in the morning, returning west in the afternoon, his face always to the sun, so nicknamed Cybi Felyn (yellow Cybi) distinct from Seiriol Wyn (fair). But most of all he must have looked to the sea. He is linked to Cornwall, County Meath and Poitiers: there are llans named after him far up the valleys of the Teifi and the Usk, and he turned numen at his holy well in Llyn. His churchyard is walled on three sides – the fourth drops away to the open water and the tide.

These are the oldest churchyard walls in Wales: they belonged to the late Roman fort on the site, probably third or fourth century, in which St Cybi set up base, and which are remembered in the Welsh name for the town, Caergybi, Cybi's Castle. At these walls the vast Roman empire ended at its north-western edge. Circular bastion towers remain at the angles, and by the gate is the fourteenth century mortuary chapel of the saint, much restored. Cybi's relics were put on display three Sundays in July, and still in the eighteenth century Rev. Thomas Ellis was speaking out against the superstition of them, asking the town to move these riotous feast days over to Saturdays.

The importance of the church is shown in its cruciform plan, which marks it out like Bangor, Clynnog and Llanbadarn Fawr as a mother church of the *clas* tradition. Like Bangor and Clynnog too, it was substantially rebuilt in the final years of pilgrimage. The high fan-vaulted porch and rich embattled walls of the south side are covered with sculpted creatures – some of the best survivals of early Tudor times, and still shot through with primitive religion. Over the doorway there is a small stately image of God the Father, crowned and bearded, with the crucified Son. Inside, there are carvings above the pillars, extraordinary heads and angels in the crossing arches, and a painting of the Tudor rose by the pulpit. There are angel musicians in the nave, and a pelican in a roof boss. The windows have glass by David Evans from the 1840s, and Burne Jones from 1897 in the south aisle, images of Saints Dorothy, Theresa and Agnes.

The south chapel is filled by a Carrara marble monument to William Owen Stanley, one of the breed of rich Liberal social reformers who swept to national power with Gladstone. He owned five thousand acres on Anglesey and Holy Island, where his amateur archaeology uncovered the 'Irishmen's huts' beside South Stack. The commission was given to G.F. Watts who passed it on to his friend and neighbour Hamo Thornycroft, sculptor of the figures of Cromwell outside the Houses of Parliament, and Gordon on the Thames Embankment, bible in hand, the very model of a Victorian general. Another Burne Jones window shows Jesus carrying a cross of great branches, the stigmata already upon him, Mary and John at his side. A luminous deep green and orange pomegranate window is the work of William Morris.

An earlier William Morris is buried in the churchyard, the customs officer, botanist, choirmaster, manuscript collector, devoted local churchman, one of the four Morris brothers whose letters light up the cultural life of Georgian Anglesey – more serious and sober than his brother Lewis, a rowdy, sociable, unbridled poet and unearther of lost Welsh culture.

Brightly painted chapels line the hill above, Tabernacl, Bethel, Hyfrydle, showing the growth of the port and the drift from the church in the nineteenth century. Behind them, Holyhead mountain rises to its ragged windswept tops.

In whom I am well pleased: a blessing at the doorway

Llanaber, St Mary (St Bodfaen)

SH 599 180

In 1215, the resurgent men of Gwynedd went south in the winter, looking for a fight. They rampaged through the Conquest castles of Cardigan, Cilgerran, Carmarthen, Llanstephan, St Clear's – all the way to Kidwelly, to stake their claim to overlordship of Wales. It was a time of new possibility, and a recognition of the leadership, right across the country, of Llywelyn Fawr. How was this heyday of Welsh confidence and power reflected in the making of a new parish church?

The answer lies on the sea edge at Llanaber: it was ground-breaking, refined – almost delicate, and it was planned in the latest French fashion. An inscription records that it was built by Llywelyn's kinsman Hywel ap Meredydd, Lord of Ardudwy. Contemporary with, perhaps slightly earlier than, the trio of castles at Dolbadarn, Dolwyddelan and Criccieth, it is a major fourth in the set of substantial survivals from Llywelyn's Gwynedd, and the most intact of them all.

Not that this is much apparent in the approach, on a path through something of a monumental masons' outdoor showroom, a glut of marble uncharacteristic of Welsh country churchyards, but which breaks out at the coastlines like the ruffled white edges on the grey sea below. The gravestones remember the lost years of maritime Barmouth, its shipwrights, sea captains and master mariners. Standing on rising ground above a ruined house engulfed in ivy, the wind-worn columns at the outer entrance of the church lead on to a greater display – an eight-shaft, yellow sandstone frame to the main door, with intricate leaf pattern carving. This sophisticated new French style, for many years traded under the misnoma 'Early English', announced the end of heavy Romanesque and the replacement of axe with finer chisel. But something happened in translating France to Wales: the toughness of the stone ensured the carving was in low relief, more pattern than ornament and sparingly applied, while an older and more local tradition persisted in the curling, upward-pushing lines of the sculpted foliage.

Inside, the whitewashed nave has solid cylinders of piers, with finely patterned and decorated capitals in the same style as the doorway, and typically Welsh idiosyncracy to the planning of the patterns. Above the capitals are rows of deeply recessed, pointed arcade arches, rising to a clerestory of four restrained windows on each side. The greatest of the interior arches leads into the chancel, which is raised up five steps by the hillside site, with a further rise to the altar. There is a sixteenth century oak roof which becomes a panelled barrel – a canopy of honour patterned with circles – at the east end, above a single light in the east wall: its tall and slender arch framed in rounded columns may be the designer's finest touch. Behind the altar is a wooden reredos of art nouveau influence, with wheat ears and sinuous vines to symbolise communion bread and wine. At the west end, below two more candle-like windows, is an octagonal font carved with leaves and roses – a Green Man in stone

61

looking out among them. A block of oak has been turned into the alms box.

In the north aisle, the church has two perhaps fifth century standing stones, one which served for crossing a stream before its history was realised and the other, one of the most important in Wales. The inscription on the first says simply and poignantly 'Aetern(us) et Aeter(ni)' – Aeternus (a man's name) and Eternity – or perhaps Aetern(a), a woman. The second appears to say 'to Caelestus, the mountain king': 'Caelexti monedo rigi'. A cross between Latin and something like emerging Welsh (the Latin word for mountain *mons*, the Welsh word *mynydd*), the stone seems to pinpoint an international Roman heritage on its way to provincial variation. Both stones may well predate the first church here – a missionary location chosen by St Bodfaen some years later, that still suggests a first foot put on shore. His name, no doubt the original name and dedication of the church, is still preserved at nearby Bodfan farm.

Gothic comes to Gwynedd

Llandanwg, St Tanwg

SH 568 283

St Tanwg's is a church on the beach, encroached by dunes from which sometimes it has to be dug out. The lychgate on the land side has an entrance way of mammoth stone and small sea cobbles on the floor. On the sea end the dune has gathered round the church in a protective curve, against which gravestones rest in the sheltered hollow. Only the simple bell turret reaches above it. There are traces of an old south doorway, half buried in the sand.

From the dune the views stretch out to Llŷn, to Cnicht and Snowdon. A marine base south of the mountains, Llandanwg seems to have played a key role in the missions of the saints, traced in the trail of fifth century inscribed stones which stretch inland from here. One of the largest – eight feet long, of Irish rock and carved with the name of Ingenuus – is kept by the altar. A sixth century stone forms the sill of the south east window, and a third – somewhat later – has an inscribed cross which shows white in the grey stone of the west gable.

Beneath it is a low stooping entrance to the church, which is a simple oblong of whitewashed, leaning walls, just sixteen feet wide. The floor is laid with huge uneven flagstones, and there are long dark benches across the full width of the nave. A roof of plaster and timber hangs over two impossibly weathered tie beams, constructions in jetsam. The supporting beams along the walls are punctured with chequerboard patterning. There is a long tunnel of darkness – no north window, a small south window – until light floods the chancel from openings on three sides.

In the graveyard are buried the wife and child of Ellis Wynne, rector here for six years from 1705, just after writing *Gweledigaetheu y Bardd Cwsc* (Visions of the Sleeping Poet), his pioneering satire of sinners going to hell. Its opening lines have all the dreaming west coast otherness, as at noon in the "silent warmth and thin clear air", the sleeping bard walks up to the mountain top and looks out over the sea, before his journey with an angel begins. Wynne had his own dreams in a famous folding bed – still to be seen at his nearby house – the cracking sound of which as it was folded away each morning could be heard from Harlech Castle. Just below the east window, with its worn remains of sculpted heads, is the grave of Sion Phylip, one of the last of the minstrel bards, whose elegy for Elizabeth I proclaimed her as heir to the royal blood of Gwynedd. Sion would take to bed to write, emerging several hours later with a complicated *cywydd*. He was drowned at the age of 77 while sailing across Tremadog Bay, and his son Gruffydd wrote an englyn to the 'gentle men' who rowed his body here.

> O fwyn ddynion bob yn ddau – cyfarwydd
> Cyfeiriwch y rhwyfau
> Tynnwch ar draws y tonnau
> Y Bardd trist yn y gist gau.

For forty years or more in the nineteenth century, after a new parish church was built in Harlech, Llandanwg was abandoned, unroofed, left to the sea wind and the fishermen. Its font and bell and furnishings were taken away. It was returned to use in 1884.

Llanddoged, St Doged

SH 806 637

A circular churchyard steeply banked and raised above the road, a stone church with a double nave, and a holy well close by, are among the customary signs of a classic ancient llan. But Llanddoged is different. The first hints are jaunty bargeboards on the gables. In 1839, the church was reinvented inside.

The timing is unexpected. Just when two centuries of interiors dominated by the pulpit were turning over to a new awareness of the altar, Rev. Thomas Davies of Llanddoged made his pulpit heightened, skylit, framed and focused by paintings, arms and exhortations: absolutely centre-stage. There is a reading desk and clerk's desk below it, and box pews range around it theatrically, spreading out over both the naves through the slim arcade of timber posts. Raked pews at the west are separately marked for boys and girls. Something like the stagy courthouse constructed in the same years at Beaumaris, it aims for shared, dramaticised experience. Yet it could only be the product of a country village.

Thomas Davies was responding early, as churchmen were only just beginning to do, to the growing threat of competition from the chapels, which were taking congregations with the *hwyl* and excitement of their preaching and modern, more comfortable and more egalitarian surroundings. His chapel-like seating and his commitment to instruction from the pulpit made a more than expansive gesture in that direction, but the words on the panels show the balance a churchman still had to strike: on one side '*Pregethwch yr Efengyl*' – Preach the Gospel, and on the other '*Anrhydeddwych y Brenin*' – Honour the King. The church had a place in the landed and hierarchical establishment which it could not push aside, and which was seriously constricting to its place in nineteenth century *gwerin* Wales. Yet Davies must have done enough to cross the ground here: his interior still serves, and Welsh is still the language.

The king's arms have been hastily adjusted to cope with the accession, in 1837, of a queen. There are older remnants: monuments of the Kyffin family, Jacobean panelling by the altar, a stone octagonal font. In the east wall are simple sixteenth century trios of roundheaded windows. They look out to the steeply-rising hills and the road to Llangernyw, where the churchyard yew has lingered on for four thousand years, one of the oldest living things in the world.

Llanegryn, St Mary and St Egryn
SH 596 057

The Dysynni valley, running down from the bleak heights of Cader Idris into Cardigan Bay, is still one of Wales's most wild and beautiful. Even in its western reaches, calmer, greener, more agricultural, it is still spiked with outcrops of volcanic rock. There is a point where, looking due south west, a sliver of the sea appears in the distance between two hilltops, and this is the place St Egryn chose to build his church. "One has a feeling", wrote a recent vicar in his loving account of it, "that around this spot, there is something more than the natural eye can see". The village has grown up in the valley below.

Llanegryn churchyard survived in its old circular form until just over a hundred years ago and was then extended, with the lychgate in a different position. Incised in the stone on the south wall of the chancel is a cross, which the sun delineates sharply on a bright day at noon.

The church has one of the finest surviving Welsh rood lofts. Attempts to date it have ranged over an unlikely two hundred and fifty years, from the early fourteenth century to the later sixteenth, extending to both the periods when design in Britain has been at its most exuberant. It has the flash, the skill, the love of nature to set it in the generation whose exotic legacies remain at Ely, Southwell or St Mary Redcliffe, whose lives ran into the shocking wall of the Black Death. But it surely belongs to the early Tudor world, in the late and final flowering of Gothic that came before Renaissance.

The screen is a textbook of the medieval patterning and filigree of international Gothic style, here suffused with Celtic tradition and even better on the east side than

Panels in the early Tudor screen

the west. Here between the ornamented true vine borders are seventeen loft panels, each of them different, some of them bursting with images of new Spring growth. One has the spinning wheel tracery so admired on the House of Desdemona on the Grand Canal in Venice. The wheels of Llanegryn however, (in another Celtic echo?) are spinning clockwise. There have been claims that it belonged to Cymmer Abbey until the Dissolution: tradition has the monks carrying it here over the mountains to save it, but Cistercians, surely, would have taken a more practical route. The story reflects a kind of truth: the tithes, church – rood loft and all – of Llanegryn belonged to Cymmer. The monks brought the dedication to St Mary, and they led the services from the east side in the chancel while the villagers stood in the nave. Thus they kept the best of the screen to themselves, a fertile and abundant garden quite free of the religion on the other side, in the long row of now lost saints: a cheerful Cistercian trait seen again at another of their churches in Llangollen. Llanegryn loft is part of the rich chain of surviving evidence that the white monks were as central to the cultural renaissance in the years around 1500 as they had been to that of the high middle ages over two hundred years before, and that on both occasions, they were right at the creative heart of those strands which were most distinctly Welsh.

The loft is still accessible, now from a small vestry but originally directly from the churchyard. Up here in the 1850s and 1860s the first High Church revival choir in Wales, fully surpliced in white, used to sing – attracting great crowds but backfiring on the patron when the local non-conformists led a strong vote against him at the next election. Higher up the valley until not long before, people travelled to search out Mary Jones, the girl who had walked the twenty-seven barefoot miles across the hills to Bala in search of a Bible, and who would receive curious visitors long into her old age, in a garden buzzing with bees.

The cross on the chancel wall

Llaneilian, St Eilian

SH 469 929

The rocky headlands of Anglesey's north coast were natural territory to the early saints. There seem to be no traces left to find now at Pant-yr-eglwys and Penbrynyreglwys, but lonely medieval churches still stand at Llanrhydrhys and Llanbadrig. By the steep edges of the coastal path at the north east corner of the island, a stream runs into the ruined base of a shelter. This is the holy well of Eilian, a saint of healing power whose cult fed the growth of his shrine church just inland.

In a farming country the well's reputation for blessing the health of sheep and cattle, as well as conjuring miraculous cures for people, must have made it especially sought out, a popularity visible in a church complex altogether grander than the hunkering stone shelters typical of lesser saints. Even well into the nineteenth century people travelled considerable distances to drink from or bathe in the well, and walk over the fields to offer prayers and donations to the church, which was still then producing substantial surpluses for local poor relief.

Llaneilian today is a rambling complex of faded buildings, chopped and changed about throughout the medieval age, then left to its quiet corner for the past four hundred years. From outside, by the crumbling base of the old stone preaching cross, the building's history can be easily read. It has a twelfth century tower, now brightly

A low-walled steep-roofed adjunct between chancel and mortuary

limewashed again after years under dull grey pebbledash, with a rare pyramidal spire of the Penmon style. Adjoining it is a battlemented, moulded exterior of expensive Perpendicular, with a substantial porch, and to the east a passageway, a low-walled steep-roofed adjunct dated 1614 which links, as at Clynnog Fawr, to a mortuary chapel on the site of the saint's cell. The plan of square nave and square chancel links it to the double squares of the ancient churches on the south side of the Menai.

Inside in the plain nave, figures hold shields at the corbels, and Mary in coronation robes has a pulley wheel in her hands. A great timber rood loft swings out from the chancel arch to fill the wall. It is stark with just two narrow rows of ornament – oak and ivy. On the central curving panel a painted skeleton holds a scythe with the message '*Colyn angau yw pechod*' – The sting of death is sin.

In the chancel there are choir stalls of 1533 and a chandelier of 1768 in the grip of a gilded hand. Above in the corbels carved musicians play various kinds of pipes, two blown with the mouth and two with a bag. The church still has a late eighteenth century clarinet and syrinx, which show its windband tradition continuing on to a late Georgian heyday. Stalls, carvings, instruments and a rood loft large enough to hold a good-sized band are evocative clues to the celebratory, music-filled wakes of St Eilian, which must have reeled through churchyard and church over so many centuries. On these days people would get into the old church chest and turn themselves round in it three times, to give themselves health until next year's Eilian's Eve. Another chest, known as Cuff Eilian, would receive their offerings.

A little low door at the far right corner of the chancel opens to the sloping passageway to St Eilian's chapel, where he has been remembered for so long. The first grant of lands came in the early sixth century from Caswallon Lawhir (the Long-Armed) who, we are told, drove the Irish from Anglesey, and who can conceivably be described as a contemporary of Arthur. Ivy intrudes into this bare space with its old wooden roof, and a curious five-panelled altar table inscribed with the first words of Psalm 115.

Piper at the gates of Môn

Llanengan, St Engan

SH 293 270

From the headland and holy well at Braich-y-pwll, the island of Enlli seems to hover on the water, its looming mass of rock a black magnet which for more than a millennium drew trusting bands of pilgrims down the winding roads of Llyn. From inlets like Porth Meudwy they cast themselves on the thin and dangerous races between mainland and their destination – an island abbey which would receive and feed them, and promise them that by being there, at the holiest place in Wales, their after-death journey through purgatory would be swifter.

The island's sacred standing, rooted in pre-Christian times, gathered along the way associations with such holy men as Cadfan, Dubricius and Einion (Engan). So many were rowed out to be buried in their company that Enlli became the 'island of ten thousand saints', and among them, some say, are Merlin and King Arthur.

To do its work, the abbey had an outpost and foothold on the mainland, the church of Llanengan, which has survived while the abbey has not, and has inherited its bells, its three-lock dugout chest, and perhaps its rood screen too. It stands close by the mountain of Garn Fadryn, from which high vantage point the local poet and vicar's son R. Gerallt Jones described looking down at the long chain of Llyn's grey churches, "small flickering places…in the pale evening". The abbey may have owned others of them, and used them for inland shelter in the stormy winters: there are farms at Bryncroes still called Ty Mair, Mynachlog, and Bodgaeaf – Mary's House, Monastery, Winter Stay. Llanengan church is placed precisely where the pilgrims who had walked the southbound roads which linked them all the way from Clynnog Fawr would look out across the great bay of Porth Neigwl, and get their first full sight of their island destination.

A yew-lined path leads to a broad double nave church on a fine stone floor. R. Gerallt Jones believed it to be the oldest extant complete building in Llyn, with one thousand year old walls. Some of it has more the early Tudor look, with the tower added in the last and most prosperous age of pilgrimage, its construction noted by a Latin script in two thin long lines over the west doorway, the message oddly starting on the lower line. 'This belfry was built in honour of St Einion, King of Wales, Apostle of the Scots, A.D. 1534 I.H.S'. The puzzle of the Scottish claim has been attributed to local confusion of St Einion with St Ninian. From here too there is a good view of the priest's room built above the porch, and the convenient provision, wedged against the angle of the tower, of an ensuite garderobe.

Light streams through the open spaces of the naves, which are covered over with ancient timber roofs. Both have rood screens, one of which has a loft, with intricate openwork carving unusually extending to the lower panels. The true vine design threads along the breadth of the screens, and as at Llanegryn, the finer surviving work faces the altar. Especially in the north aisle there are creatures and faces in amongst the flora. With eighteenth century irreverence, members of the choir nailed up their hat pegs on it. There is also a concentrated and more contemplative image of the five wounds of Christ. The choir stalls – those of the Augustinian monks of Enlli – are rougher and could be older than the screen, and the altar rail is later, presumably from the time of Archbishop Laud.

Fashioned for the monks of Enlli

Llanfaglan, St Baglan

SH 454 607

Llanfaglan is the stone walled llan laid bare, a lonely circle in a great green field by the sea. The wind turns off the long tidal beach at Foryd Bay, cutting through the seaward screen of trees on the west wall of the churchyard. Out beyond the dunes and narrows at Abermenai Point lies the low frame of Llanddwyn Island. The view changes from the flat sea to the line of hills along the Llyn and the northwest edges of Snowdonia. Past the top of the field near the farm, there is a holy well with a wide stone seat and wall, also dedicated to St Baglan.

The church in its green circle is a huddle of walls, mostly windowless, with a tall bellcote extending thinly upwards. The lychgate, a small stone building with a tiled and sagging roof and dated 1722 has slate and timber seating and a cobbled floor. The church's deep porch has a sea-weathered fourteenth century truss, stone seats and an ancient sill formed of a stone which must once have been the gravestone of a mariner. Beside the long inscription of a Celtic cross is the unexpected outline of a medieval ship. Its type turns out to be, even more surprisingly, Italian.

Llanfaglan must once have been a landmark on the trade routes, the old sea lanes which rounded north west Wales here, heading far to the south – but it has been pushed to the margins by time. A nineteenth century congregation, facing firmly landward, built themselves a new church in a more sheltered place. Their old church has been left unchanged for the past two hundred years.

An extraordinary gathering of box pews and benches fills the nave and single

Llanfaglan: a lonely circle in a great green field

transept, crowding between whitewashed walls of rough masonry and a roof of ancient timbers, its central truss veering like the line of flags along the aisle. There are crucks projecting on the south side which were for hanging lighting in the darkness of the western nave. Like all the oldest churches of the district, when first built its only natural light came from a window at the east, and from the open door. A large funeral bier is propped up against the wall. Over the doorway is a huge stone lintel with another shared connection to the distant south, a sixth century Latin inscription: Fili Lovernii Anatemori. The font is fourteenth century.

The original nave dimensions make up a double square – another authenticator of Llanfaglan's antiquity – like those of the first Capel Beuno marked out in the floor at Clynnog Fawr. The later chancel is raised on a slate-tiled floor, and its heightened east window encroaches on the ceiling, just as the two decker pulpit's sounding board is crammed against the rafter. In the seventeenth century a transept was cut into the medieval fabric, leaving the tie beam reaching tentatively over the entry. It is lit by deep uneven windows. In it, the largest of the box pews, directly facing the pulpit, is patterned with a rim of small circles. All the others round it are plainer, bearing only initials, and dates which range from 1737 to 1803. The parish population at this heyday was less than two hundred, and when the church's possessions were itemised in 1788, the list started well with "a square silver chalice", but continued to a board of Ten Commandments "most invisible" and ended shortly with "one ladder, two spades, two shovels".

Llangelynin (Conwy): no other llan seems to cut back so far into the past (see overleaf for entry)

Llangelynin (Conwy), St Celynin

SH 752 737

The mountains west of the lower Conwy are thick with the traces of ancient community. Beyond the upward winding roads which peter out at farms there are standing stones, hill forts and hut circles high above the treeline, and a Roman route which finds the pass at Bwlch y Ddeufaen. Almost at a thousand feet, between two wind-torn carns, a switchback dry stone wall snakes over the moor, marking out the llan of St Celynin.

It is an expanse of rough ground, high and exposed, with a well of water in one corner and a fast running stream along the southern wall. The church is crouched in the small fold. No other llan seems to cut back so far into the past: the life of early saints can be imagined here on the days of set-in rain, and as much when it blows clean away, opening up the view across the estuary a short way from the gate.

Five hundred years ago the church was given a stone porch with an arched wooden front, but the doorway and frame are at least a hundred years earlier, and the hinges older still. There is a threshold to step over. The interior is dark and ancient: the narrow stone-walled nave leads forward along old flagstones to the wreck of the rood screen, long ago torn from the posts and grooves which remain. Its lower panels are made of simple boards, some vertical, some horizontal. There were no windows in the south wall until the eighteenth century. Seventeenth century furnishings congregate around the chancel – tall altar railings with twisted balusters, pulpit, communion table, the older pews. There is a barrel roof above them, the frame of a canopy of honour.

On the north side a chapel has been cut into the wall at some time in the sixteenth century. It is raised up steps from the nave, in the steeper land on that side of the churchyard, and there is no flooring, just the mountain earth. Its entrance is framed by a lintel: there is no use here for arches. It is known as *capel y meibion*, the men clustering up here for worship, separated from the women in the nave.

There is a squint from the porch looking out towards the gate, suggesting the lost life of the churchyard and beyond. The well attracted people for healing, and provided water for baptisms. It had its own stone shelter, of which some straggling trace remains. Outside on the mountain are the footings of an old inn, suggesting days when the llan was on a road more travelled, and further along, of a small stone circular building, imagined as Celynin's cell.

Llangelynin thus carries all the signatures of the ancient churches of Eryri: the threshold, the absence of the arch, the double-square dimensions of the nave which pre-date the addition of a chancel or transept, the old interior darkness before the adding of windows. All these holy places of the sea-edge and high mountain are bound together by this common origin of style, a blueprint from the Celtic world still clearly marked in their fabric, most resonant here and at Llanrhychwyn and Llanfaglan.

Llangelynin (Meirionydd), St Celynin
SH 571 072

One of the classic views on this part of the coast must be the sight, framed in a rocklike lychgate, of the bell turret porch of Llangelynin with the blue-grey sea beyond and Bardsey island in the distance, looming out of the haze. Western gales have shaped the frame of this church. The sea-facing west window is the smallest of openings, and to save the bell from being rung all winter by the wind, the open turret has been turned 90 degrees and built on to the south-facing porch. The building seems to have been welded on the underlying rock: the interior floor is like the ragged surface of the rock itself. The lower walls may be as old as now exist in Wales, as near as we can get to the origins. Llangelynin is the Welsh church when it first crawled out of the sea.

The missionary saint Celynin landed here in the late sixth or early seventh century. He has connections with Snowdonia, where another of his churches stands above the Conwy valley, and he is said to be buried on Bardsey. The building now, mostly windowless walls, is mainly of at least five hundred years later. The porch has a strong fifteenth century timber roof, and a sea-stone stoup that used to have a reputation for miraculously filling with water. The miracle now will be to keep the water out: a great crack in the south west wall presages the dampness inside. But neglect and disuse have not been without their rewards.

Llangelynin has the jumbled contents of long ago: a Welsh Commandment board from 1796; two bronze chandeliers of 1845; an old pulpit and the base of a rood

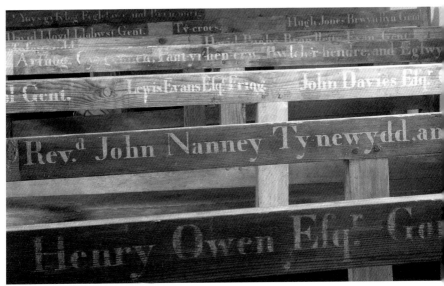

Members of one body

screen; a window for a musicians' gallery; a font in its Celtic position at the centre of the church; pews from the 1820s that still display the names of those who sat there in their organised places (Griffith Owen, David Pugh, Miss Edwards, Jane Rees…). The benches at the back have the names of farms only – for the servants and the hired hands. On the wall hangs a seventeen foot long double horse bier, from the days when in this most rural of parishes, coffins were borne for miles over hills and lanes from isolated farms to reach the churchyard. A resonant photograph survives, men standing at the horses, women at a distance behind, of its last funeral journey down the hill.

Alongside, something of a mural of Psalm 26 has been scraped back into sight. Its words, for a church built on the rock, evidently honoured by its congregation, and so noticeably preoccupied with the careful choice of company, are like a personally chosen signature for Llangelynin. "I do not sit with deceitful men…and refuse to sit with the wicked", says the Psalm, which must have made for interesting glances between Griffith Owen, David Pugh, Miss Edwards and Jane Rees: "Test me, O Lord, and try me." Into this parish with its thoughts thus directed rode an unknown gypsy in a tricorn hat and green swallow-tailed silk coat, all the buttons of which were half-crown coins – the first man, it is said, to play the violin in Wales. His name was Abram Wood. That he and his family were welcomed and absorbed is shown in the presence of his gravestone of 1800 close by the porch, and by the celebrated role of so many of his descendants in bringing their music to the local tradition, by fostering the culture of the Welsh triple harp.

Llangwyfan, St Cwyfan
SH 336 683

At a turn in the road from Aberffraw to Porth Cwyfan, the eye blinks at the sudden sight of a church in the sea. There was a time when the coasts of Anglesey could offer more of this: at Puffin Island and Llanddwyn there are only ruins now. St Tysilio's still stands in the strait beneath the Menai Bridge, remade inside its ancient door. But these three are churches *on* islands. At Porth Cwyfan the church, the llan, *is* the island.

As the sea recedes at long low tide it is possible to walk out over the rocks and swathes of seaweed to the base of the church wall. There is no more raised churchyard in Wales than this, fifteen feet up above a circular wall with stone steps at one side and a grassy floor at the top. It is still not too high for winter storms, when the waves crash over the reefs and fling their spray at the roof.

In recent years its strong and geometric profile, a triangle on an oblong on a circle, with the small outline of the western bellcote echoing the east window, became a mesmerising theme for Kyffin Williams, painting it dark against the green fields of the coast, or lit by the glowing white and grey of the winter sea. Llangwyfan is becoming Kyffin Island.

Up close the belfry is shaped like a keyhole. There is no bell, and no west

The island llan, 100 feet in diameter

window. On the sides there are small round-headed windows and a square-headed doorway. The piled stones of the walls are whitewashed inside, and filled-in arches on the north side show that there was once another aisle – part of a larger church which long since collapsed along with part of the churchyard, sending graves tumbling into the sea. There is a line of stone seating along the wall, and old timbers in the roof. Services are still held in the summer, at times that vary with the tide. Empty of the loose chairs that fill it then, it has a gaunt charm.

Due west from here, across the sea and ten miles inland from the Irish coast, is the ancient holy site of Glendalough, the spiritual bastion of St Kevin, his true name in old Gaelic Coemgen. The Welsh, perhaps, recognised him here by the name of Cwyfan, a possibility which seems real enough in the west-facing, Ireland-oriented, Age of Saints history of Anglesey. His cult extended further east to the atmospheric country church at another Llangwyfan in the Vale of Clwyd, and perhaps also to the great Flintshire roadside cross of Maen Achwyfan, both of them a few miles inland from the north Wales coast.

Aberffraw went on to be a court and capital of independent Gwynedd, and the legendary home of the wedding feast of Branwen. It is a neighbourhood of fine churches: rebuilt Llangadwaladr with the seventh century Cadfan stone and an early Tudor Crucifixion/Resurrection window; the treasurable wayside chapel of St Mary Tal-y-llyn, lovingly restored after recent disasters to its contents, and Aberffraw itself, retaining in its walls the arc of an ornamented doorway of Welsh Romanesque.

Llanrhychwyn, St Rhychwyn

SH 775 616

Llanrhychwyn would have claims enough to special status among Welsh churches for its site in the mountains which rise up west of the Conwy, and for the sunlit presence of its time-worn interior, but it adds to this the sheer antiquity of its walls, roof, font, glass and bell, all of which must be among the oldest of their kind in Wales, and a place in history as the church frequented by Llywelyn Fawr.

This little sacred place remains quite lost in winding lanes, unnamed on the map, the centre of a huge and ancient parish bounding some of Wales's most spectacular and unpeopled scenery. The churchyard stands just off the lane to Llyn Geirionydd, alongside a farm. The lychgate is a deep shelter dated 1762, from which the path leads round the eastern walls of two low-eaved conjoining naves towards the southern door.

This low, round-headed doorway in the thickest of walls is the most ancient part of the fabric, perhaps not far off its millennium, a fragment of old independent Gwynedd. The oak door hangs on wooden hinges in the leaning wall. Llywelyn must have known this slim single nave, walked through this narrow doorway, perhaps was responsible for building the chancel. He may have come here first some time around 1200, when he wrested Gwynedd west of the Conwy to add to his eastern territories.

Inside light enters on three sides to the twin naves with their limewashed walls and old oak furnishings. They fall away a little to the east with the lie of the land. The older south nave, the original church, had the dimensions of a double square before extending to a chancel with visibly thinner walls and a canopy of honour (now plastered over) below a seven hundred year old collar-beamed roof. As in all the oldest churches of the district, there has never been a western window.

The small square font where the two naves join is difficult to date but is certainly early – eleventh or tenth century. When the north nave was added in Tudor times, the line between them was marked not by arches but by simple columns, massive and heavy, balancing the roofs on lintels. The use of slate slabs as at Dolwyddelan suggests the patronage of Maredydd ap Ieuan, the founder of the Wynn dynasty, and his presence is confirmed in the Crucifixion window of 1533, in which he asks in the inscription for prayers. The accompanying saints are David and probably Rhychwyn, now partly missing. Beneath them the communion rails and hexagonal pulpit with long reading desk are seventeenth century; old oak chests and benches spread beyond them. The roof in this aisle is arch-braced, and there is a stone seat across the west end.

The finest glass belongs to the small east window of the older chancel, brown line and yellow stain, a Virgin and Child, and Holy Trinity. Mary is among the oak and acorns, and the face of Jesus, as newborn and crucified, remains unchanged. The Trinity is close-grouped, with Father, Holy Ghost and Son in a descending line, as in the later brass depiction at Beaumaris. But whereas there the Father is enthroned with hand raised up in general blessing, here the picture is more intimate and personal, with more focus on the hand wrapped supportively beneath the bar of the Cross. The installation of this York-style glass around 1460 was perhaps a payment of respect to the Yorkist seizure of power, and it may have been here, inspired by this window, that the Wynn family embarked early on their honouring of the Trinity, one hundred and forty years before they gave it its improbable vernacular apotheosis in red, white and gold, on the ceiling of Gwydir Uchaf.

Intimate and personal: the Trinity at Llanrhychwyn

Llanrwst, St Grwst

SH 797 616

The magnificent setting of Llanrwst can be seen at its best on the heights above Trefriw, from where the town spreads out beside the winding river Conwy in its deep green valley, curved around on three sides by hills and thickly wooded slopes. The quality of the land, at a point where the Conwy can be bridged, produced the riches of the church: a great landowning family here would have much to trade, and much opportunity to do so.

The family were the Wynns, and in 1633 they were riding their fortune at Court, where Sir Richard was Treasurer to Henrietta Maria. That year he attached to the south side of the church a chapel which was to be stuffed full of family memorials, heraldic badges and playful surfaces of intertwining diamonds and circles. There are claims that he used the court architect Inigo Jones both for this and for the elegant neighbouring bridge, but there is no evidence, and the chapel is stubbornly late Gothic – manifestly not in Jones's style.

The Gwydir chapel is rectangular and lit by high clear windows, through one of which there is a memorable view of the grouped gables, roofs and chimneys of the almshouses and the Eagle Hotel. The family would have sat lining the walls as in a chapter house, their own heads making curious company with the ten carved heads whose wide-eyed faces protrude at each end of the stalls. Their sightlines diminished through the years as the clutter of memorials increased: stately pyramidal columns of variegated marble; an alabaster effigy of one month old Sidney; an apostrophe to Margaret Vaughan, heiress of Caergai, described as the Sappho of her age; and to Sarah, Sir Richard's wife who came from Chirk, caught in William Vaughan's superb perspective brass of 1671. A freestone memorial interrupts the floor of alternating black and brown stone diamonds to proclaim 'Funus, Fumus, Fuimus, Ecce' – Death! A vapour! Behold! We have existed – a brief epitome of the years just after Shakespeare and the Morgan Bible: St Paul meets Hamlet, and the medieval and the modern mind conjoin. Two more bearded faces look out from a higher rail. There are heraldic bears, and over the door the winged eagle of the Wynns. After forty years of this, the family decamped up the hill to Gwydir Uchaf, to sit among a new range of equally excited images – but this time finally focused on religion.

The chapel also holds the bare stone coffin of Llywelyn Fawr, who died in 1240. Its quatrefoil niches must have framed some decorative images, probably carved in bronze. The lid has not survived. Perhaps it had a portrait effigy destroyed as too dangerous an icon in a conquered Wales. The effigy nearby is of Hywel Coetmor, who fought for the Black Prince at Poitiers.

The greatest treasure of the nave is the rood loft, expansive enough to be a town commission although others claim monastic origins, pointing to clues such as the monk's head descending from the fretwork in the arches. The emblems of the

Passion, the IHS and the wreathed Cross mingle in the carved oak with emblems of secular power: Tudor roses and dragons, and Catherine of Aragon's pomegranate badge which dates the work as early sixteenth century. In among both are pigs, rootling for acorns. The front of the loft retains the canopies that must have held a full array of saints, and the screen's combination of openwork on upper and lower panels with a vaulted arcade mark it as a fusion of Welsh and English styles.

The nave was rebuilt in 1470, following destruction in the Wars of the Roses, and a tower and north aisle were added over four hundred years later. But the site, on a bend in the river, goes back to the twelfth century when a son gave it in expiation of his father's sin of murder. The victim was Prince Idwal, son of Owain Gwynedd, and brother to Prince Madoc who is said to have reached America three centuries before Columbus. He has a monument at Mobile Bay in Alabama.

Out in the churchyard, there is a grave with iron railings for Robert Williams, a writer of englynion and lyrical sentiments who was born up the mountain at Llanrhychwyn. His bardic name was 'Trebor Mai' ('I am Robert' backwards). The white stone with the Lamb and Flag, the sign of St John, now set in the wall of the almshouse range, came here from Ysbyty Ifan, a base of St John's Knights Hospitaller in the mountains to the west.

The empty tomb: Llywelyn Fawr at Llanrwst

Nanhoron, Capel Newydd

SH 286 309

Towards the western end of the Llyn peninsula there are two small churches, a little less than five miles apart, which retain the simple, rural interiors of late Georgian Wales, an outlook over fields sloping down to the sea, and a form and dimensions as readily used for a cowshed. In between them the wooded ridge which spines down above Sarn Meyllteyrn preserved the separate spheres of Llyn's north and south: Capel Newydd at Nanhoron belonged to the great bays and headlands of the southern shore, sheltering sea-trade along St Tudwal's Road, while Penllech church looked north to a blank and open sea. So it was that – to confound the standard narrative of richer church and poorer chapel – here the church was poorer, filled mostly with the simplest benches, while almost all the chapelgoers sat in gated boxes.

Penllech is the most modest of churches – little more than a barn in a farmyard. Its isolated setting in the fields and moor is resonant of medieval Wales. When seen as a link in the line from the six hundred foot highpoint above to the landing place

The gift to be simple: non-conformity in 1769

83

of Porth Colmon below, there may be something older lingering on. A gateway leads into a small churchyard surrounded by stone walls, and a simple oblong of a building with the bell turret at the far end. The bell chain hangs down against the west wall. Inside, the church is a soft grey, the wash of the pulpit, reading desk, box and bench pews infusing the whole space. Electric light and heat have not intruded here, where candles must have lit each winter service, the candle holders nudging up from pulpit and pew as pattern and shadow in the grey space.

When Capel Newydd – the oldest intact non-conformist chapel in the north – was licensed on 6th October 1769, to such men as William Jones of Rhyd-y-clafdy, Griffith Griffiths of Aberdaron and John Williams from the nearby farm of Saethon, these early independents breaking from the Church were not much concerned with new design. Only the omission of altar and bell, and the inclusion of a second door, suggest a chapel rather than a church. Their converted small stone building stands in a harp-shaped field inclined to turn to miry clay in winter, even in the green mossy floor of the interior which forms an ordered passageway between the boxes and the elders' seat, linking one door to the other. The few open benches are banked on the short wall. The three-decker pulpit is placed at the centre, facing across to the largest of the boxes which is graced also with more daylight: the positions of sitters and preacher influenced in this way the irregular placing and dimensions of the windows. Candlesticks descend on pulleys from the pegged roof timbers. All else is whitewashed and plain: the eye drifting from the pulpit can rest only on the funeral bier.

The same visitors' book – kept with the key at a nearby farm – has sufficed since the 1950s, opening with the names of those who helped restore the chapel then, after the last congregation had gone: a plaque marks their work with a couplet from the glint-eyed local poet and *eisteddfodwr* Cynan. A few modest memorial slates and stones rest outside in the grass, as for 'CW', aged 81 in 1825, who may have been among the first to gather here.

It may seem as though nothing but quiet ritual ever disturbed the peace of these places – but both were engines of independent thought and change. Penllech's humble interior was one of the earliest grammar schools in the country, a day school from the sixteenth century when Henry Rowlands got his education here: he went on to Oxford and the Bishopric of Bangor – a more orthodox career than his Griffith neighbour at Cefnamlwch who became a celebrated pirate. He was one of the new breed of Protestant leaders whose tradition-breaking ways and passion for the Bible spurred on their urgent sense of need to drive away the superstition of the past. The spread of education in Tudor times was inseparable from this religious impulse, which powered the church's role as maker of opportunities for those in rural parishes: the kind of empowerment which ultimately led to the building of chapels such as Capel Newydd.

Rowlands's will shows his desire to build the new society in the local community of his childhood: he is concerned to help its poor and repair the roads and churches but most of all to found a new school at Botwnnog, and send more boys from Llŷn to Oxford. The will is full of his detailed specifications and outbursts of opinion: "The schoolmaster shall be…a good scholar, a Master of Arts…and an Englishman (if it may be) for the language sake"; the poor shall be given clothing – "I do not mean white paltry flannel or black foolish cotton but good boarded frieze whatever it cost"; the way from Cefn Leisiog to Rhos-ddu needs mending – "a very wicked bad way, God wot" and Ellen Trygarn, a "fatherless girl that is without help" is to have a cow, a young bullock and a feather bed, but not marry without the Dean's consent "or else never to have a penny of it".

There were soon those whose education led them into challenge with the Church. The Edwards family of Nanhoron was firmly on the Puritan side in the Civil War, over a century before the building of the chapel down the lane. When Captain Timothy Edwards died at sea in 1777, catching gastric malaria in the Caribbean after naval battles with the French, his widow Catherine placed his memorial in the nearby parish church at Llangian, but found her stimulation and her solace at the chapel: one of her books is kept here by the pulpit.

The memorials at Penllech carry other signs of more than ordinary scholastic traditions. The gravestone of John Bodfan Anwyl remembers him as "poet, lexicographer, minister" –

> Wedi bwriad y bore – a'i obaith
> Rwy'n gwybod o'r gore
> Y daw'r alwad o rywle
> Gyda'r hwyr am dwg i dre
>
> [In the morning
> I hoped to know the answer
> – to know when the call would come.
> The evening came to carry me home.]

He was only carrying on the local imperative. An earlier lexicographer minister of Penllech, Daniel Sylvan Evans, was curate from 1848 to 1852 and compiled his English-Welsh dictionary here, going on to edit Lewis Morris's attempt at "a Critical, Historical, Etymological, Chronological and Geographical dictionary of Celtic…names of men and places", and embarking, years later, on a definitive Dictionary of Welsh. He died in 1903, having reached the letter E.

Penmon, St Seiriol

SH 631 808

Penmon is a magical promontory, jutting out from the south east edge of Anglesey. A single road leads past the curve of hills to the headland. The gaze takes in the mesh of land and sea, a blue arena where the Great Orme, Ynys Seiriol and the snow-capped mountains of Eryri dip into the sheltered strait. To the Age of Saints, it was made to be studded with churches: on the Orme the ancient llan of St Tudno; on the island the standing tower and ruin of a monastic refuge; and on the southern-facing slope Penmon. If you were sailing round the Irish Sea, fifteen hundred years ago, as other men were doing in earnest, looking for a base which would speak for the beauty of Creation, at Saint Bees or the Calf of Man you might worry about the west wind, at Howth or Killiney about the east wind; at the Isle of Whithorn about the northern cold – but at Penmon, you would know you were home. St Seiriol has been remembered, literally, as the blue-eyed boy, the memory of his face borne forward in the fair blue mountain flower known in Welsh as *Llygad Seiriol*, Seiriol's eye.

The road turns to run alongside a rambling range of buildings, half ruin, of a medieval Augustinian priory. Against the backdrop of the hill, the group rises to a tower, its second stage made harmoniously square by the running of a string course, its third stage a pyramid of stone with the outside cut to pitch, a rare precursor of the spire. It could belong in Gascony or the Auvergne, but it is part of the heritage of the old independent land of Gwynedd. Further along is a great domed dovecote with a lantern, and simple openings in the sides to let the birds fly in and out. The upward view inside is of a curve of stone, a chequerwork of ledges for a thousand birds and spiral steps around a central column, from which wooden ladders would have reached up to the higher walls. It has become a squat for swallows.

Opposite, a path runs beside a fishpond and a line of trees to a walled enclosure where the holy well of Seiriol is cut into the rock. There is a kind of outer room, with ledge seats on three sides. The inner room was probably more private and closed off, an angled squint providing light but no view in for those outside. From the doorway the distant mountains gleam on the Menai. An oval trace of stone in the ground may be the last remains of the cell of Seiriol himself.

The old way to the church was from the far side, to an ancient south doorway still unprotected by a porch. Patterns of cable and zigzag, and single stone columns with cushion capitals date it to around the 1140s. The face of the lintel has been carved into a creature once thought to be a dragon, its head turned fiercely east: the description has lately diminished to 'dog-like'. The weather is wearing it away. Beyond the doorway is a nave of the same date, early Romanesque with windows placed high, small and deeply splayed; the arch to the tower incised with figures, chevrons and chequer; a doorside stoup and a pillar piscina. An ancient standing cross at the west end has Viking patternwork mixed with carved figures, at eye level when kneeling, laid out in the Irish High Cross style. This was the cultural fusion of the tenth century islands of the Irish Sea, the air which Anglesey breathed when Dublin was a Viking base and the Isle of Man belonged to Norway. The image is of the temptation of St Anthony, assailed on either side by beasts with bird-like heads, and the patternwork includes the characteristic ring chain of Gaut Bjornson, the Isle of Man-based sculptor who sometimes signed his work and declaimed his achievement, centuries before most artists did so.

The south transept, entered through another great carved arch, has chevrons on the walls in an arcade which bunches up at the end in a typically uncalculated way. A window contains some remnants of St Christopher in fifteenth century glass, filled out by the Victorians. There is a second thousand year old preaching cross here which

One of Penmon's thousand year old preaching crosses

has affinities to Anglesey's numerous geometric fonts. Some of its abstract lines turn into serpent heads.

But the church is nowadays approached from the east side up a handsome curving stairway dated 1709, which leads into the courtyard where the cloister may have been. Ahead is the steeply gabled 'prior's house', and to the left the ruin of the monks' domain, three storeys of cellar, dining room and dormitory on top. The reading seat by the refectory window still survives, and an elongated lancet in the west wall. The way in to the church leads to a cool Victorian chancel which preserves from the medieval building only the unusual drop in level from the nave, and a tiny damaged champlevé enamel from Limoges, Jesus in a nimbus, his right hand raised in blessing. It is hard now to imagine pilgrims pressing by St Seiriol's shrine, another scene from Penmon's lost and fragile past which these interiors falter to convey. Best to come here on a summer evening, the ancient buildings casting haunting shadows, night air drifting in from the sea. Bells are ringing out in the high belfry, and in the stone, a dragon is breathing.

The old south doorway to the Priory

Tywyn, St Cadfan

SN 588 009

Tywyn is the Welsh word for shoreline, and from the *tywyn* at Tywyn, the great sweep of the west coast curves out to Enlli in the north and Pen Caer in the distant south. When, in the Celtic years, the Irish Sea was the humming centre of trade and cultural exchange, Tywyn was at the heart of things. According to the *Book of Llandaff*, St Cadfan arrived here with his own set of twelve apostles to establish a *clas* and spread Christian knowledge inland from the early sixth century. Later he moved on to Enlli, where he launched that island into the mystic holy role that so inspired medieval Wales, but the Cadfan connection kept Tywyn thriving for centuries.

The church is set back a few hundred yards from the shore. From the outside, what appears is Rev. Titus Lewis's vision of recreation – a tower, transepts and choir added just over a hundred years ago to complete again what may have been the mid-twelfth century picture. The nave is the real thing, its massive presence unmistakable on entry. Its short cylindrical pillars and low round arches are as simple and plain as the whitewashed walls. Four small roundheaded windows (one square-headed on the south) are cut through on both sides, setting up a loose, not quite in-sync rhythm with the arches below. The use of aisles at Tywyn is unusual and contrasts with the aisleless naves of other near-contemporary *clas* churches, such as that surviving some miles south at Llanbadarn Fawr.

Like Penmon, Tywyn nave is another survival of the Welsh Romanesque of independent Gwynedd, and they were both built in the time of Owain Gwynedd or perhaps his father Gruffydd ap Cynan, the native prince who made his country glitter with white churches "like the heavens with stars". Gruffydd's cross-border patronage of St John's in Chester and of Christ Church in Dublin, the childhood home of his royal Viking mother, shows the orientation of his world. The abbot of the time was Morfran, subject of a poem by Llywelyn Fardd, who relished his military qualities.

Tywyn went on to be an Augustinian college, whose members lived and worked here just as in the *clas* which it replaced. Two of its sculpted monuments, lodged on the north side of the chancel, are amiably known now as the 'crying knight' and the 'unnamed priest'.

The crying knight is a grand recumbent effigy from around 1350, in hauberk, surcoat, pointed bascinet. His right hand reaches across to grasp the hilt of his sword. His right eye is usually crying. A small black fault in the stone, at the cleft of the open eye, gathers moisture from the air which seeps slowly down across his face. He may or may not be 'Griffith ab Adda of Dolgoch and Ynysmaengwyn, Sheriff, who died in the fourth year of Edward III', which a nearby, much later Latin inscription claims.

The unnamed priest is probably a few decades older. He lies under a decorated, cinquefoil arch, carried by angels, and his feet rest on lions. He is caught in the moment of giving communion, in full dress with eucharistic alb and chasuble, his hood drawn over his head in an atmosphere of mystery. The presence of the only other such priest-image in Britain at east coast Beverley Minster, and the deep folds and long sweeping lines close in style to the early tombs of Westminster Abbey, convey Tywyn's new orientation in the time of Edwardian rule.

In the north aisle of the nave stands Tywyn's oldest and greatest treasure, a tall, slim stone incised with a cross at the top. It has two eighth century funeral inscriptions spread along its four faces: the oldest surviving piece of writing in the Welsh language. Through the wear and weathering, they record simply the names of two wives, Cun wife of Celen, and Tengrui beloved wife of Adgan, and then only, '*Erys poen*' – Grief remains.

Gwynedd Romanesque: the nave is the real thing

II

The North East

Denbighshire, Flintshire, Wrexham

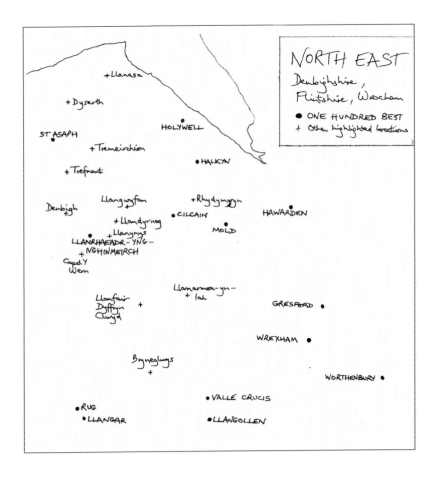

NORTH EAST
Denbighshire,
Flintshire, Wrexham
● ONE HUNDRED BEST
+ Other highlighted locations

+ Llanasa

+ Dyserth

ST ASAPH

HOLYWELL

+ Tremeirchion

+ Trefnant

● HALKYN

Llangwyfan
+

Denbigh
+

+ Llandyrnog

+ Llanynys

LLANRHAEADR-YNG-
+ NGHINMEIRCH

Capel Y
Wem

+ Rhydymwyn

● CILCAIN

MOLD

HAWARDEN ●

Llanfair
Dyffryn
Clwyd   +

Llanarmon-yn-
+ Ial

GRESFORD ●

WREXHAM ●

Bryneglwys
+

WORTHENBURY ●

● RUG

● LLANGAR

● VALLE CRUCIS

● LLANGOLLEN

Cilcain, St Mary

SJ 176 651

Cilcain is one of the large ancient parishes of Flintshire, spreading out below Moel Famau, the mother of mountains, the highest of the Clwydian range. The church enclosure, still raised by over six feet on the north side and evidently once circular, conveys its dark age Celtic origins. Set among poplars and horse chestnuts, it has a hearse house by the lychgate and stands across the road from a cottage which was once the village school, and the White Lion pub, as old a building as much of the church.

The body of the church is two naves and a western tower, its walls a rough assemblage of local rubblestone, siltstone, limestone and sandstone. Moses Griffith painted it on a day of cloud and sunlight in 1799, and called the picture 'Kilken'. It shows the rounded windows of the northern nave, which had been much rebuilt that century – the earlier version had burned down one Christmas dawn at the close of a candlelit carol service known in Welsh as *plygain*.

The south nave, not quite matching in dimensions, is fifteenth century. Its astonishing interior roof is reminiscent of Llangollen for its bold alternating hammerbeams and angels with huge folded wings. But their much greater closeness to eye-level gives them a uniquely massive presence. It is as if this roof was designed to stand on much taller walls. The way it changes style not quite at the start of the chancel, and its arcades go out of line with the arches in the wall, seem to back up the view that it came from somewhere else. But it is unwise in Wales to conclude too much from a little irregularity.

The angels bear the symbols of the Passion such as the hammer and the three great nails of the Crucifixion, but the roof also has its grinning grotesques and a curious couple on the north side, depicted sheltering by a pillar. Their wide eyes, long beards and jerkins place them with the motley crew above Llangollen nave: they may be the creations of the same wry local craftsmen, working for the circle of Cistercians and their lordly sponsors. Wall plates bear the fleur-de-lys of Mary, the favoured saint of the Cistercians and the dedicatee of Cilcain. These things suggest a link to nearby Basingwerk Abbey, which was certainly continued in later years when the Mostyn family – relatives of the Tudors who had fought at Bosworth with a troop of Flintshire miners – owned both the abbey grounds and large amounts of Cilcain parish: there are several memorials to them here. The fleur-de-lys extended a tradition of carving plantlife in threefold motifs which are also evident on Cilcain's Romanesque font and on several of its medieval tombs.

The sixteenth century painted glass in the east window has the only depiction in the country of the Virgin weeping at the Crucifixion, but it is the restraint and sophisticated use of colour which mark it out. Mary turns her face away while John gazes prayerfully at Jesus's slumped head. The vertical of the cross is barely suggested, and in most of the picture plane the glass is left stark and clear to create a stripped down focus on the drama of the figures. The royal reds and blues reserved for the Holy Family are balanced by softer greens and purples in John's clothing, colours reused across the landscape to bind the whole scene together. Golgotha – suggested by a few strewn bones and a well drawn skull – stands in curving hills evoking those outside. St Michael with a dragon, and St Peter, tonsured as a monk, look out from either side.

Cilcain's other treasures include painted boards with the Ten Commandments, and verses from the Welsh Bible, and by the west wall a propped up stack of remnants of fourteenth century tombs which contain some rare and evocative survivals. One shows a woman with a vase-like Modigliani neck, her hands held up in a gesture conveying prayer, a more primitive echo of the tomb of Joan, wife of Llywelyn Fawr, now in the porch at Beaumaris. Another has a diagonal sword and heraldic shield carved among oak foliage. Made like many other contemporary memorials in the region from a close-grained grey stone found in northern Flintshire, it would seem to come from a local workshop, perhaps just one family, who worked in the years between the conquest and the Black Death, sending their productions out by boat along the northern coast or up the Dee to places such as Valle Crucis. These carvings represent the end of an era in being among the last in low relief – the next generation expected fully sculptural effigies – and in another way a new beginning. On this stone like many of their others, there is a lion rampant on the shield. Heraldry had belonged to the conquering army, and the defeated

In the company of angels: a motley crew above the nave

Welsh had no coats of arms of their own: now they were trying to adopt the forms of their new world. On this stone too, a hand grasps the sword a little out of its sheath: it remains ambiguous as to whether it is being drawn in a warlike gesture of defiance, or being returned, like Iorwerth Ddu, the man memorialised, to rest in peace. It is hard to think of how this generation could have better represented how they felt.

John Douglas, the architect of Halkyn, restored and adapted the church in the late 1880s, putting in new pews, closing off the north nave with partitions, and adding the porch, together with wrought iron gates made around 1720 by the Davies family, which came from the church at Mold.

Golgotha in the green Clwydian hills

Gresford, All Saints

SJ 346 550

The wholly unexpected sight of this great tower and tall clerestoried nave begins the seeming mystery of a huge and sumptuous church in a small village; a border church, English-style but full of Welsh inscriptions; a Tudor arts and crafts master-piece whose ways are marked by a yew tree and an altar which predate the Age of Saints; a glasshouse church with a range of late fifteenth century painted images which remains, even after damage of time and accident, one of the finest gatherings in Wales. It all suggests a secret source of wealth, long before the modern mine which ranged underground along the Alyn seam. Its memorials are for the local gentry of Gwersyllt, Trevalyn and Llay Hall, for the lost Catholicism of medieval Wales, and for the 266 miners still sealed in their dark tunnels, who were killed in a wall of fire around two o'clock in the morning on the 22nd of September 1934, when all the neighbouring villages woke to the wailing of women.

The wealth came from pilgrimage, to see the miraculous image of Mary once held inside the church – and from the aristocratic patronage it attracted. It funded a considerable rebuilding of tower, nave and chancel in the late fifteenth and sixteenth centuries, and a pilgrim procession path within the church which can still be traced despite subsequent alteration.

The pilgrims came up the north aisle to the Madocks chapel, the morning sun lighting up scenes of the birth and motherhood of Mary, and stories from the Golden Legends, where suddenly they were face to face with their destination image in its niche (lost, presumably, at the Reformation). When they turned their eyes beyond it, the great east window blazoned Mary's place among the Trinity, her hands upheld in blessing as she rests against her thorn-crowned son. Beneath her, 108 saints and seraphim in seven rows sing out the *Te Deum*, "We praise you, O God, we acknowl-edge you to be the Lord......", the Latin words strung out among the figures in a true church of All Saints. The pilgrim path then led them on behind the altar, in an extension of the church made for the purpose, by which the base stones of the old east wall became the reredos, and a sunken passageway (now hidden behind doors) led between rounded arches. Up above was a probable musicians' gallery, the clues to which are the blocked entries on the high walls – not windows, because they have no glazing grooves, but doorways.

Out they came into the shock of the Trevor chapel, intense in its colour and its images of martyrdom, embodied in the scene of Herodias, mother of Salome, defer-ring a dish of sucking pigs to get her knife stuck in to the Baptist's severed head. The Trevor effigy below, a curiosity of 1589, is a different kind of carve up, head and legs, but nothing in between. It is as good an overture as any to Gresford's extraor-dinary collection of pre-Renaissance carving in wood and stone – the disembodied sword-wielding arm of Goronwy in the north aisle; recumbent chain-mailed Madog in the south; the octagonal pilgrim-badged font; oakbeamed angel roofs and delicate pierced or vaulted screens; the choir's figured poppyheads, crouching beasts, and angel armrests. Its picaresque misericords are themed with predators in the presence of their prey: a fox among hens, cats playing with a rat, lions with a lamb (or fox?), a devil mixing with souls and, resonating in this company, the Angel and the Holy Spirit approach the young Virgin Annunciate.

Among all this, casually positioned on the floor in the south aisle, is a Romano-British altar, fourth century or older, to Morta, the Fate who carries, as depicted on the stone, the shears which cut the thread of life. It is thought that offerings to her were placed in the hollow on the top. This is the Fate to which, in *A Midsummer Night's Dream*, Bottom – in character as Pyramus – makes his cry of comic despair beside an animated wall, an act first performed in the same years as they were topping out the tower of Gresford church. This might seem nothing more than pure coincidence, but for the curious fact that both church and play shared the same artistic patron: the courtly Stanley family who first gave Gresford's great east window a hundred years before, and for the marriage of whose newly titled earl William the *Dream* is thought to have been premiered on 26 January 1595, in the presence of Queen Elizabeth herself. The date was, incidentally, four days before a new moon, the night and time signalled by Duke Theseus in its opening lines. The Stanleys were the power and the protection behind two of Shakespeare's acting companies in the late 1580s and the 1590s: Derby's Men and Lord Strange's Men, both named from family titles. The Dream connection sheds a new and fascinating light on the older portrait carving of a Stanley – depicted wearing asses ears – on a corbel in Wrexham nave. It all suggests some family in-joke at work behind the play, which William must have looked back on pleasurably when he retired, after a life at Court, to a fine house nearby beside the Dee.

There are two eighteenth century brass candelabra in the nave, and the outside walls of Gresford church are rich with medieval sculpture. The key image of Mary is crowned above the south porch. A figure on a south west niche of the tower, once suggested as Henry VII, may be Christ in Majesty. High above them, stone figures move among the pinnacles on top of the tower: a king, a sleeping man, a pilgrim shading his eyes, looking out into the distance. The tower chamber holds Gresford's famous peal of bells. Below the battlemented parapets of the aisles, strange beasts and gargoyles, flowers and human faces, wrap around the walls. The ring of yews was planted in 1726, to accompany a grand survivor by the south east gate, one thousand six hundred years old.

Scenes from the Golden Legends: Mary glorified at Gresford

Halkyn/Helygain, St Mary the Virgin
SJ 209 712

Those who go exploring the churches of North Wales begin to recognise familiar touches of the same late Victorian architect, among the Denbighshire moors, out west of Snowdonia, as far south as the Mawddach, and most of all in a heartland by the north east borders. It is easy to come to think of him as an old friend.

He has never had the level of recognition of his leading contemporaries and near-contemporaries, the London men like Pearson, Street and Scott, all of whom built to commission in Wales over the same years, planting their style indifferently across the regions. But he can match them for sensitivity to detail and love of materials, and his work is rooted in the borders tradition of carpentry, vernacular style, of horizontal more than vertical lines, and of integrated, almost domestic interiors at a time when domestic architecture was in its golden age. He represents the best of the Arts and Crafts movement in the north.

His name was John Douglas, and he practised from the cathedral close in Chester for over half a century. He put his stamp on the cathedral approaches, buying up the east side of St Werburgh Street and building the timber-framed ranges which form one of Chester's most recognised scenes. It is only here that there is a small posthumous plaque recording his work: in his lifetime he eschewed such things, remarking once that the way of the 'old fellows' who built the medieval churches was to put their faith, not their names, into their work.

He built for the Duke of Westminster for over thirty years, a partnership which brought a characteristic look to many smaller buildings across the huge estates extending west from Eaton Hall, well into Denbighshire and Flintshire. The Halkyn estate had been a major source of Grosvenor wealth: the lead ore in the mountain attracted huge prices even early in the eighteenth century – such a temptation for Hugh Lewis, the rector of the time, that he tried to get permission to mine through the graves in the churchyard. The new church commissioned and built in 1877-78 began with great advantages: money; empathy between patron and architect, and the skills of the estate's master craftsmen – the stone mason Edward Edwards, who owned the quarry at Pant-y-pwll-dwr, and the joiner Richard Parry. Douglas's father had also been a joiner, and his immersion in these things from childhood shows in his exceptional feeling for carpentry.

Together they produced an interior which unites congregation and priest as one group, the chancel wide and visually open, slightly raised but fully accessible under a distinctive six sided roof and drawing in light through a massive east window, the lines of which continue downward to integrate with reredos and altar, where there are paintings of the Last Supper, Annunciation and Commission. The craftsmanship is at its best in the great roof, the slim carefully made windows of monochrome glass, and the choir stalls, with pierced and traceried panels and images of sunflowers and circles, which crop up on the bench ends as a modern take on medieval poppyheads.

The guiding spirit is of comfort and dialogue: the whole space seems to convey the confidence and pleasure of the makers. It is all so natural that it comes as a surprise to realise how avant garde it was for 1877. At Halkyn Douglas had come into his own, chiming with a new age and style so different from the cool High Victorian grandeur displayed not far away at Gilbert Scott's Trefnant. He went on to indulge himself with half-timber churches across the border at Altcar and Hopwas, and stone Cheshire churches such as Warburton, a clear descendant of the Halkyn plan. His finest later work in Wales can be seen at Bryn-y-maen in the hills above Colwyn Bay, more radically conceived, with its great west wall of ashlar stone broken only by a central frame of glowing glass.

A defaced crucifixion image from Halkyn's medieval preaching cross, the heads of Mary and John tilted dramatically upward, has been preserved in an outside wall buttress. A yew circle and a hidden spring are the other memorials of the earlier church.

Medieval remnant preserved in an Arts and Crafts classic

Hawarden/Pennarlag, St Deiniol

SJ 315 659

When Catherine Glynne married William Gladstone here in July 1839, the church 'crammed to suffocation with females', the Glynnes of Hawarden linked themselves to the man who would go on to save the fortunes of their estate – and of their parish church, which was to need almost total restoration after gutting by fire in 1857. Because of that reshaping, the building has come to reflect unusually closely a man and a family – and also, of course, because the man went on to be Prime Minister for an unequalled four terms. Devout, determined, and filled with boundless energy, he might be found striding the thirty five miles over the hills to Penmaenmawr to take a 'seabathe', or immersed in his library retreat, while wrestling with the not insignificant challenges of governing one third of the earth.

His memorial in the church where, when at home, he worshipped every morning is a small side chapel with a resplendent Arts and Crafts-style monument by Sir William Richmond, whose work began sombrely with a fine pencil study, now in the National Portrait Gallery, made at the death bed. The monument depicts Catherine and William, who shared a 59 year marriage, in the boat of life, a magnif- icently-winged angel at the prow, accompanied on their journey with the images of Christ and the patron saints of Britain, and allusions to Homer and Dante, the lifelong companions of his imagination.

When the family turned to Burne Jones for the church windows – there are seven here to his designs – they were turning to an old friend. They had long been in political sympathy, liberal and anti-imperial. Gladstone had made him a baronet, the first artist ever to become so. Burne Jones was closest perhaps to Gladstone's daughter Mary. He drew her at Hawarden one evening in 1879, at one of the midsummer house parties she used to compose for her father, while the group had gathered to listen to a reading of *Emma*. She leans forward reflectively, a person intimately known, her eyes intense, as though artist and model both strained against the unearthly pull of his style. Her friend Ruskin admired its somehow not quite complete serenity.

The great west window was to be Burne Jones's last work. He had lately been hailed as a forerunner by the new young generation of Symbolists in Paris, but he was looking older than his years, battered by the death of William Morris which, he said, had left him "quite quite alone". In this Nativity the mood is deeply withdrawn. The watchers at the scene look inward. There is no signature maiden looking out to capture the viewer in her cool gaze. Beyond a row of angels who have turned their backs, the face of the child is hidden. The picture's other-worldly stillness is framed in angular glass which is sometimes abstract, and carries astonishing bursts of colour, like the deep shepherd green, and angel wings of Tiffany blue. Burne Jones's colours, wrote one critic, never glow, but he can never have been standing in Hawarden chancel, on any fine late afternoon, when the sun is going down.

Outside, the view from the north looks down the long slopes towards the estuary of the Dee, and makes clear why this place would have been hard fought in the early border struggles, and has a name in old English as well as Welsh. On this north wall there is a small sculpture of the Virgin and Child, as child-like as the Child has ever been.

Time of confinement: Burne Jones's valediction

Holywell/Treffynnon, St Winefride (Gwenfrewi)'s Well Chapel

SJ 185 762

The holy wells of Wales were once as commonplace as churches, drawing every outcrop of spring water into association with religion, legend and cult. So ancient and deep-rooted was their value to communities that it seems likely the early Church had to bind them into its system of belief as part of winning souls. Most are now lost or forgotten, and those which survive for the most part overgrown. Many are in or near churchyards, and suggest that the dual location was important: Llangybi, Llandeilo Llwydiarth, Gumfreston, and Llanrhaeadr-yng-Nghinmeirch are among the most numinous.

But the greatest of them all has been recognised for centuries simply by the name of Holywell. St Winefride's Well in its (lost) heyday was a surging torrent bursting from the ground which seemed to embody fertility, purity, and the regenerative spirits of the earth. "It boils up", wrote Pennant in the late eighteenth century, "with a vast impetuosity".

All through the middle ages pilgrims flocked here in great numbers, daring the treacherous sands of the Dee, lighting torches to summon boats across the Mersey, or following from the west the route of Gawain towards the foreshore, with the isles of Anglesey away to his left. They were coming to give thanks, or regain health, or simply to see the place of martyrdom of 'sweet St Winefride', a seventh century Welsh princess, and the niece of St Beuno.

The most concise and poetic evocation of her life was written in the fifteenth century by the Iâl poet Tudur Aled. His 'Cywydd Gwenfrewi Sant' conjures up her murderous beheading by a local chief, setting off the stream of water where her head fell. Her uncle interceded by prayer to bring her back to life, and she lived on for years as Abbess at Gwytherin in the Denbighshire moors, although, says Tudur, her pure white neck was always jewelled with a scarlet, circling thread. The *cywydd* sings to its listeners to come to find blessings at her laughing, bubbling, health-giving stream which, it joyously proclaims, dwarfs the Tigris and Euphrates:

> Dyfriw gwaed, fel dwfr a gwin
> Dwyn iwch wyrthiau dan chwerthin,
> Crechwen gwraidd crychwyn groywddwr
> Coel iechyd ynt – clochau dwr

No other Welsh saint made such an impact across the border. A succession of medieval kings was drawn here: Richard the Lionheart, Edward IV and Henry V, who showed himself a devotee of Winefride by marking his return from victory at

Opposite: the vaulted canopy above Gwenfrewi's stream

Agincourt by pilgrimage first to Shrewsbury, where her relics had been taken from Gwytherin in 1138, and then on foot to Holywell itself. She was the special saint too of William Shakespeare's father John.

The rich Perpendicular well chapel was built at the end of the fifteenth century. Despite the long diminishing of its surroundings, and considerable damage of dirt and time which has given its interior a cave-like intensity, there is still nothing else quite like it. Its uniqueness comes from being built directly over the water, so that it rises up on slender cluster-pillars out of the source, which is framed in the form of an octagon. The vaulted canopy above is filled with sculpted bosses and pendant capitals, the largest of which hangs over the well centre, displaying six eroded scenes from the life of the saint, with the arms of England and Wales on the underside. Other arms in the ceiling demonstrate the rank of its patrons – the crown and three pomegranate shield of Catherine of Aragon, the emblems of the Stanleys, the head of the abbot of Basingwerk. The right hand entrance has a snarling Tudor dragon.

One corbel shows a pilgrim carrying another on his back, as would have been done to take the lame through the water a required three times, in an echo of Celtic rites. A large irregular stone on which Beuno himself once sat is still there beneath the water. In the chapel room above, from which all pilgrims once descended by an inner staircase to the luminous well below, the carving is equally prolific, with fabulous beasts, grotesques and harvest scenes alongside the emblems of the Passion and more heraldry.

Towards the 1800s, things had got more prosaic. Pennant felt that the permanent mark of the saint's blood on the stones was the product of a vegetable plant called *byssus jolithus*. The rushing water was powering new industry. Milner wrote in 1806 that "the whole scenery must have been at once beautiful and sublime in the extreme, before it was broken and polluted by modern manufactories, dwelling houses and wash-houses." But he was struck by the case of Winifred White, a 26 year old shopkeeper's servant from Wolverhampton, whose intense back pains and loss of the use of limbs had been deemed incurable by her doctor. With one bathe at Holywell on 28th June 1805 she was immediately cured, and carried half a hundredweight and walked for six miles to prove it. By 1898, Frederick Rolfe noted drily that the local church denied all evidence of cures, but the local doctor thought otherwise. Holywell had gone mad, he said: it should close the well and start a bottling plant. But another century on the pilgrims still arrive, as they have done continuously for nearly one and a half thousand years.

Llangar, All Saints

SJ 064 425

A quintessential Welsh country church, Llangar has that defining combination of serendipitous vernacular charm and serious precision of location and meaning. The place at which one river pours itself into another has held sacred power since long before the Christian era, and Llangar watches over the confluence of the Alwen and the Dee in a green and undulating landscape which seems designed for praise and for heart's ease. The body of the whitewashed nave hugs into the steep slope of the churchyard field, the ground pressing up against the base of the east window, the north wall leaning out. Lines of table tombs and small semicircular headstones tilt and sway with the hillside while staying curiously aligned to the lie of the church. These are modest graves – their preponderance of initials over names and their absence of poetry gives unusual reticence and mystery to the lost congregations of Llangar. Many are eighteenth century, like the broad stone lychgate at the entry to the llan.

There is a bench at the top of the churchyard. The novelist John Cowper Powys liked to sit here, late in life, looking out over the still tombs and roofs at the river flowing quietly down the valley, this creator of intense and febrile landscapes and fateful human complications, self-confessed "terrifyingly formidable genius", in disguise of outward calm. He was a proud descendant of an ancient Welsh family, many of them preachers, John Donne among them. From here, it is possible to see the former fording point on the river where some of the congregation had to cross to attend services, and across the valley the roof of Gwerclas, the house from which the local squire and his family came by boat, disembarking no doubt at some small lost jetty down below the church. Once on a day of rising flood, one of the family was drowned.

The church door has an englyn carved into it, dated 1654, which evokes the white deer (*garw gwyn*) said to have been found here and to have given the llan its now abbreviated name. The old single-chamber interior has been preserved by the congregation's decision, one and a half centuries ago, to move to a new church nearer where most of them lived. Under the framing arches of the wooden roof is a close-packed gathering of eighteenth century furniture, faded medieval murals and a deep gallery approached by a twisting back stairway.

All the box pews are on the north side of the nave except for the one by the altar, which was for the rector's family. Four are dated: that of 1711 for the family of Gwerclas is the earliest and grandest, and recycles some seventeenth century panels. It has their coat of arms and the motto *Cymmer yn Edeirnion*. Simple benches for the poor line the south wall, either side of a three decker pulpit. Also eighteenth century are the columned altar rails, the painted cupboard above them watched over by a cherub, the ten commandments boards in Welsh – and a royal arms of c. 1730 which

was once in the church but is now displayed at Rug. At that time too, the ancient stone font was moved to its curious curving hollow in the wall.

The surviving wall paintings accumulated, overlaid on each other, from the fourteenth to the eighteenth centuries – a patchwork collage of holy images, exhortations and warnings. An image of Death looms at the entrant through the door. He stands over a pick and shovel, raises a winged hour-glass and jabs with an arrow at a painted inscription which contains a rector's name and year of dying. One series of murals on the south wall, unique in Wales, is of the Seven Deadly Sins riding on animals. These images first appeared in Austria in the fourteenth century and as they spread across Europe took on differing ideas for which animal should symbolize each sin. In Llangar Pride is a lion, Gluttony a boar, and Lust a goat or perhaps a stag. Some parts of the wall have the remains of large red decorated frames, their contents hopelessly faded: experts suggest the customary narrative images of Christ and Mary. The oldest survival is the outline of a bishop in a pinnacled church. The roof was also painted above the altar with a canopy of honour.

Up in the gallery, the front of which still has some faded texts, simple benches date from 1715, and a space is reserved for the musicians who would stand to sing or play around the pyramid-shaped music stand.

Welcome to Llangar

Llangollen, St Collen

SJ 217 419

This riverside llan from the Age of Saints has been chopped about a bit over the centuries, so it no longer borders the steep bank of the Dee as it must once have done, and it has lost the rounded boundaries which must have echoed the surrounding hills. The building's history is equally chequered. The oldest part of what survives is the early thirteenth century doorway, a lonely remnant of the high middle ages. There is an unaspiring tower from the Georgian years which also shaped the houses on neighbouring Bridge Street. Then in the 1860s, as the town expanded south and west of the bridge, a new chancel and south aisle were added, a little too early for the best of Victorian rebuilding.

But these accumulations still have at their heart a small fifteenth century double nave church, with the most remarkable roof in Wales. Tradition claimed it must have been stripped at the Dissolution from Valle Crucis Abbey but when, twenty years or so ago, restorers were at work on it, they could see nothing to suggest that it had ever been anywhere else. It came, nevertheless, from the same world of patronage and resources: the church belonged to the monks of Valle Crucis for centuries.

The carving reaches its peak in the two easternmost bays which would have been directly over the medieval chancel and sanctuary: they find themselves now over the nave only because of the Victorian extension of the building. In these extraordinary panels Christian symbolism is subsumed beneath a restlessly Celtic profusion of plant life, intertwined beasts, disembodied heads and a gaping Green Man. It was a secret pleasure garden for the monks, quite probably hidden from the old nave by a lost high rood screen. On the lower, more didactic ranges are a Virgin and Child, Jesus making the sign of blessing, and instruments of the Passion like a vivid knotted scourge. There is an unusual image which conflates in one design the pillar to which Jesus was tied, the ropes which tied him, and the cock which crowed at Peter's denial – an image which turns up again at Llanrwst, another church within the orbit of nearby Cistercians. One angel with folded wings carries a wreathed cross, while others along the beams above the nave carry weapons or are playing musical instruments.

But the best of the nave roof panels are the boisterous images of ordinary folk. They form a kind of fifteenth century three-dimensional cartoon: three ages of woman as young and fashionably dressed, middle aged and pious, then old and heavy-eyed; stereotypes of women in a scolding bridle or a ducking stool, and men as grotesques or jesters or engaged in drink, as in the series of three carvings on the north side, rolling out the barrels, raising a tankard, and finally climbing in the barrel for more.

This pell-mell vision is our own Sistine ceiling – what we got in Wales while Michelangelo was working in Rome – and both of them were driven by the same urge to celebrate Creation and the yearning for the human to touch the divine. Who is to say which of them came closer to the truth, Michelangelo charged with the electric potential of the first awakening in Eden, or the fallen carvers of Llangollen, catching glimpses of heaven through the foliage and the ageing and the beer?

The north aisle carvings are of local animals like the rabbit and the pig, and a Welsh inscription which translates as 'Mary, may the doors of heaven be always open to you'. There is a Jacobean table with the inscription 'Jesus 1636', and an ancient door now redeployed to lead to the vestry.

The south aisle has a modern monument to the Ladies of Llangollen, escapees from Kilkenny, bound in their romantic friendship for over fifty years together at nearby Plas Newydd, where for several decades they made this corner of Wales essential to society and literary excursions, as the Gladstones were to do again a few miles north some years later. Their real memorial is outside in the churchyard, where they came to share the grave originally given by them to the neglected third member of the household, the equally interesting 'Molly the Bruiser', their faithful servant Mary, whose 'masculine qualities afforded them protection…in a village not remarkable for sobriety'.

Llanrhaeadr-yng-Nghinmeirch, St Dyfnog

SJ 082 634

To a nation once so famously obsessed with genealogy, and so responsive to the holiness of trees, the iconography of Jesse must have struck particular chords. It comes from Isaiah, who saw the spirit of the Lord upon Jesse's descendants in the form of a branch growing out of Jesse's roots, and it was picked up by the bardic tradition of *cywyddau*, in which a great man's lineage was celebrated as a branching tree. There are telling remains of Jesse trees elsewhere – in wood at Abergavenny and in stone at St David's and Llanilltud Fawr – but the best preserved and most complete is in the Vale of Clwyd, and in glass. The great east window of Llanrhaeadr – the finest glass image in Wales – shows the line from Jesse to Jesus emerging from the foliage like unfolding flowers.

Its emphasis is on the royalty of Jesus, as royalty was in those days a form of holy power, and shows him descended from the crowned heads of Jesse's line, hailed by prophets and evangelists. At the base, Jesse lies sleeping in a walled enclosure with Moses to the left and Zadok, priest of kings, to the right. The central light leads up to David, a portrait of a bard, Welsh harp in hand, waistcord knotted on his red tunic, buttons painted gold on the abraded glass. Above him the Virgin and Child

An effortless display of mastery

stand in a golden mandorla, watched over by a one-eyed sun.

This unremembered artist had both daring and flamboyance, throwing his complex and intricate design across so vast a space while playing Renaissance games with number, symmetry and colour, in an effortless display of mastery of the new techniques of silver staining and enamelling, to match the skill of his contemporaries at King's College Chapel, Cambridge. He simplified his image of the complex descent on to fourteen descendants, dramatising the number so stressed by Matthew in the opening chapter of the Gospels, which was the number also symbolic to David, the letters of whose Hebrew name (DVD) are also the numbers 4,6,4 – which total fourteen. He played with mirror images – the figures in the outer panes simply reverse from left to right, and with tones – weighted lower reds give way to greens and mauves, while the upward branches are winding and white, their yellow leaves huge against the blue of the sky. It was a high wire performance for 1533: the date is written in Latin next to Zadok. A fading inscription over David, also in Latin, 'I will sing of the Lord's mercies for ever. R.J.' is a clue to the donor – the church's priest Robert Jones.

This north nave also has a fifteenth century dugout chest with three locks and a poorbox, and two images of the pelican in piety – symbolic of sacrifice – one carved in wood and the other painted in the glass above Mary's head. Some jumbled glass in the west window contains a small Annunciation of 1508 which once must have belonged to something grander, but which evidently failed to get the same protection as the Jesse tree, hidden so carefully through the years of civil war.

The church was just one nave and a small west tower from the thirteenth century to the fifteenth, when the second (north) nave was added, and the two long hammerbeam roofs. The money to do this came from pilgrimage to the effigy and curative well of St Dyfnog. The long-lost effigy must have stood in the sanctuary of the old nave, which has a canopy of delicate design, and angels on the beams. In a later monument at the west end, the local squire Maurice Jones is mourned in swaggering baroque, with cherubs weeping into handkerchiefs as long as their arm.

There are other legacies: few villages in the country have a gathering of buildings like Llanrhaeadr. Vicarage, almshouses, and a neo-Jacobean hall with barns and stables cluster round the church: a grouping that might be English but for the double nave, the churchyard stream, and holy *ffynnon ddyfnog* over the bridge in the wood. A dank, leafstrewn pool now, old accounts describe it paved with marble, and decorated with small human figures.

Zadok the priest, and the date in Latin, 1533

Mold/Y Wyddgrug, Capel Bethesda

SJ 237 637

The parish church of St Mary and Capel Bethesda stand almost at opposite ends of the sloping main market streets: one on the high ground, one on the low; one lordly in origin, one built by the plain man; one in the old Gothic, the other classical in deliberate distinction. It is the story of the Welsh church in microcosm.

The churchyard is the burial place, by the north door, of the painter Richard Wilson, the son of a Montgomeryshire preacher and his wife, who was a Flintshire Wynne. He elevated the wild landscape of Wales into a subject acceptable for Art, decades before Coleridge and Wordsworth's Romantic realisation of such things. His images of Snowdon or of Cader, his views along the valley of the Dee to Castell Dinas Bran or down from Holt to the flatlands of Cheshire, have yet to be equalled, and his reputation as the father of British landscape flowed from the loving precision of his observation and from touching these views with the golden light of the classical, Italian *campagna*. In the next generation Wright, Turner, Constable and Thomas Jones his pupil all paid their tributes to him, and showed his influence in their early styles.

St Mary's takes the hill site favoured for churches in this part of Wales, as at Hawarden and Halkyn, which looks down over the wide and open estuary lands of the Dee. In both location and demeanour it is an aristocratic church, badged with the heraldry of its patrons the Stanleys, who planned with ambition but realised only its grand arcaded nave and aisles. The rest had to wait, and when the tower and clerestory were added in the eighteenth century they were considerably lower than originally intended. In the nineteenth century the commission for the apse was given to George Gilbert Scott, then the grandest architect in Britain.

When much more ordinary folk rebuilt Bethesda chapel just a few years later in 1865, they marked out a different territory. They used the same Cefn sandstone as the church and they hired a London architect, W.W. Gwyther, but they built a porti-coed façade which evoked for them the era of the early church, before the impurifying accretions of Catholic and Gothic. Bethesda's façade managed to be both proud – a declaration of the new status of non-conformism – and yet also one of the most grounded, ascetic and truly classical of the temple-fronted chapels of Wales, without any of those additions that others found so hard to resist when building in this style. Inside, the heritage of simpler, earlier interiors is what shapes the space and the plainness of its decoration, however grand the sweep of the tiered gallery and tall, splendid organ behind the pulpit and *set fawr*. The walls have the old famil-iar roundheaded windows and the ceiling the most modest of plasterwork. The only image in the entire interior is on the pulpit: wheat and vine to represent the body and the blood. Bethesda thus remains firmly, rootedly vernacular, yet its new aspira-tions are equally clear: it gave to the ordinary the same transforming touch of the classical which Richard Wilson had blueprinted a hundred years before.

The building is an exact and purposeful expression of the men who built it, empowered by chapel teaching and led by their minister Roger Edwards, who pioneered through his newspapers *Y Drysorfa* and *Cronicl Yr Oes* the breaking of the shackles then placed on ordinary men to express themselves politically – and also artistically – a venture then still so publicly daring that all of the official contributors and reader-letter writers did so under cover of pseudonyms, some of them as strikingly classical – Brutus for instance – as Bethesda's façade. Edwards, author of the well-known hymn '*Pa le, pa fodd dechreuaf*', had influence through the Calvinistic Methodist church well beyond the local town, and he laid considerable ground for the rise of that radical north Wales liberalism which was to batter against and finally to tear down some of the bastions of privilege and inequality so ingrained in the Britain of his time. It is no surprise to find that, years later, his son-in-law was an influential backer of the parliamentary candidature of Lloyd George.

His pulpit rhetoric and personal encouragement played the muse to a young tailor and would-be preacher who began to release through *Y Drysorfa* compelling fiction unmistakably set in the midst of local *gwerin* life. Daniel Owen, son of a miner killed in a colliery flood at Argoed, went on to father the Welsh novel, in his hands another elevation of the ordinary into art, his whole intent encapsulated in the lines on his public statue down the road, that centre stage belonged now to the common people. "The man was never born," he wrote in *Rhys Lewis*, "of whom the honest life-history would not be interesting." His pew is marked with a plaque, from where he sometimes dreamed the presence of his characters, Wil Bryan turning forward the clock during prayers in the hope of urging forward the end of the service, Evan Gwernyfynnon falling asleep in his own Sunday school lesson up in the gallery.

In Bethesda's close-set interior the mind reaches out for all this life and memory, for those people touched here by the thousands, as for George Evans, railwayman, soldier and Llay Hall collier, and Catherine Williams, housemaid and shopworker. They were married here on 1st September 1924. Their honeymoon was a day trip to Llandudno. He was English speaking, she was Welsh speaking. When they met they couldn't understand much each other said. He would walk the lanes from Cefn-y-bedd to her family's three-room cottage out beyond Nercwys; the boys in the trees would throw stones at him for coming to take a local girl. He had fought in France and Italy, lost his faith in the carnage of the Somme, learned while still in uniform in Egypt that the girl he planned to marry had died in the influenza epidemic. When he met and married Catherine, he recovered chapel life, became a lay preacher and eventually an elder at Cefn-y-bedd, she joined the sisterhood and was a mainstay of the chapel *parti*. They had three daughters and seven grandchildren and lived beyond their golden wedding: two characteristic twentieth century Welsh lives, of the hopelessly inadequate label 'ordinary', and they were deepened and made richer by all the communal, spiritual and sometimes comical experiences bound up in the meaning, to all those Welsh communities, of 'chapel'.

Rug, Holy Trinity

SJ 065 439

The estate chapel at Rug, in the green country of the Dee, has perhaps the most charming of the painted interiors of Wales. Comparisons can be made with the folk art of Scandinavia, or alpine Bavaria or, closer to home, the Conwy valley – and with more modern movements like Bloomsbury – but in fact there is nothing else quite like it. It is at the same time less sophisticated than it planned to be, and much less naïve than it looks; and its special paradox is both to place inside a sugar-coated, gingerbread interior a stinging set of warnings about oncoming death, and then to box them in with so many teeming images of life on seats and roof and walls that its boundless *joie de vivre* quite overwhelms the sobering messages intended.

Nothing of this can be imagined from the outside, a plain grey stone façade with a bell-turret top now approached through a winding path bordered with lavender. Inside the west entrance door, in a second gesture of theatrical restraint, is a narrow hall with the first steps of a winding staircase leading off it, and a small wooden inner door to push open. Most of what we see survives from 1637, almost exactly contemporary with the Gwydir Chapel at Llanrwst, but Rug is both more intimate and more eccentric. Roof and walls – almost every panel, every beam – are covered with carved and painted angels, strange and familiar creatures, flowering plant life, mock effects of marble, clouds or starry heavens, memento mori, symbols of religion.

There are two lines of benches, each line gouged out of great oak blocks to make a structure like a sleigh. The base of each line has a carved row of creatures, several of them dragons, caught from one end in the gaze of a marvellous quilted sheep. The slender wooden seat-backs were added later. They face forward to a chancel screen added in 1855, original canopied pews, a sanctuary chair, an altar and a red and black lectern-pulpit painted with the Lord's Prayer in Welsh. On the north wall the messages of death are framed in a mural of candles, hourglass and skull. In a typical Rug touch, the skull is haloed in a wreath of irresistibly flowering buds and roses. They stand on a table beneath which a skeleton leans comfortably back on a coil of rope. It raises its knees slightly, to accommodate itself within the columned space. Inscriptions in Welsh warn that 'every strong one is weak in the end', 'life, however long, will come to an end', and 'like the flame consumes the candle, life perishes daily', a line which derives from an Elizabethan carol.

The carving is at its most intense and closely detailed on leafy friezes which run along the pew canopies and most of all along the upper wall, underlined with curling vine stems and interspersed with small crowned angels and symbols of the cross and IHS. There is more meaning up here than has yet been deciphered: the messages thin out noticeably in the poorer quarters of the gallery where the occupants would not have had the education to decode them. More angels hang like cut-outs on the trusses, Welsh mams with speckled wings, intricately carved and red and green and

gold. Above them the great wooden roof beams make quatrefoils and trefoils in the air, and an extraordinary wooden candelabrum topped by four cherubs hangs in two tiers with vertical pendules to catch the falling wax.

The chapel is the striking creation and memorial, on his family estate, of the singular Colonel William Salusbury, pikeman in the Netherlands wars, privateer in the East Indies, epic defender of Civil War Denbigh against everything Parliament threw at him, a sometime writer of religious poems who kept the company of Eos Ceiriog, the most breathtaking word-spinner and elegist of his age. His family had made other ventures into national life, producing in Elizabethan times the first translator into Welsh of the Book of Common Prayer and the New Testament – as well as a Catholic conspirator hanged on Tower Hill. Centuries later Rug would spread its influence in some surprising places: Sir Edwin Lutyens recorded its effect on the Viceroy's House in New Delhi. But its visual vibrancy and colour represent the road not taken for the next two hundred years in Wales, where plain interiors of undistracting whitewash became the moral standard, belying the seriousness of Rug's intent, a might-have-been which did not make new roots.

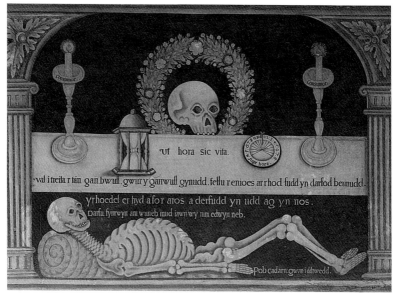

Say it with flowers: Rug's warnings of oncoming death
Previous page: Colonel Salusbury's vision: the west end and gallery

St Asaph/Llanelwy, Cathedral

SJ 039 744

The rolling farming country between the border and the Conwy river was a regular battleground for centuries. Part of the itinerary for passing soldiery was to do a bit of damage to St Asaph. That misfortune, coupled with a destructively violent storm in 1714 and subsequent decay, means that what we see now has more to do with rebuilding than with ancient mystery. But St Asaph rewards some lingering. There is much in the detail of its polished, open spaces and, given its explosive history, some surprising survivals. Of all the grand High Gothic churches which once spread across the north, it is the only one still fully standing: all the others are in ruins or were rebuilt by the Tudors. And this is William Morgan's church: he ended his days as Bishop of St Asaph and was buried underneath the altar, the boy from the mountains of Penmachno who went on to translate the Bible into Welsh, the greatest single landmark of the culture.

From the west front, Britain's smallest cathedral has still the look and feel of its thirteenth century origins, when a century of rebuilding began after a wrecking by Edward's conquering army. It had not been finished long when Owain Glyndwr burnt out the whole interior again. The destructive impulse is embedded in the walls: the west front is mottled with huge blocks of red Rhuddlan sandstone and a lighter yellow stone from the banks of the Dee, a combination which chemically reacts against each other. The deep receding doorframe and tall curvilinear west window have a kind of restraint and simplicity that shares something with the smallest churches, a spirit continuing inside in the arches of the nave, notably unbottlenecked by capitals, and in the transept crossing, all of 1310-20.

The corbels are alive with faces. One bent like a hunchback is a depiction of a deaf man, and opposite, a soft-capped man with a toothache has his finger stuck in

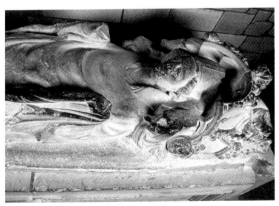

Bishop Anian, who got on the wrong side of Edward I

his mouth. There is a stillness in the sleeping face of Christ nearby. The light-giving clerestory above is fifteenth century. In the north aisle are two ancient memorial stones: the once-fine tomb of Bishop Anian, who got on the wrong side of Edward I, a sadly mutilated effigy with its blessing hand cut off, and a later stone of around 1330 which shows a hound catching up on a hare, over a diagonal sword and shield of fleurs-de-lis and lion rampant.

The chancel and the grand oak roofs are mostly the recreative work of George Gilbert Scott. The main attraction here in medieval times was the shrine of St Asaph, unusually not the founder saint but his successor, after St Kentigern had gone back north to his lasting base in the Welsh-named city of Glasgow. The canopied choir stalls go back to 1482: fine late Gothic crocketed and pinnacled creations of William Frankelyn, Master Carpenter of the Counties of Flint and Chester, who carved his face into the south side. Only those at St David's outdo them.

There is a chest dated 1738 by the Davies brothers of Bersham, and in a niche in the north transept an ivory Madonna and Child thought to be part of the loot from the Spanish Armada of 1588. In that same year William Morgan was down in London supervising the final proofs of the first Welsh bible, painstakingly guiding the English printers through the unfamiliar words and talking over the day's work each evening in the cloistered grounds of Westminster Abbey with his host the Dean, who happened to come from Ruthin. He interwove the differing vocabulary of north and south, used old roots to make new words as Shakespeare was about to do in English, and stepped into Latin only to record his dedication to 'illustrissimae, potentissimae, serenissimae' Elizabeth herself. He died in St Asaph on 10 September 1604, leaving in his will from among the flotsam of his life five flower pots, two peacocks and two swans. An original edition of his defining work is on display, alongside a first Welsh New Testament and the Triglot Dictionary of Dic Aberdaron, an eighteenth century St Asaph-based linguist who tramped the roads of Wales in a coat lined with books, and in the company of his cat.

In his cathedral William Morgan, the man of these familiar thousands of words, is memorialised in the company of two people remembered mainly for a single line: Felicia Dorothea Hemans, author of "the boy stood on the burning deck", and Henry Morton Stanley, of "Dr Livingstone, I presume." Felicia lived in St Asaph with her five children and elderly mother, winning compliments from Byron and evoking wild Wales in poems on such heights as Cader Idris, but her portentous style combined with romping rhythms, and her cheerful facility for rhyming kings with things and God with sod, destined her legacy for music hall instead of the academy. Stanley was famously cryptic about his personal life: a Civil War Dixie grey at Shiloh, expeditionary against the Sioux and later New York journalist, he went on to map and unravel East African geography by gunshot, while only late in life admitting to his St Asaph workhouse childhood.

Master Frankelyn's choir: the sons of Asaph take their places

Valle Crucis / Glyn y Groes

SJ 204 443

Perhaps the most human and direct in appeal of all the monasteries, Valle Crucis still evokes its former days of work and prayer, secluded in a bowl of hills, the white monks moving through the clustered buildings, reading in the cloister, fishing in the fishpond. Even in its ruins now the half vaulted roofs, dark thoroughfares, interiors of chapter house and dormitory, rafters and fireplaces bring home the attractions of its scale and the closely integrated, purposeful spaces of a small community.

From the cloister, which is now just a line of stone in the grass, there is an engaging view of the monastic buildings. From left to right the early rubble walls progress into finely finished ashlar for the later work, with five arched doorways each quite different and expressive of their age and role. On the left the round arch to the barrel-vaulted sacristy was part of the original early thirteenth century complex. Next comes the ornate traceried entry, more air than wall, to the monks' miniature library – their copy of the *Life of St Brendan* is now in the Bodleian in Oxford; then a sober Gothic archway to the vaulted chapter house, the place of discipline and business; then the little door to the stairway to the dormitory. The last on the right is the great ribbed entry to the passageway which led through to the east side of the complex, continuing the cloister's line and scale. On the north side of the cloister is the entry to the church, through a finely sculpted arch with foliate patterns on the capitals.

There is another striking view from the far side of the complex by the fishpond, where all the east faces of the buildings can be seen diminishing in scale from right to left. On the right is the extraordinary massed east wall of the church, so sharply cut and so modern in look with the flat stone buttressing which wraps itself around the lancets as it climbs. To the left are the domestic roofs and chimneys of the abbot's lodgings, then the open windows of the chapter house.

The church had a five bay aisled nave, leading through a choir to a presbytery at the east end, with vaulted chapels in the transepts either side. The south transept is the most intact. Each of the spaces of the church and the feel of the dimensions can be understood from what survives. From their dormitory above, the monks entered the church for prayer in the early hours by a night stair whose upper entry doorway, marked by shafts and decorated capitals, still remains. The mid-thirteenth century west front has another more fully decorated doorway, with a triptych of windows in a single spanning arch, and the smallest of rose windows in the gable.

This atmosphere of modest seclusion, so seemingly persuasive, is some way from the truth: Valle Crucis was a palace for its day and an expression of the power of Powys Fadog, a recently established mini-state which spread broadly up the eastern borders from the Tanat valley to the estuary of the Dee. Cut off from the ancient base

A palace for its day

of Powys princes at Mathrafal and Meifod, its ruling prince Madog was looking for a place where his body could eventually lie and the souls of his dynasty be prayed for. The claims of the narrow valley of Nant Eglwyseg, which had been marked for several centuries by a tall stone cross raised to honour God and the warrior prowess of Eliseg, an earlier prince of Powys who had made the borders 'a swordland by fire' against the English invader, had all the resonant symbolism he needed. The place came to be known as Valle Crucis, the valley of the Cross.

Power marked out the ways of the monks from the start, as they gathered lands along the Dee and its tributaries from Gwersyllt in the north to Mwstwr in the west, building up great business in wool and hides and wheat. When the citizens of Llangollen gave them fishing rights they built such an all-consuming cross-river trap that in 1243 the donors took them hungrily to court, but the presiding judge – the abbot as it happened – came down in favour of the abbey. When in the fifteenth century poets such as Gutun Owain and Guto'r Glyn conveyed its famous feasting and conviviality – on one day a thousand apples for dessert washed down with metheglin, a liquor made from water, honey, herbs and sweet-briar leaves – and the strikingly unspiritual gifts to guests of swords and bucklers – the poems, intended to be celebratory, seem not so, depending as they did on the tithes extracted from the poor of seven parishes in Llandysilio-yn-Ial, Llansantffraid, Bryneglwys, Ruabon, Wrexham, Llangollen and Glynceiriog.

The tomb slabs of the princes, once in the church, have now come to rest in the dormitory. Most are thirteenth century, fine designs of crosses, swords and foliage, including the stone of the founder. The most admired is for Madog ap Gruffydd, the founder's great-grandson (and the great-grandfather of Glyndwr), with incised spear, sword and fierce shield with the name inscription. It dates from 1306. A celebrated exchange, prefiguring the eventual taking of the throne by the Tudors, is said to have taken place between Glyndwr and the abbot, when out walking in the hills: "You have risen early, Master Abbot", "It is you who have risen early, a hundred years before your time". The story is the most memorable record of Elis Gruffydd, a Welsh soldier author at work in Tudor Calais: like so much of the best prophecy, it was written after the event.

Worthenbury, St Deiniol

SJ 418 462

The dedication to Deiniol, shared around here with the churches at Bangor, Marchwiel and Hawarden, reaches back fourteen hundred years and honours a local saint whose cult and influence is still remembered in Gwynedd, Ceredigion, Herefordshire and Brittany. Along with the raised level of the churchyard and the riverlet boundary it indicates the ancient foundation of this site, and it survived the conquest when the land was taken by the Pulestons, who set up home at Emral and soon naturalised into patrons of Welsh culture.

Over four hundred years later when Thomas Puleston died in 1735, "mightily lamented" at a funeral which cost £1,000, he left a large bequest towards rebuilding this church. Its total cost was never quite to equal that of his sending off. The new church was of brick and dressed stone with huge clear glass windows. It matched in style the newly added front and wings of Emral Hall, and came from the same architect. Richard Trubshaw belonged to a Staffordshire family of builders and designers: downriver at Chester they would later raise the Grosvenor Bridge, the greatest single-span of its day. Trubshaw built with the casual confidence of a man who was also a champion wrestler, and he gave to this quiet village of the Maelor the finest Georgian church in Wales.

But his design was already retro when new, quite out of step with the new generation of porticoed temples which had been rising in London for some twenty years. Its progenitor is the distinctly pre-Georgian Wren, whose one church outside London was on the Staffordshire estate of Ingestre. St Andrew's in Holborn, and especially its tower, looks like one of its models. And by putting the entrance in the south wall like a medieval church, ignoring Wren's transition to west doorways, it was even slightly retro for Wren.

What Worthenbury may have lacked in modernity or grandeur, it more than makes up in its sure sense of classical harmony. Seen from the outside, the nave leads to a chancel with a semi-circular apse, setting up a series of echoed shapes which integrate the whole design: its pilastered corners and balustrades link to those on the tower and its roundheaded windows and doorframes repeat the groundplan of the building. The western tower, twenty feet square, is precisely scoped to stand the belfry clear above the roof of the nave. At the top there is a symmetry of decorative balustrades, and urns supporting weathervanes on all four corners.

Inside, the church has a glorious full set of box pews, increasing in spaciousness as they rise towards pulpit and chancel, where the leading families of Emral and Broughton congregated in the warmth of their private fireplaces. Royal arms, funeral arms, and family names and badges on pews – such as for Nathan Spakeman who in 1791 owned "half this seat" – convey the rungs of social hierarchy, but this very gentry interior, with its fine chandeliers and plasterwork, has an unmistakable sense of neighbourliness, everyone together in the same room – no aisle arcades nor deeply recessed chancel – in a way that anticipates the rise of the non-conformist chapels. There are charity bread shelves and a board listing the tithes once due to the parson: 'One penny is paid for every stock of bees, one penny for a garden…'. A gallery on cast-iron columns, added in 1830, is entered up the steep and narrow tower steps and through the ringing chamber, a route which makes clear it was not part of the original design.

Worthenbury's best remembered preacher was in Cromwell's time, in a predecessor church of brick and timber. The Puritan Philip Henry was said to have increased the congregation three for one in the parish and five for one from beyond. People abandoned the alehouses on Sundays. He gave the most quoted eye-witness description of Charles I's execution: at the instant of the blow, "there was such a groan by the thousands then present as I never heard before, and desire I may never hear again." When the Restoration came, the bishop and the new young Royalist Puleston threw him out. His son Matthew, who spent much of his childhood at nearby Iscoed, went on to write the most lucid and personal of Bible commentaries, an inspiration to the revivals of the next two centuries – the key link perhaps, along with Bunyan, between the early Puritans and the first generation of Methodists – and still a publishing phenomenon after three hundred years.

More of Trubshaw's work can still be seen nearby, at the church at Bangor on Dee where, among other things, he built the tower, and at Emral. In its grounds he added a fine double row of stables and a bridge over Emral brook. They remain while the house does not, demolished earlier last century after, it is said, the last of the Pulestons went to Monte Carlo, and bust.

Classical harmony at Worthenbury, 1735

Wrexham/Wrecsam, St Giles

SJ 336 502

The definitive example in Wales of town church as architectural showpiece, a church such as this *was* the town centre, its awesome tower marking out the destination from the small farms and hill country to the west. All the markets and meetings of town life happened in the church and churchyard under the protective gaze of its gallery of saints, as in any Italian hill town or Flemish *markt*. It was not built to be as it is now, screened behind gates and railings, displaced from the hubbub, its once vast churchyard halved by the cutting through of a railway and road, and the river which once bordered it culverted and hidden underground.

Wrexham is a church of its moment, when centuries of Welsh exclusion had been suddenly replaced by the most astonishing acquiring of power. The Tudors had seized the crown, blazoning the red dragon on the royal arms and on the holy shrines of Westminster Abbey, bringing all their Welsh network to power at court. In parts of the country like this, controlled through family ties, they shouted out their praise to God for what they had been given in a series of triumphant new churches stretching north to Mold and Holywell. The Welsh, ingrained for so long with the ways of those deprived of power, must have found their minds in a spin. The church of Saint Giles is the blueprint of the times, at once the most royal, and the most subversive, of all the churches in the country.

The saints on the tower are the same who crowd the inner walls of Westminster Abbey, keeping watch over royal Tudor tombs. St James (on the north wall) and St Catherine (on the east) are a celebration of the Spanish connection – the weddings first of Prince Arthur then of Henry VIII to Catherine of Aragon. The west wall has St Barbara, protectress of towers, above the window, and above her a Virgin and Child, with perhaps St Giles on crutches to their side and St Lawrence at the upper right, all weathering badly.

The source was surely Lady Margaret Beaufort, mother of Henry VII, grandmother of Henry VIII, whose fourth husband owned much of north east Wales. She was a portent of the dynasty to come: at thirteen, already twice widowed, she had given birth to a future king. Her tomb in the Abbey is one of the finest: the hands alone are priceless. But in Wrexham her carved

With wings as eagles: the early sixteenth century lectern

head is bowed beneath a corbel, and her husband has been given asses ears. This is a strange dress for Thomas Stanley, the man who placed the crown on Henry Tudor's head at Bosworth, in the mocking guise of the fool-king Midas (but the metaphor, perhaps, was that this crowning touch turned his ordinary corner of the country into gold), and there is some forgotten and as yet unravelled strand which carried it down the generations

Bishops and kings among the judged at Wrexham

until the family, the great patrons and protectors of young Shakespeare, saw it re-emerge transformed by his imagination in a whole play devoted to the world turned upside down, in the unlikely form of Bottom the weaver. Above them in the nave the remains of a large Last Judgement occupy the high wall. There are kings and bishops among the judged, and in subversive Wrexham some of them are bound for hell: not even the Virgin Mary, baring her breasts to plead for mercy, can save them. In the chancel, the intricate canopies of the priests' seats have been mischievously filled with the spirit of pagan woodland.

This grand Tudor church came from building up and out of the earlier, simpler nave already there. The roof and walls were raised, adding the top rows of windows and a polygonal east end to give mystery and depth to the view towards the altar. Then at the west end the new tower was planted, the date 1506 inscribed into the south wall beneath a surging vault. Wrexham steeple was long ago claimed as one of the seven wonders of Wales (all suspiciously local to here). It has its mysteries: every face of it is different and sometimes oddly asymmetrical in design. Such a massive separate presence on the outside, inside it has been daringly integrated by cutting in its outer wall the great west window for the nave, giving the interior its high, unhindered view from west to east. The transformation into grandeur was spiked with curious reminders of its humbler earlier status – as though the workers would not let the new church get above itself. The corbels of the older, lower roof were left protruding from the walls above the columns of the nave, and there are broken stone remnants of window tracery left hanging from the arch before the chancel, stating bluntly that the old church ended here.

The chancel railings are early eighteenth century, made by the Davies family who also made the celebrated churchyard gates. The nave has a fine wooden roof and a pre-Reformation eagle lectern like the one in Chipping Campden, Gloucestershire. Among the sculpted tombs in the north aisle are those of Cyneurig ap Hywel, a longhaired knight with his name on his shield, and Mary Myddleton, a lively piece of Roubiliac: the deceased emerges from her tomb to greet the trumpet call of Judgement Day, sending a frisson through the neighbouring plant life in a nod to Bernini in the Piazza Navona. The last window by the door is by Burne Jones, a recent arrival from a now demolished church in Hightown.

There is another way to come to Wrexham steeple, driving down Route 95 along Long Island Sound. A replica was built on Yale University campus to honour Elihu Yale's origins and burial place, and it contains one stone from here. A stone from New Haven, by return, has been placed in the west wall, near the tomb with its famous inscription, '…much good, some ill, he did, so hope all's even…'. But perhaps the most extraordinary part of the story of this steeple is how, almost uniquely in Britain, it should have survived with so little damage through the times of iconoclasm, when holy images were smashed, so that it carried on proclaiming high over town through all the anti-Catholic centuries its honouring of Mary and her gallery of saints – Wrexham church's most subversive gesture of them all.

Eighteenth century revival: Roubiliac at Wrexham in 1751, capturing the new sense of spiritual drama shared by his Welsh contemporaries

III

MID-WALES

CEREDIGION AND POWYS

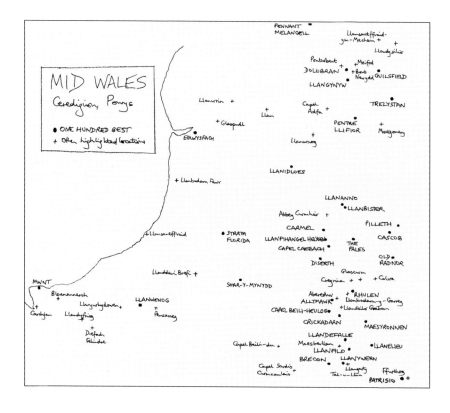

Alltmawr, St Mauritius

SO 073 469

South of Builth Wells the Wye runs through a gorge with the mountains rising to one
thousand five hundred feet on either side. The slopes on the west side are steep and
unbroken – *allt mawr* in Welsh – but on the east the river Edw cuts through the
mountain like a gash. Alltmawr church is positioned, with surely deliberate precision, to face across to this one point of eastern access, a grandly calculated setting
for one of the smallest churches in the country. The church is approached now down
a narrow path between high hedges and through an iron gate badged with the letter
M for its martyred patron saint. The churchyard is like a small enclosed garden, lined
at the top of the slope by the backs of cottages and on the far side by an orchard. Its
graves, some dating back to the mid-eighteenth century, are clustered on the east
and south sides, and have much to do with the families of two houses – one at the
gate with the large Palladian window and another, Abernant, which is just out of
sight down below the river road.

Alltmawr, eglwys fach

129

Standing off-centre in the field is a building not much more than ten feet wide, thirty feet in length. It is thought to date from the thirteenth century. Inside are beams and box pews and an ancient font, a pleasing mix of wood and stone. A hundred years or so ago, a three-sided apse was added to its original rectangular plan, with attractive window seats and a simple altar rail. The pulpit, and the windows' wooden frames, are eighteenth century.

On the south wall is a large monument with portraits of a husband and wife in relief. It dates from 1936 and is by Ernest Gillick, a medallist and sculptor who lived and worked in the old Moravian chapel just off the King's Road in Chelsea. His work can be found in London, Scotland, India, New Zealand – and France, where he made the memorial to The Missing at Vis-en-Artois. The inscription records the long marriage of two cousins, Jessie and Alfred Lawrence, who lived at Abernant. Alfred, born in Pontypool, was legal adviser to the court of Queen Victoria, the last judge in London to ride to work on horseback, and at the age of 77 Lord Chief Justice of England and Wales: the appointment was made by Prime Minister Lloyd George, who it is said as a young solicitor on Llyn had first worked with him more than thirty years before. One of the Lawrence's sons was to be the presiding judge at the Nuremberg trials, and their love of horses passed down the family to a grandson, Lord Oaksey, who rode in eleven Grand Nationals. Alfred was drowned while salmon-fishing in an upriver tributary of the Wye. He was 92.

Across the gorge the wooded banks and high cliffs of Aberedw, marked by stone circles and the traces of burial mounds, are resonant with the last days of the last Welsh prince, and with a moment of epiphany six hundred years later for the twenty-four year old curate of Clyro, Francis Kilvert, when he walked there alone over the high moor with the morning sun swinging round to the south, transfiguring Llanbychllyn Pool into a silver shield. His wrapt description of intense joy surging through him is one more captured instance of the mystical and endlessly regenerative power of Welsh landscapes, and was shared in those same years with two other preachers at work in the borderlands – Gerard Manley Hopkins at Tremeirchion and Yardley Warner at The Pales. But Hopkins, filled with the angst of his faith and his fierce poetic gift, and Warner, his idealism channelled into practical fundraising, had their sights on achievements beyond the thoughts of Kilvert, whose gentle picture of the life of his parish seems rooted in the slow and solitary pace of his observing mind, as when during his service at Bettws he holds the gaze of a foolish-faced cow at the chapel window, or another time is mesmerised by a bumble bee meandering across the altar: he has the watcher's reluctance to shake up the unfolding narrative which, for his shy love for Daisy Thomas, would ensure the unhappy ending.

Brecon/Aberhonddu, St John the Evangelist
SO 045 290

All through Europe in the thirteenth century, a new urban landscape was taking shape. Towns were expanding and rebuilding on a new scale, and at their heart were a castle, a church, a monastery, and a friary. Especially in Britain, most of this has been lost to reformation, war and time, and for a place to have preserved something of all four is close to miraculous. It has happened in Brecon.

As its Welsh name makes clear, Brecon is where two rivers meet, where the Honddu flows into the Usk. The centre of the town has grown up on the east bank of the Honddu, but it all began on the ridge which rises from the west, where the road leads up from old castle walls to the grandest and plainest of Benedictine survivals. The hill site is walled and wooded. Just through the gateway is a tithe barn with a queen-post roof. On the left is an almonry, behind which the west front of the monastic church rises undemonstratively. Beyond it the canonry and deanery carry traces of the medieval monastery ranges.

Beginning around 1200, St John's took more than a hundred years to build, reaching the crossing in mid-century and the nave after 1300, but it is consistent and integrated in style. The tower is a fortress, the outside transept walls sheer and protected, with windows high up beyond reach. The rubble walls of the north porch have niches for statues, and two carved heads projecting. On the south wall there is the quietest of entries, through a passageway where the cloister used to be. The nave is suddenly high and engulfing, and leads on into aisles and arcades and chapels through which the light and shadows shift. Tombs and monuments and small flour-ishes on capitals and mouldings are scattered through them, playing against the ancient masses of the walls.

The chancel is a towering and intricate arrangement of shafts and high lancets, one of the best things to survive from the reign of King John. John held the lordship of Brecon in direct possession for almost half his reign and his dark, impulsive presence may lie behind the grandeur of conception and the urge to rebuild a church dedicated to his own name saint. There is a triple piscina and triple sedilia, and a c.1400 stone relief carving of the Crucifixion with Mary and St John and four kneel-ing figures, very spare and gaunt with the Cross omitted, but presumably once painted in. It may have been an altarpiece: the figures with arms raised in praise probably depict the monks. The Crucifixion was the primary image of the priory: in medieval times a famous Holy Rood stood at the chancel entrance, attracting prayer and pilgrimage and money. In the adjoining Havard chapel, the Crucifixion appears twice again on a tomb from 1312 of a husband and wife from Abercynrig – between them on the pillow and gripped in the husband's hands. Around them hang the emblems of Brecon's Zulu wars.

The colonising thread runs through much of Brecon's history. The great Roman camps at Y Pigwn and Y Gaer stand above the valley to the west, and by the fifth or sixth centuries the place was dominated by the Irish, their influence still embedded four hundred years on in the shaping of the royal crannog at Llangors. It was not so long after that when Bernard de Neufmarché, William the Conqueror's relative, came riding in to claim it for yet another Outremer culture, building the castle and a first great church affiliated, appropriately, to Battle Abbey. There are two survivals from it at the west end of the nave. The font, thought to be by one of the carvers of Kilpeck, has Romanesque relief arcading at the base but gets wilder as it rises, with strange creatures and restless intersecting lines and circles. The cresset stone is thought to be the largest which survives. Its sculpted hollows would have held the oil for thirty flames to burn in the interior darkness of the Norman church, an image evoked in the Coverdale Bible of the words of Elias as a cresset, a fire.

So it is not without irony that this French building in a Welsh market town should house the regimental chapel of a band of men who in January 1879 found themselves 6,000 miles from home, goading a fight in territory that was not theirs, and being dealt the single worst defeat by a native army without guns, at the terminal spur of Isandhlwana. The saving flight of the Queen's Colour, swirling

A priest at prayer in the shoemakers' chapel

downstream among the riderless horses and speared and bloodied bodies of the 24th Regiment, on a day still marveled at for the blind, redemptive heroism of both sides, once made it the most famous single flag in British history, and here it hangs, as threadbare now as some of the ideas it once epitomised. Out in the churchyard, the nineteenth century gravestones are uniquely full of Britain's global empire reach – men and women born in India, America, Australia, New Zealand, along with Brecon natives occupying every trade imaginable: tiler, clothier, cooper, coroner, cordwainer, hatter, nailer, saddler, tallow merchant, flour merchant, bricklayer, mantua maker, bellhanger, glazier, blacksmith and baker: ninety-seven in all, counted out admiringly in *Cronicl Powys* several years ago.

There is some notable woodwork: an early Tudor screen to St Keyne's chapel with what clearly used to be roof bosses stuck on it; a pulpit made of pieces from another older screen; two sixteenth century panels of the Baptism and Deposition (fitted up sometime later to a cupboard), and an extravagant chest in the nave.

Behind the church the woodland leads down to the river, by which the monks had their mill. Their chapel of ease in the town has evolved into St Mary's, the parish church. The friary was in another direction, on the south bank of the Usk. The

Crucifixions in stone on one of the earliest of Wales's husband and wife tombs

chancel of the friary church, another thirteenth century classic of clarity and restraint, has become the school chapel of Christ College, and the antechapel has some stalls from 1400, with the most primitive of misericords, an angel, animals, a skeleton.

The restless lines of southern Welsh Romanesque

Brecon, The Plough/Aberhonddu, Capel Y Drindod
SO 046 284

The Plough has one of the finest of the grand chapel interiors: a manifestation of the pride and confidence in town and church in the 1890s, and a triumph of the carpenter's art. Its closely clustered pews and steeply raked and encircling galleries draw the congregation in towards the near vertical rising layers of pulpit, choir and organ, creating a sense of event and occasion which is unmistakably theatrical. There is an exuberance in the carving, the touches of expensive ebony, the perfect oak leaves and acorns, daringly fashionable sunflowers, the effortless demonstration of skill in the individually graded curve of each side pew, the good humoured pretence by paint that its cast iron pillars are carpentry too, and the clever way that functional ventilation is disguised in the punctured line and colour of a decorative ceiling.

But its purpose was, of course, deeply serious. The woods chosen for this forest of carpentry were pine and oak, both associated, in the books of Joshua and Isaiah, with the Sanctuary of the Lord. The centerpiece pulpit, with its two staircases curving up out of the elders' *set fawr*, has sides carved into roses and lilies. They are the flowers of the Song of Solomon, whose Temple, whose Jerusalem, was being symbolically builded here – an act of intent evoked again outside in the pediments of the façade. The ebony columned, carved squares which recur at regular intervals on the gallery front may seem merely decorative from below, but up in the gallery they are revealed as grand-fronted reading stands for Bible verses, to draw in the upstairs congregation to take part in the Word, as well as in the singing of praises. These are the keys to the excitement of ideas in which Rev. John Bowen Jones and his congregation set about reshaping their church – and reaching out for the first time to hold services in English alongside those in Welsh. The remarkable carpentry came from the local firm of Benjamin Jenkins. In the chapel schoolroom there is a photograph of the men standing with casual confidence, hats on, in the midst of their achievement.

The Plough had one of the earliest independent chapel congregations in mid-Wales, dating back to 1699, and taking its name from the house in which the early meetings were held: it may have been an inn. The name has an added meaning to a Welsh-speaking congregation, for whom Y Drindod means the Trinity, as well as the plough. Their first purpose-built chapel rose around 1730, and the current structure replaced it in 1841. An old print, also in the schoolroom, shows the clean lines of its façade of roundheaded windows, set back behind a little garden, before the later awkward aggrandisements of porch and balustrade. It had a wall tablet with name and date in the pediment, which is now kept in the back vestry.

An early minister is recorded as sharing his work between here and Cwmyoy: the ministry is partly shared now with Sardis in Cwmcamlais, one of the most precious and evocative – along with Capel Beili-du at Pentre-bach – of the small rural chapels in the western tributary valleys of the Usk.

Cascob, St Michael

SO 239 665

Between Knighton and Radnor, Offa's Dyke makes a path through the mountains, which rise rapidly another thousand feet to the west to the heart of the Radnor forest. Here more than anywhere in the country the deeply wooded world of dark age Wales can still be felt.

Cascob is missing from most road maps: a couple of miles to the west of Discoed there are some scattered houses and an ancient church, a river running at the foot of the churchyard, mountains rising on all sides. The last Welsh dragon is said to be sleeping in this mountain forest and four churches dedicated to St Michael, archangelic victor over dragons, were built around the edges to imprison it. If any of these churches – Cascob, Nantmelan, Cefnllys, Rhydithon – is lost, the dragon will escape.

Cascob churchyard is large and wild, overgrown with tall grass and huge trees. The church is like a mound on the sloping hill, a medieval bunker of ragged stone, with a few small openings cut in it. It is as though the minds which built it were under siege. The north side, traditional shield against the devil, is virtually unbroken wall. People huddled to be buried on the sheltered south: not a gravestone at Cascob has been ventured on any other side. Even the east window must be no more than two feet by four. The tower is squat and solid, on a rise formed from older building ruins. A very ancient yew stands nearby, and an apple tree rubs up against the wooden belfry.

Inside, the church is simple enough. Only the tower holds the atmosphere the outside walls suggest. Looking up from its straw-covered floor, belfry timbers stretch across the space haphazardly, a narrow corner stairway goes winding up, and occupying birds disturb intruders.

On the north wall of the nave is an abracadabra charm, which gives an awkward glimpse of local belief around 1700. A long and rambling prayer asks for protection from witchcraft and wizards and hardness of heart. 'O Lord Jesus we beseeth thee for thy mercy grant that this holy charm abracadabra may cure thy servant Elizabeth Lloyd from all Evil Spirites and from all their desesis. Amen'. The church's fine and simple screen is fifteenth century.

All quiet at the dragon's lair

Crickadarn's fifteenth century porch

Crickadarn/Crucadarn, St Mary

SO 089 423

Crickadarn has the feeling of an English country hamlet, a few old houses gathered at a junction of three roads, with church and chapel on each side. Hebron chapel is neat and upright, with bright red door and window frames. St Mary's sinks into its ancient churchyard among the trees and rambling bushes, pressed on the west and south sides by old gravestones. Beyond it across a small stream, the remains of a connecting causeway lead to a ridged field surrounded by a ditch – all that is left of a medieval castle, and presumably the 'strong mound' (*crug cadarn*) that gave the place its name.

No one knows whether this began life as a Welsh or Norman settlement, but the church more than the castle may hold what clues there are: at certain points there seem to be beguiling hints of lost roundness in the churchyard, but the main absence of roundness, the closeness of church and castle as at Skenfrith or Grosmont, and the dedication to St Mary all suggest Norman presence. The surprise in this case is that the site protects from danger from the east more than the west – it stands above the access route up the tributary river Clettwr from the valley of the Wye below. Crickadarn is one more reminder that borders in medieval Wales were changeling things, and often far from the place we now know as 'the border'. While the Normans were entrenched here in west bank Cantref Selyf, some time around 1160 the Welsh retook command of the east bank of the Wye, and held on there again for more than a century.

St Mary's earliest surviving walls – the irregularly placed long stones and narrow lancets of the north nave – appear to date from somewhere near the end of this time. More of the nave, and the timber-fronted porch with decorative quatrefoils and trefoils, are fifteenth century, while the tower is probably later, battlemented and Tudor – a home now for horseshoe bats. The main interior space has a simple oblong plan, a white ceiling, and a tie beam – remnant of the rood screen – hanging oddly through. Into the walls old tombstones have been plastered, retaining their colour and inscriptions. There are angels on David Morgan's stone from 1788, and china doll faces with red and green on another from 1780.

There is a fireplace, and an almost miniature musician's gallery strung across a doorway up in the tower. A most un-medieval oval window feeds the flow of light between the nave and tower. The impression is of comfort, charm and whimsy: Clough Williams-Ellis was here restoring and adding his distinctive touches, 'Cloughing it up' in his friends' phrase, just before the Great War. The spirit of Portmeirion was budding in his brain.

The vestry has a benefaction board of 1830, which states the charity required of parishioners on every feast of St Thomas, and Good Friday. It reminds them that should the payments not be made as stated, the sums owed immediately double.

Diserth, St Cewydd

SO 034 583

The interior of Diserth is the past in an unadulterated dose. The church door pushes open on a long nave of ranked box pews, just about patched up for something like three hundred years, where the small pomposities of Georgian Wales are ridiculed by time and dust. The new congregation of Diserth, untroubled by the absences of artificial light and heat, is small, nocturnal, and winged.

The ancient churchyard is deep in a valley close by the river Ithon, which curves around it on the north and western sides. It first belonged to Cewydd y Glaw, the mysterious St Cewydd of the Rain, who is said to have walked here past Maengewydd (Cewydd's rock) from his other church at Aberedw, casting his particular blessings along the way, and he must have sought it out for the uninhabited remoteness – in Latin *desertum* – which gave the place its name. The first view through a canopy of yews is of a long whitewashed barn-like nave pressed up against a massive tower. There is no decoration, no show, no variation of wall or roof: a typical oblong Radnorshire box, but the scale is untypically grand. The porch is lined with seats and patterned panels and has a cobbled floor.

The interior is framed by heavy rendered walls with a few, deep rectangular windows and a high oak roof – fifteenth century or perhaps even earlier – with massive cross beams ranged right down the nave. There are wall posts from a great lost screen, painted fragments of the Creed and the Commandments, a large faded arms of Queen Anne after the Union with Scotland, and the remains of old bell wheels in the nave. A bell of 1609 says "Attende unto Godlyness, Draw neere to God" and another, simply inscribed Iohannes, dates from 1300, not long after the year when Edward I passed by one June day, with his invading army. The east wall is deep enough to hold an altar cavity – a local feature also seen at Rhulen – and has a second taller recess, the purpose of which is now a mystery. Fleurs-de-lys and the repeated symbol IHS remain in faded paint around it.

The three hundred year old pulpit is a grand three-decker, placed well down the nave and taking the preacher toweringly high. The well-to-do faces would have stared up at his solitary figure, not so much commanding as strangely suspended, like this troublingly speechless house. He would have looked down at the two great banks of box pews, separated by a narrow aisle of cracked flagstones and smaller at the back for the servants and the poor. Some are patterned with Jacobean-style diamonds and circles, and many have dates – the oldest 1666. Each one is badged with the name and sometimes the house of the owner. The most spacious was for Mrs Crummer of Howey Hall, who against the expectations of her time ran her own large regional banking business. Another, equally unexpected, was for James Watt, a father of the Industrial Revolution who seems not to have brought his inventions with him. From 1805, when his Lunar Society and engine-making days were over, he spent the summers at nearby Dolfawr, pondering his new idea of a machine for making multiple copies of a sculpture, and turning down the offered post of High Sheriff of Radnor. A lost pew in the chancel belonged to Thomas Jones of Pencerrig, the now-celebrated groundbreaking painter who is buried some miles north at non-conformist Caebach. In his later days as landowner and magistrate he evidently felt the need to be seen in more Establishment surroundings. Diserth, it seems, is not what it seems, but a place where the pioneers of science, art and commerce came to congregate.

The past in an unadulterated dose

Dolobran Meeting House/Dolobran Capel Y Crynwyr

SJ 124 124

This small house in a fold in the fields of the Efyrnwy valley is the oldest surviving place of non-conformist worship in the north. In the southern half of the country only Maesyronnen is older, and as Maesyronnen was first a barn, Dolobran can claim to be the oldest purpose-built structure of them all. Its importance extends far beyond Wales to the founding of Pennsylvania, so much so that around 1850 its interior, oak gallery and all, was acquired by the family of William Penn, and shipped to Philadelphia.

Small lanes lead towards it from the Pontrobert road, but no path leads to its door, and even from a hundred yards away it is completely hidden in a screen of trees. There seem to be nothing but green grazed hills rolling away towards Y Berwyn over the beautiful, praise-giving country of the saints of Meifod and the plygain tradition. A stone wall with an old mounting block built into it surrounds the burial ground, but the meeting house itself is made of brick. The right-hand door, which appears from the brickwork to have been originally planned wider, leads into the main room, and the left door into a caretaker's house, which also served as the women's meeting room. The dividing wall is made up of four removable wooden shutters. The house is built into a sloping bank, which provided easy entry from the back at gallery level. The interior now is completely modern: the meeting house was restored to use in 1975 after long obsolescence.

Dolobran was the home and estate of the Lloyd family from around 1400, and it needs to be imagined in the late seventeenth century as a mixed estate, with livestock, a fish lodge, courts and gardens, and an early industrial iron forge. When the Quaker movement was still new, dangerous and persecuted, the brothers Charles and Thomas Lloyd risked everything to commit themselves to it. Charles suffered ten years' imprisonment for his beliefs – the Quaker founder George Fox was among his visitors – and in 1681 was one of the thirteen, along with close compatriot Richard Davies of Cloddiau Cochion, who signed the framework of government for Pennsylvania drawn up by Penn, and bought large acreages there in the Welsh tract. Thomas crossed the Atlantic, becoming Deputy-Governor & President of Pennsylvania from 1684-93, the key man in Penn's long absences.

A decade after the Toleration Act eased the risks of persecution, the members of Dolobran meeting resolved to build a permanent meeting house, for which "friends make a subscription of whatever each friend is willing." Charles's heir, also Charles, gave half the money. The first meeting in it was held on 20 April 1701. The building also served as a school, which at one time had 50 pupils. The first schoolmaster, who lived behind the left door, was a London orphan called John Kelsall. His careful diaries survive, and record the early Quaker life in the district. He writes of Quaker preachers such as Ellis Pugh of Dolgellau, author of *Annerch ir Cymru*, the first Welsh book printed in America, who came to Dolobran on a return trip to Wales from the new Montgomery County, and he also documents, wistfully, the decline of passion in the movement, admitting early on to using a pin to keep awake in long meetings. In 1724 he noted that the gathering had "gone very thin and small...few seek to be acquainted [with] the inward and secret exercise of Truth". The Lloyd family interests shifted east to Warwickshire, where they went on to found their bank.

The truth is that the first generation of devotees was dying even as the meeting house was built, and mass emigrations took most of the movement out of Wales to America, where its ideas spread into the commonwealth of progress. Its physical memorials are few: they include the monument stone beside Llyn Celyn in Meirionydd to the brave Quaker farmstead of Hafod Fadog, now under the water; the houses at Neath, The Pales and Dolobran – and an older, and finer, Welsh Quaker meeting house than these – but it is not in Wales. Welsh immigrants built it on arrival in Merion, Pennsylvania in 1682, where it still stands, a gabled, cross-shaped house, its interior of old wood intact, its long graveyard full of Welsh names, and some stones marked with flags for those who fought in America's Civil War.

Off to Philadelphia in the morning

Eglwysfach, St Michael
SN 686 955

Over the opening frames of an old BBC documentary on R.S. Thomas, the voice of Huw Wheldon talks of his role as priest in a remote part of Wales. In fact Eglwysfach, though not on many road maps, is right on the main road from Aberystwyth to Machynlleth. Around a bend or two from the ruins of the great eighteenth century ironmaking furnace, the church comes into view between steeply sloping hills and estuary meadows, set back in an expansive churchyard.

R.S. understood the character of the building better than most, emphasising its chapel-like spareness by removing colour and clutter, having the box pews painted charcoal black against white walls, and commissioning great black wrought-iron lights to hang low from the high ceiling. It has subsequently been listed. It makes an interesting match to the Huntingdonshire church of Leighton Bromswold, where another Welsh-born poet-priest, George Herbert, over three hundred years before, had also rearranged his church towards simplicity.

CADW calls it Tudor Gothic, with Regency character, but these styles are hints in a simple oblong cut by tall narrow windows, with a chancel bay added eighty years later in 1913. It has height and elegance, with simple lines rising up through lights and candleholders from the huge flagstones. Like the box pews, the gallery also remains from the original 1830s interior. Beneath it by the entrance, a kind of baptistry has been created, railed off, with antique chairs beside a font which looks Norman, and is of unknown origin. There is the most astonishing acoustic.

R.S. was vicar here from 1954 to 1967, the time when he emerged into prominence as a leading new poet, publishing some of his best-known volumes, *Song At The Year's Turning* and *Poetry for Supper* among them. Immersed in nature, he could smell the sea in the tidal river and watch the wild birds circling over Ynyshir, and he carried it into his poetry, imagining the swifts rip the silk of the wind, sending unseen ribbons trailing on the air. Yet it was in some ways a dry time for him, and everyday parish life did not chime much with his visions of a transfigured Wales. Often he found himself lost, fumbling for new themes, while the past called him back to an earlier time in the hills around Manafon. His faith began to shiver. It was here in this church he pictured himself in the darkness and silence after the congregation had gone, nailing his questions one by one to an untenanted cross.

Outside, the churchyard is full of flower, and many eighteenth century gravestones, wonderfully carved and some very small. They date from the time of the predecessor church on this site, called Llanfihangel Capel Edwin, where Shelley's great friend, the poet and novelist Thomas Love Peacock married a Meirionydd girl in 1820, almost a decade after last meeting her, having proposed by post. R.S. must have pondered about him, felt some fellow feeling for this challenging, aloof, warmhearted radical, so dismissive of contemporary taste and so romantic for ancient Wales. But Peacock's pastoral affinities were joyously pagan, and his best remembered legacy is only doggerel:

> The mountain sheep are sweeter,
> But the valley sheep are fatter;
> We therefore deemed it meeter
> To carry off the latter.

The silver grey lychgate also belongs to the earlier church: it is a building in itself, with a long arched entranceway, and sheds to either side. Across the wall is the old vicarage, and a church hall of deep green corrugated iron.

Healed by sunlight: R S Thomas's church of shadows

Guilsfield / Cegidfa, St Aelhaiarn

SJ 219 117

The Marches are rich in the country craftsmanship of the fifteenth century, a time when churches were being made grander, airier and lighter. Wood and stone were used with instinctive skill, and a sense of alignment or symmetry that was still wayward and irregular. St Aelhaiarn's church at Guilsfield seems to carry all the spirit of the time: its new aisles and clerestory, emboldened tower and tall two-storeyed porch are part of an expressive outer frame made up of miscellaneously piled up stones, some singularly large; a massive nail-studded door of huge bars of oak and fleurs-de-lys iron hinges right across the width; and a muscular timber roof. The considerable engineering skill required to raise its great spanning beams into place sits all of a piece with the offcentre line of nave and tower, and the out of square east wall of the chancel, which wrongfoots the rhythm of the internal arches down the nave.

The building's largely unrecorded history muddies attempts to understand how such a fine expansive church should rise in a small border village, but the keys must lie in the sheer size of its fifteen thousand acre ancient parish, the richness of the soil in its hill-sheltered, floodplain location, its place at the junction of roads, and the grandeur of the gentry estates gathered round it at Garth, Trawscoed, Trelydan and Varchoel. It was also, being in a part of Powys which backed Edward I, a place where succession passed peacefully, and long after the conquest, by the simple court device of ordering a last Welsh heiress to marry an English lord, connecting the parish to greater wealth in Shropshire.

The sense of continuity is echoed in the building. While its seventh century saint takes its origins far back, the first visible connections to the old Welsh lordship of Ystrad Marchell are the probably twelfth century font carved with beast heads, fleur-de-lys, a rose and a cross, and some say also the interior stonework of the tower. The ancient iron-bound oak chest, over seven feet long and roughly axed from a trunk, may be almost as old.

There are curious carvings on the timber roof of the south aisle – beasts and faces, one an owl, which was a heraldic figure for the family at Garth, but these are small preparation for the vast new canopy which in the sixteenth century was hung above the chancel and east end of the nave. It contains two hundred and forty carved wooden panels with more than a hundred variations of interlaced circles, triangles and quatrefoils, a masterpiece of snowflake delicacy the patterns of which were played on by G.E. Street when he added his nineteenth century screen. Oddly propped up at the back of the nave is a carving of St Christopher and a four hundred year old cupboard with complicated scenes of Resurrection and Nativity, bordered by women in the same strange pose as those on the walls of Plas Mawr in Conwy. They arrived, apparently, from Trawscoed Hall.

By the seventeenth century the church was surrounded by some fine old houses and the country's largest churchyard gathering of yews. At the gate the yew trees begin and beneath the first a weathered tombstone memorialises Richard Jones of Moysgwin, gent, who died at the age of 90, in 1707:

> Under this yew tree
> Buried would hee bee
> For his father and hee
> Planted this yew tree.

This is a churchyard with a fondness for quatrains of doubtful literary quality, whether in the nineteenth century displaying faith and hope, or earlier, sounding deadeningly final. Someone put it with touching directness for Esther Lewis of Moelygarth, who died in 1767, aged 84.

> Sixty one years she has been his wife
> Without either frown or blow
> Now here she lies down by his side
> In this cold earth below.

'Be diligent' says the warning on the tower clock, 'Night cometh'.

Country craftsmanship at Guilsfield

Gwenddwr, Capel Beiliheulog

SO 048 435

The Nant yr Offeiriad springs from Eppynt mountain, and its name, the Priest's brook, suggests religious associations going back beyond memory. There was an outpost of the Cistercians of Abbey Dore at the small settlement of Gwenddwr (Whitewater), and from its ancient church two roads wind towards the isolated farms in the hills to the west.

The northerly road stays high above the valley stream, curving round to reach an old farmhouse with window frames of fading blue, and a long range of barns. From here an old trackway leads steeply down the hillside to the Nant, between a gnarled line of wind breaks and a wooded tributary stream. Sheep graze in the field beyond the mountain ash and hornbeam. At the valley bottom, the mountain streams meet; Beiliheulog may originally have meant a place among the willows, but over time the words have pleasingly transmuted to a place in the sun. The track emerges on something like a house, with a fenced southern garden filled with gravestones.

One of the most secluded early chapels of Wales, Capel Beiliheulog is a rare and precious survival of a stage of chapel-building which came after the first converted barns like Maesyronnen but before the late Georgian box chapels with their trade-mark symmetry and roundheaded windows. It was first built in this guise, perhaps, about 1740, for a membership which had reached 150 as early as 1715. Unsigned

A place in the sun: the lane to Nant yr Offeiriad

148

and hidden in this little dip in the rolling green landscape west of the Wye, it was not, of course, as isolated as it seems to travellers' eyes, but took its place among the small farms of the neighbourhood. The people would come on foot or by pony, refreshing themselves from the small streams alongside, just as at the waterside llans from a thousand years before. Its rural simplicity seems to hold the essence of the country's old dissenting culture, the kind that was taken to America in the years around this time: among the emigrants of 1712 was Beiliheulog's minister, Howell Powell of Maesyclettwr.

Through the eastern door are half a dozen rows of pews, all facing firmly west as though to make a point about their breach with the east-facing traditions of the church. Beyond them are the elders' seats, a small communion table and a raised pulpit with two stairways. The two tall windows behind are low and deep, while those on the south side are irregularly set, their clear glass flooding with afternoon light. There are a few early nineteenth century memorial tablets on the walls.

A steep wooden staircase climbs up to the small gallery, just three rows of simple benches. From here the poorer members of the congregation could look down towards the preacher, but they could also see and hear the river, and look out on the day and the gorse in the field. As Gwenallt observed in another country chapel not far from here, there was only a wall between the Saviour in the chapel, and the Creator of the world outside.

Something like a house

149

Llananno, St Anno

SO 096 743

A mile or so north of Llanbister on the road along the Ithon river valley is the lonely setting of Llananno, down in a dip and as close to the river edge as any church could be. Water rushes by, churning as it runs over larger stones. The land rises steeply to the east, and all the tops are marked with ancient tumuli.

The older church has gone: this is a rebuilding of the 1870s, although its simple plan, rough stone walls and arching timber roof perhaps evoke what went before. The oldest gravestones rest against the south wall.

The medieval screen and loft are almost the whole of the attraction: their delicacy and complexity astonish. What are they doing in a small wayside chapel, founded as a simple outpost of the church at Llanbister, which can never have had many in its congregation? Of all the surviving lofts it is closest in design to Llanegryn's in Meirionydd, which shares exactly the same structure of a gallery of saints under canopies, narrow borders of undulating plantlife, one above, two below, and all supported by airy vertical partitions and a flat receding decorative undercroft.

Llanegryn's is connected by tradition to the nearby Cistercian Cymmer Abbey, and some similar associative connection seems likely, if only in the shared patronage of craftsmen, between its sister Abbey Cwmhir and Llananno, over the hills just a few miles to the east. The façade of the Llananno screen outdoes its west coast companion in the Gothic intricacy of its canopies and the Celtic complexity of inter-lacing lines which play in the fronded undercroft and trellis window panels, the high beam water plants and low beam true vine which is threaded through with echoing pomegranates and spiked at both ends with knot-tailed wyverns. Over the entrance way to the chancel the work looks from a distance at its most transparent: a design of ten ornamented circles diminishing in size from left and right. Such lofts, display-ing dazzling use of line within confining borders, are the visual counterpart of the compressed and interweaving poetry of *cynghanedd* and *cywyddau*, which shared the patronage of the abbeys and a golden age in the last years of the fifteenth century.

But on the east side of the screen, where Llanegryn blooms again, Llananno changes personality, most of its panels plain, its spare leaf pattern suddenly giant-size like William Morris wallpaper. There is a strange carved head on it with two faces merging together, and nails driven through its eyes. It is as if no eyes would see the east side of the screen, another odd echo of its neighbour Abbey Cwmhir, where the east side choir was never built.

The saints on the west side, replacing lost originals, were added in 1880 and probably much else has been renewed. When Rev. John Parker visited in 1828 he noted that one border, many crockets, and some panels had gone missing. He rooted about in the rubbish on the floor and found some fragments of the patterning. As he tried to piece them together, they crumbled in his hands.

A churchwarden's pew dated 1681 stands at the back of the nave, David Lewis's name carved with a fine disregard of line endings. R.S. Thomas used to like to visit here: his poem 'Llananno' is on display near the door.

Victorian figures on Llananno's medieval screen

Llanbister, St Cynllo

SO 110 734

Llanbister church stands on its hill like a ship on a slipway, its west end shored up where the land falls steeply away towards the village and the Ithon river valley. On such a site a western tower made no sense, so this fortress of a tower, heaped up in craggy stone, was built at the higher east end to command the hill with much less effort. The nave is an upper deck, reached by climbing seventeen steps up from the entrance. Its long broad barn-like interior is dominated by a huge oak roof and heavy walls which are punctured by cuts of great depth to the windows. On the north side these are small and ancient. On the east, because of the tower, there is no window at all. Only in the late middle ages was the south wall broken through by two great openings, one of four lights, one of five. The overall effect is still true to the thirteenth century fabric, and is of half-light, and cave-like defensible shelter.

St Cynllo's is the best surviving evocation of the final years of Welsh Maelienydd, more than the wrecks of castles which stud the neighbouring hills at Tinboeth and Cymaron – a doorway in the mind to the Marcher era, dramatically entered through the deep, high porch with ten massive stones leading up to the door and using as its threshold a graveslab. The princes of Maelienydd and Gwerthyrnion had the singular misfortune to find stationed on their eastern border the Norman family of Mortimer, who were to prove themselves for close on two hundred years the *ne plus ultra* neighbours from hell, attacking, killing, blinding and kidnapping their way to take more for themselves of the lands to the west. By the thirteenth century, when St Cynllo's nave was built, the forces of Gwynedd had entered the fray and Llanbister must have changed hands half a dozen times, leaving us to wonder whether these walls were a proclamation of Mortimer gain, or a home-grown propaganda honouring of the great Welsh saint of this ancient upland kingdom once known by the name of Cynllwig, the territory of St Cynllo, Cynllo's *cynefin*, still marked by mother churches here and at Nantmel and Llangunllo. Traces of Llanbister's Age of Saints status may still linger in the earthworks on the north side of the churchyard, and in its memory of healing sulphur wells.

In later times the church acquired its many pleasing old fittings: a fourteenth century font, sixteenth century screen, seventeenth century bench pew, eighteenth century pulpit and a most unusual early twentieth century walk-in baptistery, an ingenious use of the ground levels. Older than all these is the parish chest by the north wall. The wall has several faded traces of paintings and a case holding the remains of double basses and a bassoon, used by the little church band to accompany the singers in the 1716 wooden west gallery, before the arrival of the organ swept all that away. The area beneath the gallery was the parish schoolroom.

From west to east the church rises in steps at the screen and again at the altar reflecting the rising ground, but in typical local style there is no other marking of the chancel, no entry arch or variation from the nave in height or width. Inside the tower there are four old capitals carved with foliage – possibly from Abbey Cwmhir – and above them a bell frame dated 1752. Two of its bells bear the date 1701. There must be more inscribed dates in Llanbister church than almost any other, and they give clues to changes and to restorations. The greatest structural change was a reduction, in 1701, to the height of the tower, after which the wooden pyramidal belfry was added, and topped with weathercock and vane.

Total surveillance: the view from Llanbister's truncated tower was once even more commanding

Llandefalle, St Matthew

SO 108 356

There may be at Llandefalle no single object remarkable enough to set this Breconshire country church apart: much is damaged, lost, eroded, or rudimentary enough to begin with. But there is something about the sum of it – setting, fabric, the fine small details of tomb and glass and screen, a kind of rustic grandeur with which few churches seem so comprehensively endowed.

Even the lane which leads to it, a true Welsh *lon coed* uphill and tunnelling beneath a green canopy – 'tree-shrouded', one visitor described it – seems to mark it out, merging into the stonewalled lychgate with its timbered roof and the old stone steps and stile. The land has started rising steeply, so that coming into the open ground of the churchyard the view opens grandly out to the Black Mountains ranged across the valley. High above Brecon at the seven hundred foot line, Llandefalle hill climbs on behind us almost twice as high. The llan preserves remnants of its early raised and curving embankments. It is scattered with yews and fine eighteenth century tombstones like the one for Mary Jones, aged 3 in 1767, on the church's east exterior wall. There is an overgrown well-stream on the north side and the ground drops down to another small stream on the south.

The church has a high tower with small windows at three levels and then a bell loft with projecting stone guttering and a pyramidal roof. From it extend the long nave, the south aisle, the deep and slightly narrower chancel. There is the puzzle of the church's founder saint: perhaps Maelog or someone unrecorded called Tyfalle, whose dedication was corrupted or simply changed to Matthew at a later date. And there is the puzzle of its size in this location, suggesting wealthy patronage, a local lord or prior. Clifford Priory, about ten miles north east up the valley of the Wye just beyond Hay, held the living at least some time before the Reformation and this would seem to point the connection to the Clifford family, leading barons of the southern march for generations, in their own territory here as lords of Bronllys and Cantref Selyf. Around 1300 when the oldest parts of the surviving building were put up, the place belonged to the last of the Cliffords, Matilda Longspey, a grand-daughter of Llywelyn Fawr and one who interceded with the church to give the last Llywelyn proper burial. Just before the start of the fifteenth century when this more expansive church took shape, the land had come into the hands of Henry Bolingbroke who seized the throne violently to become Henry IV, and whose resulting need for good works to expiate his sin still, in Shakespeare's telling, haunted his son on the eve of Agincourt. It is tempting to think that Llandefalle's church was such a work.

In the flagged porch there are stone benches on both sides, and a water stoup half scraped away by children, long ago sharpening their knives on it when going to school inside, which they did until 1904. Their games in the churchyard may account for the traces of external shutters on the windows – iron hinges and one surviving S-shaped shutter catch. They would have entered through the ancient iron-studded door, past the remains of the bolt log and the deep cavity in which it could be lodged in the wall during times of fear.

The huge barn of a nave is lined by four Gothic arches, and the cross timbers are crooked trunks. There are faint remains of paintings on the walls and some jumbled old stained glass in the south aisle east window. Writing two hundred years ago in his *History of Brecknockshire* Theophilus Jones, the Archdeacon of Brecon enthused about the old stained glass still then surviving, a beautifully coloured Crucifixion in the south aisle, in which his eyes were most drawn to the elegant binding of a book in Mary's hands. The wall below is lined with patterned panels dated 1687. There are old flagstones at the west end, an original window head and an extraordinary scooped-out stone for a font. "The pewter basin is disgraceful, like part of the furniture of a barber's shop", recorded the Archdeacon. The crypt can be glimpsed through a grille.

A simple rood screen survives, with steps rising and falling either side to form a threshold to the chancel, and dragons at either end. Their attributes include triangular teeth, a knotted tail and a wing like a cape. One is foreshortened, squashed up against the wall on tiny feet, more frightened than frightening: the carver simply ran out of room for him. The steps to the rood loft are still open, the loft entrance there, but the loft is gone. A high panelled wagon roof continues at a lower level into the chancel, which has whitewashed walls lined with tablets. The Jacobean altar rail has twisted baluster columns and unusual raised doors. The parish chest must be eight feet long.

Rustic grandeur at Llandefalle

Llandegley/Llandegle, The Pales Meeting House/Ty Cwrdd y Crynwyr Y Pales

SO 138 641

Wales's oldest complete surviving Quaker meeting house is hidden up a country lane at the edge of the Radnor forest. Its low stone wall and thatched roof face the narrow lane, from which a path leads through a small gate and around to the porch. The land falls away steeply below, opening out the green view across the valley of the Mithil and the wooded slopes below Llandegley rocks. The site evokes the urge for both beauty and seclusion.

Beyond the porch is the warden's cottage and a small graveyard with rounded gravestones, simply inscribed. Burials may have been the first purpose for acquiring the land in 1673, as Quakers would not be buried beside the church. It was originally fenced with wooden palings which gave The Pales its name. The meeting house itself is thought to date from 1717.

Inside the house two doors with dates above them – A.D. 1745, and 1828 – lead off into plainly decorated rooms with tall windows which bring in the view. The slightly smaller of the two is the meeting room: it is lined with narrow eighteenth century benches, and has a stand for the minister. The larger, with a fireplace and edged with flagstones, is the women's room, for worship and business – often carried out by the women of the movement – and it was for many years a schoolroom. Some old inkwells remain propped on the mantelpiece. The dividing wall, as at Dolobran, contains winged shutters so that the conduct of a meeting could be shared and opened up across the whole space.

The beauty of the place filled the diary of the man who lived and worked here in the 1870s, another Kilvert who immersed himself in nature, let the children in his day school run wild over Coed Swydd, "the distant hills and clouds all teeming with evidences of divine goodness", sympathetically recorded the privations of his farming neighbours "Alas for Welsh life, and the hardship of women" and the workaday details at The Pales, "the thatcher rethatching the roof of my schoolhouse in the rain – a wet, difficult thing", while the birds in the eaves became his friendly companions.

His name was Yardley Warner, and the pattern of his life brought together threads which had run through the history of The Pales for the previous two hundred years. His life's work was in pursuit of the emancipation of, and then the difficult providing for, the four million slaves of America's southern states. First working on the "underground railroad", the undercover freedom route that ran escaped slaves up to Canada, he turned after 1865 to fundraising for their livelihoods and education. He set up forty negro schools in Tennessee and North Carolina: one of his still-surviving legacies is the suburb of Greensboro where he provided ex-slave families with land to till and a school in which he taught, living among his new community as a pariah to many neighbouring whites. A freedman carpenter named Harmon Unthank took a spar of wood and worked a namesign for the place: he called it Warnersville.

Warner came from Pennsylvania and carried out his work through the Philadelphia Society of Friends. When he preached out in the open on Penybont Common down below The Pales, he was following in the footsteps of the first Quaker, George Fox, whose own diary records in moving terms his great preaching meeting there in 1657, accompanied by John ap John, the Ruabon-born first Welsh Quaker, who carried the ministry into Welsh – telling the large crowds that every man is equal, and every man is free. John ap John was to be one of the funders of the Welsh tract, the great Quaker land purchase in Philadelphia, and thus the revolutionary message of Penybont Common sowed seeds for Yardley Warner down the centuries. After his few years in Radnorshire, combining local ministry with frantic fundraising trips around the British Isles, Warner returned across the Atlantic, where he died of typhoid in Bush Hill, North Carolina in 1885 (although his English wife Anne was to return and carry on the work here). A museum in Springfield displays his hand-carved model of Noah's Ark, complete with all its passengers, looking very much like The Pales.

The view from The Pales, "all teeming with evidences of divine goodness"

Llandrindod Wells, Capel Caebach

SO 058 623

Caebach Chapel is one of the secret treasures of mid-Wales. It was founded in 1715, one of the earliest non-conformist buildings, and may have reused in its walls the stones from Capel Maelog, a nearby ruin from the Age of Saints. It stands above the river Ithon, a country chapel built before the town emerged, in the small field which gave it its name. Now filled with yews and huge gravestones elegantly carved, it has the look of a diminuitive churchyard. The whitewashed long wall of the chapel faces the path. It has a central door, on either side of which is a tall clear window, set unusually low. Each has a kind of ogee curve at the top, a rare chapel flourish.

Inside, the half-octagon pulpit is against the short wall, placed as though it were the altar of a church, and lower in height now than it would once have been. Rows of mid-nineteenth century putty-coloured gated benches face it, varying in size and height and rising in steps at the back, from where a small window looks out to the green hills across the valley. Each bench has a holder for candles. A gallery above was added in 1804 on simple wooden columns, and it may have been then that the chapel acquired its hipped roof, which adds to the height and raises the space for windows, making the interior unusually light. From it hangs a large chandelier, a signal of gentry patronage, no doubt from the occupants of the chapel's one box pew.

In 1954 some 30 sketches, made in oil in the 1770s and privately kept since then, came up for auction in Christie's, London. They were small and undemonstrative, but they had a photographic clarity not known before the 1800s. They captured the sunlight as freshly as a Monet, the geometry of form as intensely as Cezanne. It seemed as though, in an age when art was mythological, academic, full of superfluous flourish, it was enough for this artist to paint the light as it fell on a whitewashed wall, a door, a window, and evoke the simple materials from which they were made.

The painter was Thomas Jones. He was born in 1742, into a family which owned the estates on which Caebach was built, and on which the spa town was to rise. He is buried in the chapel vault, and his name is on the family monument above it. It records him as a magistrate, not a painter, and the year recorded for his death (in fact 1803) is wrong by several years. His grandfather, Rev. Thomas Jones, was "the pious founder of this chapel" but a later minister drily noted the absence of religion from his progeny. Young Thomas took the road to Bohemia, taking up with art and with a Danish mistress – below his station and Catholic to boot. Offered the chance to sail with Captain Cook on his southern voyages, he joined instead the artists' colonies in Italy. It was there that his artistic vision flowered, but its unmistakable roots were the vernacular simplicity of Caebach and Radnorshire, first caught in airy paintings from his terrace at Pencerrig.

One of the first independent chapels in this part of Wales, Caebach attracted the dissenting preachers such as Howel Harris, who recorded that the crowd in the churchyard sang with "great gales of life". Congregations would travel here by pony: the outbuilding by the gate was the stable. Later congregants have left their presence here by many pencil scribblings on the backs of pews, including, up on the far end of the gallery, an englyn.

Pure and simple: early non-conformity at Caebach

Llanelieu, St Ellyw

SO 185 342

East of Talgarth the old lanes follow the lie of the land, sinking into it, winding their way through wooded slopes and undulating fields, their progress finally deflected at the dead end head of Cwm Rhyd Ellywe. Llanelieu still feels like the end of a long road. Beyond a cluster of old stone houses, stone steps lead up through a screen of trees into a large loping field with an ancient building stranded on its further side. There are sheep grazing, a few random gravestones on the south side, almost none of them upright, inscriptions mostly worn away. A stream rounds the churchyard on the east and north, meeting another at the angle, deeply banked, islanding the llan in its own enclosed world.

This raised and sacred island at the end of the long tunnelling valley is, as at all the old llans, just the outer ring of enclosure within which the concentric secrets of a saint are encased. Within it is the church, a rough box of almost unbroken walls, piled up from the sandstone which lies beneath the soil. In the church's enclosing darkness, a wall to ceiling screen marks out the third inner layer, within which, no doubt, there were yet further layers, of tomb and grave and reliquary, of the mysterious St Ellyw. In this poor and isolated place at the Black Mountains' ragged edge, the landscape and its wood and stone were drawn upon to make a holy place to be approached with awe, as though, in the mind, it was something as powerful as a pyramid in Egypt. It is intended to bring you to your knees.

The way in now is marked by a few small signs and remnants. The bells in the wooden bellcote are seven and eight hundred years old, among the oldest in the country. There are circles incised on two small grave markers which are propped against the leaning porch wall, their primitive Celtic crosses perhaps fourteen hundred years old. The ribbed church door has a sanctuary knocker. It opens on misplaced hinges, to steps leading down in to the darkness.

At dusk with candlelight in the interior, the great rood screen and long arcades cast surging shadows down the nave. The screen is blood red, pockmarked with stencilled white roses and open quatrefoils through which eyes in the loft could follow the priest's work at the altar. It still bears at its centre the unpainted ghost-mark of the cross. There is a grandeur to its presence unexpected in a place which may never have had more than fifty people to inhabit it, but there are traces of links to the patronage of Llanthony, and the see of St David's itself. To these roots may also belong the late medieval roof, with tie beams and cinquefoiled windboards; the fading west wall painting of Adam and Eve, the serpent and the Tree of Life; and the late intrusion of the paired west windows, a fifteenth century attempt at introducing light, hesitantly deep silled and low set.

After the Reformation the church continued to be cared for: texts and a large royal arms with lion rampant were painted on the wall, an altar rail added and the font given a cover which is almost baroque. Two back pews date from this time. A square-faced sundial dated 1686 was placed outside just by the porch. These are the gifts of families whose memorials occupy both church and field, like the Prices, Vaughans and Awbreys, the last of whom lived well here for centuries, while also sending sons as early colonists of Virginia. When they settled there in the northern neck, in what was later to become Westmoreland County, they must have been among the first white men in the territory. One descendant is recorded a century later, owning 140 acres on Machodoc creek. They had better fortune perhaps than the blind harpist Thomas Jones, whose memorial is inscribed here in Welsh, or than Walter Watkins, whose tablet in the north east window leaves a bequest in 1773 to 'two of the poorest children lawfully begot', but a later enquirer recorded 'it is not paid, and the will has never been proved'.

Llanelieu: Arcadia of ghosts

Llanfihangel Helygen, St Michael

SO 046 644

St Michael-in-the-Willows is encircled by oaks. It could be an old longhouse in a clearing, but for a small bell turret and a few scattered gravestones. Windows are small and domestic with blackened timber lintels; walls are built in tiers of long flat stones up to the mossy roof.

Inside, through the nailed door, it is almost like an early chapel. The pulpit – a high three-decker – is on the long wall half way down the flagstoned nave. Box pews and double-backed benches are gathered around to face it. There is no west window, but a small stone-floored vestry behind a barn-like wall of huge horizontal planks. Pegs protrude from the beams in the late fourteenth century roof. The parish chest is of the six plank type. Oldest of all is the font, cylindrical and miniature, probably very early Norman, like the dedication of the church. The choice of St Michael, lover of mountains, may also reflect or have influenced the location, on the crest of a small hill.

Not beside a river, still apart from settlements and absent from most maps, its origins remain mysterious. In the Radnorshire vernacular, houses, barns, churches and chapels all draw from a common currency of pattern and material, simple rectangles of wood and stone, and make them difficult to date. For most of its history Llanfihangel Helygen was a chapel of the mother church at Nantmel, without burial or communion rights, and the building in this form may owe much to the seventeenth or eighteenth centuries, the time of the Jesus Chapel north at Llanfair Dyffryn Clwyd, which also did not have an altar. The ecclesiastical east window was added only in 1854. This sole non-vernacular touch was, strangely enough, the result of an appeal begun by perhaps early nineteenth century Wales's greatest champion for the vernacular – Thomas Price, Carnhuanawc, vicar of Cwmdu and curate here, whose proud Eisteddfod speeches in the 1820s declaimed, against the pressures of the age, the international value of Welsh life and language and inspired, in addition to his own poetry and classic *Hanes Cymru* (History of Wales), the work of a new generation of literary women, from Charlotte Guest's first published translation of *The Mabinogion* to Lady Llanover's lifelong sustaining of *gwerin* music, dance, poetry and dress.

The 1851 census records a parish population of just 97, mainly Morgans, Lloyds, Morrises, and Hamers. The parish reaches east to the banks of the Ithon and the remains of Castell Collen, once the primary Roman base in mid-Wales, a fortress, religious centre and early spa. A silver ring has been excavated there, with the roughly made inscription '*Amor Dulcis*'.

Farm, church or barn? Llanfihangel's Radnorshire vernacular

Llanfilo, St Beilo

SO 119 332

Llanfilo eases into the hillside, a few farms and cottages along a climbing, winding lane. Up on the ridge the traces of an ancient settlement mark out an elongated circle. The views from the high south side of the churchyard stretch out to the Black Mountains and across the falling valley to Llandefalle hill, a great sweep of territory in which the stone-tiled church of St Beilo slopes and steps down in a descending line of tower, nave and chancel, following the flow of the land. There are some characteristic signs that there has been a church here for fifteen hundred years: raised and rounded boundaries; a site surrounded by springs and on a gentler stretch of slope below the brow; and a dedication to a saintly daughter of Brychan, the fifth century king from whom the name Brecon derives.

The lychgate by the roadside is among the oldest in the country, dating from around 1700. It carries simple memorials to the Great War dead. From there a path leads through the llan towards a medieval porch with deeply splayed windows and a flagstone floor. There are consecration crosses incised in the arch and a fifteenth century wooden roof. The door is packed with nails and still faintly inscribed in red from the date of its last repair – 1767. Above it, the stone lintel is carved with the diamond-pattern of the Normans, one of the earliest signatures in a fabric rich in the craftsmanship of many centuries.

Inside the door, a small nave rises in low steps towards the tower to the left, and drifts slowly downwards to the right. The font is old beyond dating, perhaps from the Celtic church before the Normans came. There is a fifteenth century wagon roof with ribbed panelling and one great tie beam, and across the east end a rood screen and loft of c.1500. Pomegranates, vines and roses trail among the patterned ornament, with a dragon at the north end of the head beam. The loft has unusual three-sided pilasters across the front, perhaps originally arrayed with saints. The saints in between them now, carved in relief, are insertions of the 1920s. There are some pews from 1630 and signs of much renewal towards the end of Charles II's reign, including a new pulpit and a tall adjacent window cut to light it. The walls, inside and out, are lined with memorial tablets, mostly Georgian, remembering the families whose rituals centred on this church for centuries, the Vaughans of Tredomen and Pengoyffordd and the Havards of Penmaes, a farm which still preserves its old stone cider press, a memory of the orchards which once covered much of these slopes.

The chancel is half-secret, separate, revealing itself only on entry through the tracery and a nave end-wall deep enough to suggest a lost role as the eastern limit of the church. Flagstones mark the further stages of descent. In here the ceiling and the east side of the loft are utterly unornamented. Rectangular windows with wooden frames add to the vernacular spirit which pervades the whole interior. A beautiful deep window is cut into the altar wall, from which the green landscape of the eastward-turning Wye reaches out into the distance. The cracked bell on the floor once rang the Angelus: it is cast with the royal heads of Edward III and Queen Philippa his wife, and a Latin inscription 'Missi de celis habeo nomen Gabrielis' – I have the name of Gabriel sent from heaven. A cross-slab with a floral border, by the altar, is late thirteenth century. The stone altar tables are older still.

The pilgrim roads of a second daughter of Brychan, St Eluned, weave along this ancient upland, pausing at the well outside the churchyard wall (now capped) and crossing westward beyond Llechfaen to Slwch Tump where her lost shrine chapel stood. Another route led through Llanddew, passing by Gerald of Wales's front door. He noted her healing power and the trance-like actions of her devotees: Eluned, he wrote, had triumphed "in an ecstasy of self-denial". The Normans had taken up her cult on their arrival, servicing it from Brecon priory and settling in Llanfilo in some numbers. Earthworks of house platforms and sunken lanes spreading to the east suggest the village was much larger then.

At home in its landscape

Llangynyw, St Cynyw
SJ 127 091

In a green landscape of rising hills, St Cynyw's churchyard has been lifted even
further by the burials of fifteen hundred years, so that a stone wall now holds it up
above the natural slope. A circular wall, a circle of seven yews and a church within
them map out the characteristic Celtic llan. No village has ever grown up around it,
leaving it open to the wide and undulating view. There is a scattering of eighteenth
century slabs among the stones and crosses, and a sundial with a plate dated 1616
and the inscription 'Sunny Tyme Only'. A path between the yews leads to a deep and
well-preserved oak porch of the fifteenth century: weathered wooden panel walls,
arched roof, bench seats and an arrangement of concentric cobbles.

The church is a simple whitewashed chamber, much from the time of the porch.
At the western end is a tiered gallery from which carols are still sung by candlelight
at Christmas. The bell rope intrudes through the wall. The view from up here is
splendid, the whiteness of the plastered walls and ceiling contrasting with the dark
oak below. The screen still stands before the chancel, with some patterned tracery,
winged dragons, flowers and pomegranates, and a fragment of true vine. A part of
the tracery is not the oak original, but a well-disguised replacement made of iron in
Mathrafal forge.

Behind it is a polished wooden altar and reredos with painted angels and symbols
in gilded panels, and above them on the walls, two darkening mid-Victorian paintings of the Nativity and Resurrection. There is a hooded reading desk, a litany desk,
and an eighteenth century benefactions board. These are High Anglican touches but
with a homely charm in keeping with this modest and human interior which, in such
a landscape, carries the distinctive hallmark of the Welsh aesthetic, and its too readily
under-estimated meaning and value.

A panel in the screen

Llangynyw is one of the cluster of small parishes at the spiritual centre of ancient Powys. Its boundary line winds along the river Banwy past the old court of the Powys princes at Mathrafal, and pours itself into the Vyrnwy at Bont Newydd, where one of the oldest surviving Calvinistic chapels stands on the banks, built at a river-fork as if through ancient instinct by the early elders. The northern boundary turns upstream along the Vyrnwy, a district full of other old survivals – Capel y Crynwyr, Saron Ty'n-y-rhyd and the Upper Chapel at Pontrobert – all outbreaks of early non-conformity and renewing spiritual seriousness, the last of them the home of John Hughes, the preacher and friend of Ann Griffiths.

Ann was standing right here in Llangynyw church, on 17 November 1798, for her brother Edward's wedding, at which she signed as a witness. Her much-loved hymns and letters still burn through the fogs of two hundred years, opening the heart of a young woman whose swings between joy and vulnerability were caught in her intense and soul-baring lines, sometimes revelling in her Lord, sometimes troubled by him, more often troubled by herself, wondering how much to trust the pleasures of her life. She held in her mind the story of the Shunammite woman, prepared and expectant: the view of things to come seemed good "through the lattice", with her spinning heart "swiftly travelling through a world of time to the world which lasts forever". She died at the age of 29, living on for just a few days after the death of her first child.

Fifteenth century timber and stone, ancient yews

Llanidloes, St Idloes

SN 953 846

The grandest church buildings ever planned in mid-Wales were the four Cistercian abbeys which began to take shape from around 1200. Strata Marcella, Cymmer, Cwmhir, Strata Florida: there is not much left of them now. Strata Florida has its famous arch, rounded with a Celtic twist, and Cymmer a few strewn walls beside a farm and river. Strata Marcella has disintegrated, leaving speculative traces maybe in a nearby parish font, or Llanfair Caereinion's triple-shafted doorway.

Cwmhir was the most ambitious of them all. The nave was the longest in Wales, twice the length of St David's – and only exceeded in Britain by Winchester and Durham. Some have seen it as Llywelyn Fawr's intended cathedral to his new vision of the country, a cultural and religious powerhouse at the centre of the map. It was never finished. Some of it has nevertheless survived – but not where it was built. Nearly five hundred years ago, it migrated to Llanidloes.

Llanidloes is a melting pot: an early llan from the age of saints adjoined in the late thirteenth century by the grid plan of a conquest colony. Then in the 1540s, the pieces of the great Cistercian abbey arrived for reassembly. In the eighteenth century John Wesley came to preach from a stone in the open-sided market hall, and in the nineteenth, chapels rose on almost every street, some colonnaded like temples, Heol China still sustaining the plygain at Christmastime.

The last medieval angel roof in Britain

The parish church has seen it all. Hard by the river and on a slight rise above it, the old approach route came straight from the Severn through the single gateway on the churchyard's north east side. The tower is the oldest part of the current building, a massive, probably fourteenth century bastion topped by a typical Montgomeryshire timbered belfry. Inside it is surprisingly elegantly vaulted. It was built to stand well above the nave originally alongside it, but the dissolution of Cwmhir must have offered the chance for a nave of new height, breadth and ornament. The parishioners planned the disassembly of the stones of its south doorway and parts of its arcade, and their perilous transport by cart through the pass at Bwlch-y-Sarnau and down the beautiful tumbling valley of the Marteg.

For many years the spectacular nineteen-bay hammerbeam roof was thought to have made the same journey, but in 2003 tree-ring dating was used to prove that the timbers were cut in the late summer or early autumn of 1538: the town had commissioned for its grand new nave the last medieval angel roof in Britain. There are images of the instruments of the Passion, an archer, a bird of prey and stranger creatures carved on the brackets. The date 1542 was carved on an angel shield to mark its completion.

The doorway, with shafts and Corinthian capitals, and the nave arcade – five arches of Cwmhir's original fourteen – are from the first decades of the thirteenth century, and close in kind to those at the contemporary Haverfordwest. They still bear the original masons' marks. Each column is a cluster of triple shafts, those at the east being shorter, suggesting they came from the raised east end of the abbey nave. The arch nearest the tower is narrower than the others, as though insufficient space was left for it, and it had to be squashed in.

The capitals had an even more unlikely reassembly. They are of the French type known as stiff leaf, which was new around 1200 and evolved through subsequent decades with the leaves becoming more unfolded and full, as if through a long slow Spring. There are examples here of each development of the style, matching the years through which the Cwmhir nave was built, some of them arguably early enough to pre-date Llywelyn Fawr's extending power. But the separate stones that made up each carved capital were not put back together as they had been taken down: they were shuffled together without thought, to make a row of accidental, composite capitals of jumbled pieces from across the years.

Llanwenog, St Gwenog

SN 494 456

The upper valley of the Teifi is broad and green, a different world from the wooded defiles through which it runs at Cilgerran and Cenarth. From the hills on either side, a thousand feet up, the great fortress towers of its churches are the landmarks of the countryside. The best of them are at Llandysul and even more, Llanddewi Brefi, ancient and rich in the early history of Wales. But St Gwenog's church has the edge: the medieval fabric – thirteenth century walls and a fifteenth century wagon roof – has survived here better than anywhere else in the county, and its exceptional nature reflects at least one patron of more than regional standing. The tower, built just five hundred years ago to mark the Tudor winning of the English crown, carries the badge of Rhys ap Thomas, Lord of Dinefwr and Carew, the man who by tradition gave Richard III his death wound on the battlefield. No tower is more enclosed, its walls broken only by the narrowest of slits, its few carvings small and isolated in great banks of stone.

There is something about a church entered through the western tower, and St Gwenog's, on a strong slope with the view ahead barrelling down the long nave towards the altar, uses all the dramatic potential. It is like entering a deep cave in the rock. An ancient stoup projects to the right and carved faces watch over the descent into the body of the church, under heavy masonry arches with great cuts through which bell ropes hang. The ten commandments are written in black on the walls. Only then are there windows, very deeply set. It is all massive and primitive, and its signature piece is the font.

This extraordinary sculpted stone, probably twelfth century, has a circle of twelve heads massed against each other, their features as broad and strongly incised as African masks. They are presumed to represent the twelve apostles. There is nothing else like it in the country – a neighbouring font of similar date at Pencarreg across the valley, with typical monks and kings, underlines its powerful difference of style.

But the centrally-placed carving in the church is the Crucifixion, originally in an outside wall but lately brought inside for shelter by the altar. It is a small, elongated oval, fifteenth century perhaps, from which the image is scooped in relief. Weather has worn away the detail. As in the paintings of medieval masters from Giotto to Memling, Christ hangs on the cross, towering over Mary and St John, their hands here clasped in anguish or in prayer, his arms outstretched like a blessing. It is another legacy, most likely, of the courtly warrior Rhys ap Thomas and his cosmopolitan artistic patronage, no doubt inspired by his formative years in Burgundy.

Around a hundred years ago all the church's bench ends and its screen were locally designed and carved by an enterprising team of five – Rev. John Morris, his curate Henry Jones, Colonel and Mrs Davies-Evans and their estate carpenter William Evans – and during the Great War they had expert help from a Belgian refugee, Joseph Reubens of Bruges. They made a kind of rural diary spreading out over more than thirty years from 1889, connecting events far distant in time or place with the current preoccupations of the parish: the two local men who died in Gallipoli in 1915, the acreages ploughed by each farm in 1917, the only visits to Llanwenog by Archbishops of Canterbury – in 1187 and 1902, the choir leaders and musical prizes, the signing of the Peace of Versailles.

Outside, the churchyard falls away towards the river, looking out to the mountains of Llanybydder and Pencarreg. Among the scattered graves are many marked with very small and simple stones. David Lloyd and David Davis (Dafydd Dafis Castellhywel), Unitarian preachers, suspected Jacobins and purposeful upsetters of the status quo, are buried here alongside one another near the door. Davis was a poet too of life's fragilities, and translator into Welsh of Thomas Gray's Elegy on another country churchyard. For centuries here on New Year's Day or Christmas morning, violent village football games poured out down the valley towards the church porch of Llandysul, which was the other goal. It took fifteen minutes, in one nineteenth century account, from the first throw of the ball for it to surface again between the scrambling bodies.

Llanwenog: massive and primitive, and its signature piece is the font

171

Llanywern, St Mary the Virgin
SO 103 286

It says something for the territory when the names of two neighbouring villages, Llangors and Llanywern, are variations on the phrase "the church in the bog". But while Llangors at its green village centre looks well-drained and comfortable, Llanywern, at least in the wetter months, is exactly what it says on the label.

From here the line of the Black Mountains coming down towards the Wye looks like a high tide of falling waves. Small eddies of streams pour in along the lanesides, running into a spreading, reedy pond spiked with tall bulrushes, then out again to curl around the ancient churchyard, and ooze and squelch across it until saturation. Pools of damp seep up into the nave from under the flagstones. Services once held in the mire of an earthen floor — and burials here — can be only queasily imagined.

Llanywern is as simple a rural church as survives in Wales. Its pleasures are of atmosphere, of ancient community and irregular vernacular, in which it is still

As simple a rural church as survives in Wales

172

totally immersed. It harks back to sixth century St Cynidr, and to four hundred years looked after by the monks of Brecon, whose sub-prior had a house here. A cluster of four farms immediately around it seem unchanged over centuries, their traditional stone barns the homes of small gatherings of jackdaws and collared doves. It is a church filled with birdsong.

The building is fourteenth century, stone, wood and tile, a linear sequence of porch, nave and chancel with the small interruption of a belfry, enclosed with a pyramid-shaped top. The ground from the outside appears to fall away slightly to the east, but inside the effect is different, as steps rise to the chancel, and the roof lowers under an oak wagon ceiling, giving the altar more intimate focus.

The north wall is pressed and buttressed with two huge and primitive triangles of stone: the south wall leans outward as though in incongruent consequence. On that side there is a blocked up priest's door, and a small memorial tablet to William Watkins, who died in 1728. The stone is mauve or reddish grey, many of the pieces flat, and above it the roof beams rest on a pole of wood as long and slender as those which support the open barn across the road.

The porch is lined with stone seating and has two angular and tapering openings in the walls. Two standing stones are the pillars which frame its entrance, with another at the left of the nave door, and a riverstone underfoot. The wooden arch beams overhead have pegs at the joints.

Inside the floor rises beside a stoup and a thirteenth century stone bowl font with a curious wooden cover ringed with bottle top circles. It leads on between two rows of simple wooden pews, the seats made of great broad planks that also serve as ledges for the row behind. The interior walls are limewashed, the roof unceiled and hung with oil lamps, and the windows scattered and deep. The pulpit is reached as though by mounting block.

In the chancel are more eighteenth century wall tablets, locally made, their borders garlanded and graced with angel wings. A little of their colour remains – green leaves, yellow flowers, red in an angel's trumpet. Beneath the altar are six tombstones of some grandeur, with coats of arms and floreate roundels, clearly made to match. They are seventeenth century, and their inscriptions are brief portraits, as of 'Owen William ap Richard Gunter, paternally descended from Sir Peter Gunter, knight, who married Gwervil, daughter of Meredith John Jenkin, they had issue ten children living, viz Lewis, John, Meredith, William, Thomas, Richard, Mallt, Juan, Lleici and Gwenllian'. Owen died in 1615. Behind these are oak altar panels decorated with flowerheads in interweaving circles, and a date, its numbers spread out to left and right: 1657. While Puritan rule was stripping out church decoration, deconsecrating altars, life at Llanywern carried on – then as now – regardless.

Maesyronnen Chapel

SO 177 412

Up the hill from Glasbury, set back down a lane, Maesyronnen Chapel stands alone among the fields. It started life as a barn, long and low and earth-brown, with a sixteenth century farmhouse adjoining it. There is a sundial in one of the gables, and beyond the cruck wall a small keeper's or minister's cottage, part of its adaptation for chapel use. Maesyronnen is the closest we can come now to the first chapels of three hundred years ago, wonderfully intact with early furniture and a many-stranded tie-beamed roof: Welsh vernacular at its sociable and unpresuming best. Yet the essence of all later chapel design – the positioning of pulpit, *sedd fawr*, congregation, windows, doors – has already taken shape here.

Light comes in on three sides through simple, deep set windows. An extraordinary assembly of old tables, pews and benches stretches in a long row down the flagstones. At the centre two communal seats face each other across a plank table, all joined at the base and dated 1728. This was a statement of belief: communion had been placed at the heart of the congregation, not railed off at an altar, and they too were at the heart of things, independent and free to worship as they chose collectively, without instruction from others elsewhere. Beside them on the long wall was the pulpit: it has since been cut down from its original height, and is painted with the names of all the ministers since 1645, among them David Price, the teacher of Howel Harris. There is a reading desk with cupboards for books, and a *sedd fawr* – the big seat – for the deacons.

Maesyronnen (which means field of the ash) was registered as a chapel in 1697, but was probably the congregation's meeting place for some good while before. The wall memorials offer clues to the better off among them: one for Mary Lloyd, the daughter of a gentleman; several remembering the deaths of children; and one late Georgian with a Latin inscription, 'Vita mihi mors est, Mors mihi vita nova est; Nam dilexit multum' – Life is death to me, and death to me is new life for it delights me much. According to a survey of 1715, there was a thriving attendance of two hundred and fifty.

Cromwell is said to have come here, and Whitefield to preach. One August day just after the Second World War R.S. Thomas sought it out, and finding the doors locked, lay down in the field to imagine the first worshippers entering the dark interior, rustling the pages of their Bibles. He recorded how the mystery of Creation overcame him, like a fountain welling endlessly up, and he took to his knees in praise. The novelist and traveller Bruce Chatwin, a modern pilgrim to the spirit of place, must have visited some forty years later, imagining the urgent preaching, the harmonium wheezing to the hymns of William Williams, and communion shared across the table, as though this was the Upper Room and the Last Supper itself. Maesyronnen is the unmistakable original of 'Maesyfelin' chapel in his novel *On The*

Black Hill. He recognised a place where men affirmed their world in speech and song, foreshadowing the songlines he would go on to find elsewhere: he was a writer who slipped confidently through the borderlines of continents or cultures, and unreliably from document to fantasy, but he was earthed by the power of this old interior, and of Welsh hill farming life, as truths which needed no embellishment.

Mwnt, Holy Cross
SN 195 520

There is a point on the road to the coast where suddenly the sea bursts into view above the hedges. A startling headland hill rises sharply above the line of the cliff edge, in the full blast of wind and weather, while the sea swirls in the races between the shore and Cardigan island. Entrenched on its lower slopes is the bright white church of Mwnt.

Mwnt is a survival of the ancient urge to worship where nature is most elemental. A mortuary chapel lay higher up the hill, and there used to be up there a stone preaching cross, from where the preacher's words must have been blown out to sea like the small birds that fly into the cross-currents. Those who go round to Mwnt's seaward side walking sometimes come back on their knees, so sharply can the gusts drive across the drop. Many were buried here; many more were embarked from here to Bardsey for pilgrimage or burial. Just to the south of the hill is a small beach, reached by steep steps leading down, from where the old voyagers in their oxhide boats must have edged out over shoals of mackerel and curious passing dolphins.

The little church enclosure is embanked like an iron age fort. The west side has a small bell turret but no window, only a wall of worn white paint. A short path leads like a gully from the gate to a door so low it must be entered stooping, until surrounded by solid walls of leaning stone. It is like entering the chamber of a dolmen.

There are plain deep windows, all square headed. The present building, late thirteenth or fourteenth century, was primitive even in its time, hunkered down to weather the Atlantic storms. The stone for the font comes from the nearby Preseli hills, which were also the source for Stonehenge.

One relic of a grander interior remains, stone steps which led to a rood loft, and two crumbled shafts of its parapet. A trail of roses, and a few damaged faces, perhaps of the Apostles, can still be made out.

The church of the Holy Cross, entrenched on its headland hill

Nantmel, Carmel Chapel

SO 054 665

The roads that lead north from the Dulas valley wind upwards to a few small farms and cottages, and stop. Beyond is the wooded country where white monks came eight hundred years ago to build at Abbey Cwmhir. At a bend in the road, there is something like a cottage, a white-fronted chapel in a field by a fast-flowing stream. It is set back behind a screen of holly and wild roses, and two yews gripped in ivy. Another stream used to run through the middle of this small grave-field, but has been now oddly buried under the turf.

Carmel Chapel was built around 1829. It is made with loose assembled stones but the chapelfront is symmetrical, with two central windows flanked by two black doors and smaller windows aligned above them to light a gallery. The only decorative touches are the arching tops to the window leads, and the small wooden pinnacles at the top of each gable, although one of them is down and lying on the grass. Three martins have made nests under the eaves. Against the southfacing, suncatching whiteness of the stone, the windows present intense contrasting blackness, a visual accident explained by there being no openings, no other light entering, in any other wall.

Inside it is so small and intimate, just four rows of seats facing a simple pulpit. No preacher would have had to raise his voice above conversational pitch. The pulpit is raised and stands between the windows with the elders' seat arranged below. There is a brass lampholder ornamented with ivy leaves, and a single candleholder on a gallery post. The hat rack is a row of long nails in the wall. The clock has no hands. To the left a steep staircase leads up to a three-sided wooden gallery with benches. A certain WB spent the service carving his initials up there one Sunday in 1853.

Carmel must have been modestly conceived, a meeting house for a few members of a small community, a few families who wanted to worship in one particular way – and in this it is a wholly characteristic and moving expression of a rural Welsh tradition. In the absence of a congregation, the families are remembered in the small gathering of stones on graves, each with their own row in the grass, the Morgans of Glandulas a mile and a half south east, the Lewises of Bwlch Bryndinau half a mile north east, their distinct grey stones fading under lichen, the Williamses who lived in the mill on the Dulas, Griffithses of Court Gwyn just down the lane, Davieses of Cae Edward, and the Rogers family, who had two or three miles to travel.

They made their choice to be here, in an Independent chapel, from a patchwork which offered Calvinistic Methodism at Gwystu, General Baptist at Dolau, Particular Baptist at Fron, or Anglicanism at Nantmel or Llanfihangel Helygen; the religious map of nineteenth century Wales in microcosm. Walking or riding the Sunday roads the families' choices must have made a web of crossing paths, these few in the quiet conviction that it was at a place called Carmel Elijah discountenanced alternative prophets.

Their graves are a stark record of how the lives lived in these communities in this time were traumatised with early deaths – 'in memory of 2 daughters', 'in memory of two sons', 'We mourn the loss of one / We did our best to save / Beloved on earth, regretted, gone / Remembered in the grave'. These deaths, before the ages of twenty or thirty, in Victorian Wales, are a counterpoise to those of a next generation, and a reminder that those were not, as it can sometimes seem, uniquely doomed. There are three of them remembered in this single field, who died at much the same ages, but in Egypt, Palestine and France. Two were from the same family: Private George Rogers of the South Wales Borderers, killed just six weeks before the Armistice, and Private David Rogers of the Herefordshires, a few months earlier, whose body is not here at Carmel, but in Jerusalem.

Carmel: a moving expression of a rural Welsh tradition

Old Radnor/Maesyfed, St Stephen/St Ystyffan

SO 250 591

The old Welsh borderland was an uncertain place, full of shifting currents, cultures meeting and not meeting, strange marriages and hybrid forms – and Old Radnor is its quintessential church. A medieval church on an old Celtic hill, a vulnerable glass church with a strong defensive tower, a church full of light with arcades and aisles but flat-roofed and without a clerestory – not quite the whole Perpendicular and not quite the Radnorshire county, a country church studded with royal emblems and more-than-ordinary traces of high altars, a church that looks English to a Welshman and must feel Welsh to an Englishman. At Old Radnor baptism happens in a shard from a stone circle, images of wyverns trade with dolphins, a window of St Catherine in glory is shadowed over by a small, horned, disconcerting devil, and the name of the local Welsh holy man Ystyffan has been transmuted to a distant St Stephen. And all this strangeness is wrapped around by the reassuring five hundred year old companionship of church and pub, both sharing the original churchyard, the ancient rounded boundary making a scarp through the pub garden.

Glyndwr, probably, attacked the predecessor church and burned it down: the rebuilding seems to have spread across the fifteenth century and more than one patron. The lands and castle belonged first to the Mortimers who by this time, in a borderland epiphany, had merged in their dynasty the blood of Marcher barons – William Marshal, de Braose, de Clare – with the blood of all the ancient royal line of Gwynedd and second, from 1424, to Richard Plantagenet and then the Crown itself. Thus, for their church in Radnor, Arts and Crafts of a rare richness – and sources of artistic innovation which cannot now be quite pinned down.

Most intriguing is the organ case of c.1500, distinctly Renaissance decades before the new style had infiltrated Gothic this side of the Channel. Around the keyboard it is slim and subtle with linenfold panels in Mackintosh dimensions, but higher up the lines begin to veer and dance, becoming dolphins and wyverns and foliage – Celtic images but carved more lithely, like something from the Mediterranean south.

The one remaining panel of medieval glass is rather hidden behind the organ: a portrait of St Catherine with a martyr's wheel. She is red-robed and crowned and her golden hair flows down her back, lit up by images of sunbursts and white roses, a royal badge of Edward IV. The window's hovering devil-presence and its patronage are shared by another work of the same artist, in the little church of Llanwrin outside Machynlleth, where one black halo at a Crucifixion scene marks out from his companions the soul-deceiving angel of the abyss. On the next wall is an eighteenth century painting of Moses and Aaron, Moses depicted with horns as in Michelangelo's sculpture.

There is a full set of screens, running the whole breadth of the church and dividing chancel from side chapels. On the main screen two narrow bands of curving vines rest on a simple vault with lace-like patterning in the arches below, one of the most uncomplicated, open and expansive of the Welsh survivals, though perhaps there was more density of carving on the lost loft above. In fact it is English-style, and has a virtual twin at Cirencester. Without a chancel arch the choir feels similarly open. It has two rows of sixteenth century stalls, a medieval book chain and memorials of later centuries, among them those to the Lewis family from whom came the scholarly Victorian Cabinet minister George Cornewall Lewis. He is buried in the vault below.

The floor of the church has many medieval tiles, mostly at the west end of the north aisle and in clusters through the south aisle. There is an Easter sepulchre, and two old chests. The nave is covered with an oak wagon roof with Tudor roses in the foliage on the bosses, and the north aisle roof is older still. Most remarkable of all may be the font, perhaps the oldest and the largest in the country, big enough for baptism by immersion. A date of 800, even 600, has been suggested, and some believe that before it came into the church it was part of the prehistoric 'Four Stones' still standing in the wide flat plain by the Walton to Kinnerton road.

The devil in the detail: Old Radnor's St Catherine window

180

Patrisio, St Issui

SO 279 224

Patrisio church is a stone building in a sea of green hills. From an opposite slope it appears as a small disruption on a steep field, the old stone wall on the southern side propping up the churchyard edge's near-vertical drop. It looks as separate a place as any farm in the Welsh landscape, and in many ways as indistinguishable. The view twists round to the Sugar Loaf and the unexpected gap at the foot of the Black Mountains where the river Honddu breaks out below Skirrid Fawr. Below the churchyard field in the wooded hollow of Nant Mair, St Issui's holy well spills out above the stream, and its banks are still lined with simply-made crosses of bark and twig.

In such a setting Patrisio's mysterious shrines, its thousand year old walls blanketed with bible exhortations and its accumulated throng of ancient contents make of this extraordinary place the definitive Welsh mountain church. Each of the eras of the church – the Celtic reverence for spirit of place; the Catholic screened rituals and relics; the Protestant plastering with the Word – are encapsulated here in a way which tells the spiritual history of Wales with especial clarity.

There are rewards to approaching on foot. One way comes from the Tabernacle Chapel, a simple, intact, very early Victorian survival, just across the Grwyne Fawr in Ffwddog. The path climbs from the road through a tunnel of trees, is soaked by a stream heading downhill across it, passes the stone ruin of a farmhouse as the view opens out to the south east. A hill field leads to another full of Welsh mountain sheep, customarily retreating, and rabbits scatter in the deep lane which runs through the ancient farm of Tyn-y-Llwyn, the revenues of which have helped sustain the fabric of the church over the centuries. Then a gate into another steeply rising, thistled field in which, in the far top corner, the church appears.

A stone bench runs along the nave's exterior wall, facing out to the churchyard preaching cross – a church in a landscape in miniature. The churchyard was small and contained within the field until the last century, when it was enlarged to reach the lane. A then-new lychgate, deeply set and arched with tapering stones, frames the view back to the church and its fourteenth century double bellcote. The building in between was a stable for the parson's pony. Some of the gravestones scattered in the high grass around it are finely carved with moving inscriptions.

The westernmost door in the southern wall leads to an enclosed chapel which contains St Issui's shrine. It is a plain and private space with high walls and a fourteenth century roof. Its off-centre stone altar is unusually marked with six consecration crosses. Above the stone steps to its side is a niche, now once again holding an image of the saint, this one made in 1995 by Frank Roper. From here, through a squint in the wall, the screened interior of Patrisio can first be seen.

It is strikingly lit. High in the west wall is one small splayed window with a sloping sill, while the long north wall, traditional barrier to spirits of evil, lets in no light at all. A large window with a wooden lintel, put into the south wall only in the fifteenth century to light the new screen, suggests how dark the interior of the medieval building must have been without it. The great wall figure of Death, with scythe, spade and hourglass, belongs in spirit to this shadowy candlelight.

Below it, the parish chest and font are among the most ancient in the country. The bowl of the font is encircled with a Latin inscription, 'Menhir made me in the time of Genillin', the G like a figure of 8. Cynhillin ('Genillin') was lord of this region in the mid-eleventh century.

One of the finest of all the surviving oak rood lofts and screens divides the nave and chancel: traceried panels echo the designs of windows, and dragons eat at an undulating vine above the most refined and subtle line of waterleaf and flower. Patrisio's late fifteenth century dragons are large-winged and rabbit-eared, with just two feet and wildly individual tails – one vigorously circling, knotted and barbed, the other relaxed and meandering. The turn of the grain animates their bodies as they feed. Stone steps in the wall lead up to the loft. Beneath it there are two bare shrines with no mark of whose bones they once contained. The wagon roof is ceiled and panelled, with linenfold sides: it was probably made at the same time as the screen and the rather hidden chancel arch.

Onto this Catholic nave in a later century came the whitewashing and Bible-

primacy of the Protestant age. Worshippers could look to the right to see the vast panel of God's commands from Sinai and beyond it, the small and touching inscription which acts as a key: 'If yee love me, keepe my Commandements'. To their left, a huge Royal coat of arms from around 1700: at first sight, secular authority seems to face across to spiritual. But again, the small inscription is a key: 'the powers that be are ordained of God. Whosoever resisteth…shall receive…damnation' – precisely the verses chosen by King James to bolster the Divine Right of Kings. Crammed in by Holy Writ, the nave spelt out obedience as the strait and narrow way. But with their wayward spelling, corrections and omissions (a forgotten "cattle" sits forlornly between the lines), the writers' carefree imprecision gives it an appealingly human frame.

The chancel is Elizabethan, with Jacobean altar rails and a 1620 printed Bible in Welsh. Among the memorial tablets are a number by the Brute family, local stonemasons from Llanbedr in the 1700s, who added flowers and eccentric angels in the borders, coloured in with vegetable dye.

The porch is a fourteenth century room in itself, flagged and raftered, with a stoup and splayed windows. From its stone benches, the green south opens out.

Pennant Melangell, St Melangell

SJ 024 265

Several miles along a single track road, occasionally wooded, lead to a valley head enclosed by sharply rising hills which wrap around it like an apse. Almost at the end, a lychgate of ancient stones leads to an expansive churchyard field spreading out over more than an acre in the rough form of a circle. It contains huge and extraordinary yews, some thirty feet in girth, which seem to date back to the bronze age. The field slopes steadily upward, looking down on the meeting of two rivers – the Ewyn and the Tanad, river of foam and river of fire, tumbling from the waterfall at Blaen-y-cwm. Up above it and across the valley is a rock shelf, an exposed, ascetic place known as Melangell's bed. Pennant Melangell has Celtic sacred lore in concentrate, drawing on every element the Age of Saints knew to give a place a sense of holy power. They marked it, like a capstone, with a small shrine church, burial place of a saint.

The more remote, ascetic, lost in nature a Celtic sacred site aspired to be, the holier it became, and – the paradox is – the more it was sought out. The pilgrim trails to Pennant Melangell wound over the mountains through moorland, mist and bog, leaving traces of ruined shelters, seeking out the healing and sanctuary of Ffynnon Ewyn and Melangell's care and intercession, to be wrapped in her llan's enfolding cloak like the throbbing, dew-bedabbled hare of her legend. The paradox ensured the creation of an international shrine which draws on the art of Ireland, France and Spain, and enabled also its survival – the earliest Romanesque shrine in northern Europe.

The church is long, narrow and limewashed, one end with a bell-tower, one rounded with an apse, a stone building which seems to have begun in the time of Rhirid Flaidd, a late twelfth century ruler of Powys hailed in the poems of Cynddelw. Its unaligned walls support a fifteenth century wooden roof. The nave is less than half the length of the building, stressing the importance of the east end shrine: to the right of the door we are already almost at the screen, which is carved with oak leaf and acorns, and images of the defining episode of Saint Melangell's life. Brochwel Ysgythrog, Prince of Powys recognised her saintliness when, out hunting a hare, he saw it run for refuge under her robe. The carver puts Melangell centre stage in the foliage, the prince and huntsman one side and the hare on the other pursued by dogs, all pelting towards her. The images date from sometime around 1500.

Through the screen we are into the shrine chapel, which has a wagon roof and a large wall painting of the Creed. The relic chest is in the centre of the floor, raised on an arched platform supported by short columns with deep capitals. Fluent foliage in many variations is carved in its sandstone walls, breaking out at the gabled edges like stylised wings of birds. It would originally have been painted and its striking visual effect would have been to swathe the relics of Melangell in the leafy sanctuary she symbolised, a local deity of the regenerative earth and of the sanctity of life. This is twelfth century regional style – the steepsided gables match the 1134 roof of Cormac's Chapel in County Tipperary or those in façades such as St Brendan's at Clonfert – but some of its influences are older, recognisable in the interlacing leaves and swirling capitals.

These Celtic patterns have acquired new twists from designs used at the great mosque at Tudela in Navarra, swept back by conquest into Christendom not long before, and they may have been spread north through the high demand for reliquaries from Limoges – another source for Pennant's gables, which are echoed in a Limousin shrine at Moutier d'Ahun. They survived the Reformation iconoclasm only by their broken fragments being hidden in the walls, reversed to hide the ornate patterns of the surfaces. Around the reconstructed shrine now are two stone effigies

Twelfth century regional style

from the 1300s, one for Prince Madoc ap Iorwerth and one thought to represent Melangell, the faces of hares at her waist primitive after the animated creature of the screen.

Beyond is the curving continental-style apse, recently recreated after archaeological discovery of the original foundation lines, another insight in this land of square-ended churches to the internationalism of twelfth century Powys. It replaced an old east end addition with chimneypot, doorway and window which looked more like an eighteenth century cottage, and had at one time been used as a school. In the apse is the saint's grave itself, marked by a massive stone: all the churchyard's oldest graveslabs, some dating back to the early 1600s, cluster around this outer wall.

People were evidently still here in numbers in the eighteenth and nineteenth centuries – recorded uses of the churchyard are for ball games, cockfights and the curious *anterliwtiau*, mixed bills of satire, poems and morality of which the Denbighshire actor Twm o'r Nant, who died in 1810, gave the last performance at Pennant, his audience spread out around him on the slope. The building was still kept fresh – the small porch with rough wooden benches is dated 1737, its wooden gate 1763 and inside, a new pulpit, painted reredos, wooden candelabrum, royal arms and benefaction board. In 1723 someone scribbled a nameplay in the registers '*Mil engyl a Melangell/Trechant lu fyddin y fall*' – A thousand angels and Melangell /Will defeat the massed forces of hell.

Chaser and chaste: Brochwel and Melangell on the fifteenth century screen

186

Pentre Llifior, Wesleyan Methodist Chapel

SO 147 978

The oldest Methodist chapel in the northern half of Wales stands at the roadside between Bettws Cedewain and the timberframe village of Berriew. A circular plaque on the wall records the date of construction as 1798. It is a small rectangular building made of red brick baked on site and laid in Flemish bond style. There are roundheaded windows on all four sides, two on each, which fill it with more light than its southern forerunner at Earlswood, Monmouthshire, and look out to the green canopy of trees at the field edge. The stable is opposite. It has timber walls, and was no doubt originally thatched. There is one surviving stall inside.

The chapel has preserved its Georgian interior: rows of box pew seating with enamelled numbers, some seats grouped about the central pulpit, hat pegs on the wall, and an altar rail like a church. Wesleyans had begun administering communion in their services only three years earlier in 1795, a landmark step towards their breaking away from the Church. A gallery supported by two slim iron columns extends along the back wall, which has surprising little panes of bright blue glass, apparently original. Pentre Llifior embodies all the modesty and clarity of a serious new movement.

The chapel belongs precisely to the period – not much more than the couple of decades either side of 1800 – when Wesleyan Methodism rooted itself into the culture of the country, and when it first had its own buildings. It was still under attack, not least from the press gangs: the roadside windows have the added precaution of shutters. Wesley himself had been unsure of his appeal in Wales both because of language and of powerful alternatives from Welsh evangelists. But, especially nearer the border, the number of Wesleyan congregations grew from just a handful in 1770 to over 100 by 1810.

Because the preachers were organised on itinerant circuits, these early chapels have no minister's cottage attached. The minister who led the building of this chapel is most connected with Llanelli, where he is buried in the parish church. James Buckley's name has survived into unlikely current use through the 'Reverend James' brand of beer, and a pub of the same name in Loughor. His Buckley's Brewery continued in business all the way to 1998. He came to Carmarthenshire from Oldham as a preacher, stayed with a local Methodist leader and brewer, and came into the business by marrying his daughter. In April 1798, at the age of 28, he paid ten shillings for the land on which to build this chapel. The accounts for the building survive – the cost was just over £200, including sixteen and fourpence on bread and cheese for the workmen, and nearly three pounds on beer (brewed on site).

The links between brewing and preaching in those times had interesting roots: something to do with the appeal of non-conformism to self-made tradesmen ill at ease with the social hierarchies blessed by the church, and also to the needs of purposeful men for more purposeful embodiments of faith. But as D.J. Williams remarks in his much-loved memoir *Hen Dy Ffarm*, speaking of his grandfather Jaci Penrhiw who after a long hard week of labour would be in his place at Rhydcymerau chapel on Sunday morning, fortified by some strong home-brewed: "At that time something stronger than lemonade was needed to make a Methodist elder". Buckley's own biography of Rev. Thomas Roberts shows how hugely demanding itineraries undermined a preacher's strength, as do the diaries of his Denbighshire contemporary Rev. Robert Humphreys. On 31 May 1822 Humphreys reviews his recent past "I have traveled about 528 miles and preached over 70 times in about 76 days." He was to die of cholera – a water-borne disease – in Beaumaris, where he had gone to minister to the sick.

All the modesty and clarity of a serious new movement

Pilleth/Pilalau, Our Lady
SO 256 683

A few miles upstream from Presteigne there is a bowl in the hills where the river Lugg cuts between Bryn Glas and Llan-fawr, and turns ninety degrees to the south in the face of Gilfach Hill. The path of Offa's Dyke runs over the eastern tops, and there are castle mounds and earthworks in the valley bottom. On the lower slopes is Nant-y-groes, the estate of Dr John Dee, magician to the Tudor court.

This is the borderland of Pilleth, place of pilgrimage, holy cure and battle, and when the church was built it was Mortimer country, a base for the harrying of Maelienydd and later of Gwynedd, the last prince of which their war party killed in a gully at Cilmeri on the far side of the Wye. A century later, the Welsh under Owain Glyndwr rose again to defeat a Mortimer army here on this hillside, a pitched battle victory that lit the blue touch paper, sparking the rising all across the country. But in the strangest final twist, the family that had defined itself for centuries as an oppressor of the Welsh ('I have subjected Wales,' said one boastful epitaph in the family chapel, 'to torment') made its last fling on the national stage by joining up with their victors in the war for independence. This was Shakespeare's Mortimer, the bordersman mediating between Glyndwr and Hotspur as the latter stuck the pin in Glyndwr's more otherworldly claims, a parody of Anglo-Welsh relations in a few short lines. So many bones were found on the steeper slope a century or more ago that the place was marked with the planting of four Wellingtonia firs now towering and visible across the valley. Not far below them, reached by a long and grassy track which curves around the slope, is the Church of Our Lady of Pilleth. Glyndwr torched it, and must have pondered on his future as the sparks flew upward.

It stands heavy and ancient on a shelf in the hill, a rubblestone tunnel bookended by a fortress tower. Its facing doorway and easternmost south window suggest that it was built in the fourteenth century with a certain style, but it is a visible reduction of a former self, the tower shortened, unbattlemented, scarred by older rooflines. Inside and out the walls have no protective rendering, the north side veers outwards alarmingly, window stones are flaking. A temporary roof which has lasted a century is thought to be exhausted*.

Yet the morning light sifts in through clear glass windows on to the long rough lines of wall, taking the eye down the steps of the nave and out to the frame of green enclosing hills beyond the altar. In the tower the great assembly of loftbeams and ringing wheels and bells seems to hang uncertainly suspended. There is an atmosphere and an impressive power which must in part derive from the damage time and chance have done.

Stripped of content by an accidental fire in 1894, the church has no distracting monuments, unsympathetic glass or pews: it stands as though in stark recreation of Glyndwr's moment. Only its small piscina and octagonal font, a tentatively ornamented block of lead-lined stone, survived of its medieval fittings – and one poppy head bench end which was taken down the road to Whitton, a journey also taken by its seventeenth century pulpit and an Elizabethan monument to a man called John Price.

A century ago Sir Walter Tapper, once a pupil of Bodley, was the man entrusted with the restoration. He added the steps up the churchyard slope, with their pleasing stone and elegant inscription. In the church he made the stone altar, the base for the font, a new floor and the temporary roof, all with marked restraint and understanding.

Around by the north side of the tower, some steps lead down into the remains of a walled well, partly cut into the rock. This is all that survives of where the pilgrims came to bathe their eyes in holy water. Their honoured effigy of Mary is long gone.

*Pilleth Church has since been restored and limewashed, with a new roof and ceiling.

Place of pilgrimage, holy cure, and battle

Rhulen/Rhiwlen, St David's

SO 138 498

Between the Radnor forest and the valley of the Wye the mountains climb above a thousand feet. The little rivers of Edw, Clas and Bachawy swing away to the west while the Arrow and the Glasnant tumble east towards England. Farms have emptied of people, roads seem to peter out into tracks. The pattern of settlement may be thinly returning to the days of the saints, when a *clas* established at Glascwm was founding churches, determinedly remote, in the surrounding hills. All of them – Glascwm, Cregrina, Colva, Rhulen – were dedicated to St David. All ancient, neglected, much restored and rebuilt, the most plainly appealing is Rhulen.

It is built of whitewashed stone, a long barn with tiled roof interrupted only by a small wooden belfry with a pyramid top, and a functional porch on the south side. The churchyard is large and bordered with tall maples. It stands at a curve in the road on the edge of farmland, and feels like a long way from anywhere.

One of its mysteries is to seem on entry even smaller than expected. There is not much to the simple room which forms both nave and chancel. It has a floor of stone slabs and an ancient font. A beam in the east wall once held the rood: there may never have been a dividing screen. The altar was recessed below it so there is no window. Prospects of much extension to the east were always blocked by the presence of an ancient yew against the outside wall. Twelfth or thirteenth century dimensions are consequently more or less intact, but windows like the large one on the south have been intruded much later. It has a square-headed wooden frame, with the inscription 1723 – the only thing in Rhulen it is really possible to date. The plastered barrel ceiling is two or three hundred years old, the heavy door in its narrowing doorway, as old again.

The surprise is not that places like Rhulen are barely sustained, but that, over more than a millennium, they have been sustained sufficiently to survive. At neighbouring Cregrina, a small free mission in a private house continues after one hundred years, in addition to the church, and the grander building at Glascwm is still maintained, deep in its wild and overgrown woodland of graves. The future of old churches may amaze us yet.

Rhulen: alluring blend of timber and shale, rural setting and modest scale

Soar-y-mynydd: the chapel of the soul

Soar-y-Mynydd

SN 785 533

Somewhere between Tregaron and Mynydd Eppynt, in the high mountains and empty moors of the true *Gwalia deserta*, the spirits which haunted twentieth century Wales were born. This is the land of depopulated farms, Pantycelyn and his hymns, villages drowned under reservoirs, Twm Sion Cati's hideaway, the ranging red kite, the pathetic endgame of the last native prince, the drovers' road, the forestry commission, the Cantref Mawr into which the Welsh resistance, centuries ago, would melt. At Soar-y-Mynydd, all the compulsions of the culture meet. Approached from any direction, bare mountain to the west, steep wooded gullies to the east, tracks for men or ponies to the south, this is a journey to a different place – as far away as you will ever be, wrote the poet Harri Webb, from the world's madness. Up here, with no other building for miles around, is R.S. Thomas's "chapel of the soul". It is a simple enough little place.

From Abergwesyn, the road towards it passes another old stone chapel, dark and galleried among the trees. Lichen and mosses and the forest floor itself are subsuming the worn stone graves behind it. Pantycelyn's name is carved above the door. In these parts he and Hywel Harris and the others, back in the 1740s, brought preaching out of the churches and into the homes on the farms. In these hills too, Dafydd Morgan Ysbyty felt the surging sense of the moment which launched the 1859 revival.

Soar-y-Mynydd is in the moorland to the south, signed at the turning, and on for another mile or two. From a distance it can be picked out, behind a little wood of copper beeches, a chapel and house sharing the same roof. A stone slab bridges a stream on the path to the wooden gate. On a bright February day, the sun sets right in the dip on the ridge, lighting up the mountain stream, coming in through the window to the message on the wall: '*Duw Cariad Yw*' – the favourite of the Welsh Presbyterians. The interior, a forgotten brown, is filled to the walls with pews. Rev. Idris Owen remembers coming here as a visiting preacher in the 1930s, travelling on horseback through the hills from Pont Llanio, the snow on one March day settling in high drifts which forced him to return, in near exhaustion, on foot. Dr. Martyn Lloyd-Jones, a direct descendant of the farmer who gave the land for the building, preached here often: his wife Bethan recalled the lines of ponies streaming down the hillsides to a service and being stalled in the great stable underneath the chapel, from which their heat rose to warm the farmers and their dogs in the pews above. A schoolroom as much as chapel, Soar played both parts until 1947 when, after the worst winter of the century, the last farmers sold up to the forestry commission, and headed down to the valleys below.

Rev. Ebenezer Richard of Tregaron had it built in 1822, for the few in each generation who farmed up here, and for the drovers who passed this way on a lost road from Llanddewibrefi. It is an irony, and quite untrue to the man, that it should now be in a wilderness. Born in Trefin in North Pembrokeshire, a preacher's son, his life's work was to organise across south Wales the building of new causes and new chapels – he believed they should be small, and as close as possible to people's homes. His was the third generation of Welsh Methodism, after the *hwyl* of the first great gatherings and the remote, defensive siting of the early chapels, and he combined the reckless dedication and travelling in all weathers, the poor health and tearful, combustible emotion of the earlier generations with the organisational skill and permanent engagement with communities that was to form the pattern for the future. His monument is in Tregaron churchyard. His son Henry was to travel much more widely, playing a part in remaking the peace across Europe after the conflagrations of 1848, launching the Peace Union, and pioneering, decades before the emergence of the League of Nations, the notions of international law and a system of arbitration between states. War, he said, came from governments, not from the people, a way of thinking with deep roots in his father's chapel, which still draws to it from across the mountains people who want to hear preaching, and in the native tongue.

> Ar lannau afon Camddwr
> Mae teml i'm Hiachawdwr
> Pwy bynnag ddaw dros y fath dir
> Rydd brawf o wir addolwr
> > Cerngoch

> [On the banks of the river Camddwr
> There's a temple to my Saviour.
> Whoever comes over such country
> Gives proof of being a true worshipper.]

Strata Florida / Ystrad Fflur

SN 746 657

Come to Strata Florida as a stranger, on a day when the rain sets in, and you may wonder what draws people to these few broken stones in a flat valley soaked in cloud. On a bright day the backdrop of green and empty hills from which the Teifi flows down beside the ruins gives the place a remote, uncertain charm. It gives up its meaning only to those with a forensic interest in the differentiating details of the stones, or those who have known it first in the mind, as a touchstone of Welsh thought and culture, a bastion of Cymru Cymraeg.

Strata Florida was at the pumping heart of Welsh-language culture and leadership throughout the medieval centuries. The courts of Lord Rhys, one of its earliest patrons, and of Llywelyn Fawr were among those who gathered here. Its lands extended for 6,000 acres through the high country to the north and east, through which the ancient road can still be traced, twenty five miles and almost two thousand feet up across Elenydd to Abbey Cwmhir, sometimes still empty of any other soul. Its spiritual writings, with their fierce love for all natural things and their Creator, were central to Welsh thought. Its 130 year chronicle of the life of west Wales stopped dead at the killing of Llywelyn Olaf, as if, wrote Bradley a century ago, "black chaos had fallen, and the hearts of the historians had broken with this snapping of the thread of Welsh national life". When they reached the abbey, already wrecked by firestorm, Edward I's men finished the job, erasing the memorials of the princes of Deheubarth as they had those of Gwynedd at Conwy. More than a century later Henry IV, in fruitless pursuit of Glyndwr, stabled his horses at the high altar.

The surviving stones bear out its Celtic state of mind. The unexpectedly round arch of the west doorway, which dates from 1220 and marks the end of the main building campaign, is roped across by thirteen bands of stone, each curling at the edge into a shell-like spiral, unique in Cistercian architecture. The monks' graveslabs in the shadow of the south transept have cross-shaped headstones with interlacing ropework. The diagonal tiles in the transept have interlocking patterns filled with three-stranded triskels, as well as curious images like a man with a mirror. The stones of the walls are animist, bursting into flower in the Spring as though in celebration of the abbey's name: Ystrad Fflur, the Valley of Flowers. The stepped stone hollow in the choir was a healing holy well. The capitals of the interior, as told from one survival, swirl and intertwine: early Cistercian austerity (still to be seen at Margam, and as French as the hostile marcher lords) was overthrown here in an urge to express more westerly traditions. Parts of the design share features seen across the Irish Sea: a separating screen wall between the nave and aisles as at Baltinglass in Wicklow; polychrome vaults as at Dunbrody.

It is as though time has had selective memory, erasing all the traces which integrated more with French and European tradition. The truth is, it was a blend, like the poetry of the greatest of the local poets, Dafydd ap Gwilym, mixing the *cywydd* and *llatai* with the language and ideas of French Romance: Dafydd, the comic, irrepressible, self-parodying master, devout and irreverent by turns, always bursting with yearning love, calling the wind and wild birds to his aid, a would-be Prospero without a staff. He is said to be buried here under an appropriately burst yew, one of the last survivors of a sacred grove – there were thirty-nine still here in the sixteenth century. Recently it has been plausibly suggested that the tree now so honoured is the wrong yew, a touch of farce which Dafydd would have surely relished.

Because of all this, Welsh poets of the twentieth century have been drawn to Strata Florida more than anywhere, as though to try to touch here the pulse of the culture – "desire running like sparks in stubble," wrote Gillian Clarke, "through the memory of the place". R.S. Thomas, contemplating with a friend how visits such as this affect the mind, cut drily, as ever, to the nub.

> Time, I said. Place, he replied,
> Not contradicting

The unique thirteenth century doorway: Cistercian with a Celtic twist

Trelystan, All Saints

SJ 263 039

The great Shropshire ridges of Long Mynd and Long Mountain run on a south west parallel into the Welsh border. Their summits watch over the narrow valley in between, long a route for trade and war between the two countries. On Long Mountain, almost a thousand feet up, are the ancient ditched enclosure known as Beacon Ring and the little church of Trelystan, the only surviving medieval wooden church in Wales.

A track, marked by a signpost, leads down through fields from the nearest road to a point where the land begins to fall away. From the south side of the churchyard the views take in the forest edge and the steeply rolling grazing land spreading out for miles below. Six ancient yews frame the hills and the small, steeply-roofed black and white chamber of the church. This ancient site carries associations with the early life of upland summer grazing, with the myths of Arthur and the seventh century victory of Cadwallon over a Northumbrian army, but is first recorded as a burial place only in 1010, for Elystan ap Cyhelyn, Lord of Builth, who carried the title Glodrydd (the Renowned).

Here on the mountain in August 1485 Henry Tudor, having marched across mid-Wales from Milford Haven, gathered his armies together to launch his bid for the crown. Eight days later at Bosworth Field he won the kingdom, and the Welsh dragon was back among the symbols of power. Did he make his prayers for battle in this small devotional shelter?

The fifteenth century church was restored and encased, for protection, in a modern brick and timber frame in 1856. From this time date the porch with its rough benches, and the small vestry on the north side. But the medieval plan and structure still survive, visible most in the blackened arch-braced roof of the interior, although its low timber tie beams have been cropped down and reinforced by iron rods. There is a remnant of the oak screen on the south side of the nave, five openings with individual traceried heads and unusually curving bases, and on the south side of the vestry there are fraying timbers of original medieval walling. The chancel is flagged with old memorial stones and has a Jacobean altar rail. Two metal ten commandments boards hang either side of the main east window – a scene of the Agony in the Garden framed in wooden tracery, which is sometimes described as Munich painted glass and sometimes attributed to David Evans, a local Montgomeryshire artist with windows at Meifod and Llanwnog. Parts of old box pews have been used to line the walls, and carved panels on the north wall have images of vine trails and wheat stems. The church has a bell of c.1500 inscribed with "Sancta Maria Ora Pro Nobis", and its most curious possession is a decorated 1827 barrel organ, which can be worked by hand to play thin renditions of twenty hymn tunes, among them the Old Hundred and Rock of Ages.

High on Long Mountain, the last medieval wooden church at Trelystan

IV

THE SOUTH WEST

CARMARTHENSHIRE, PEMBROKESHIRE, SWANSEA

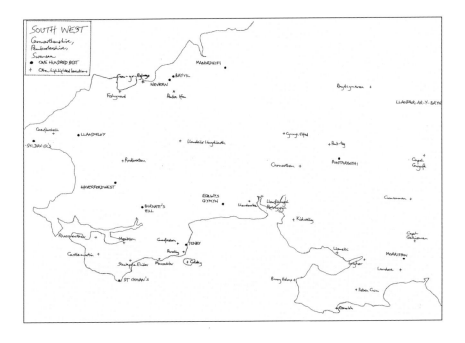

Bayvil, St Andrew

SN 102 406

This small country church east of Nevern is the most complete and authentic Georgian survival in the south. An avenue of trees – a true country *lon coed* – leads down beside a farmhouse to the churchyard gate. The church is an island among ferns, flowing green over all the outbreaks of gravestones, a haven for owls and ground-nesting birds, and for the bats which leave their mark in the interior. From the west door, the view rolls out to cliffs and the sea. Above the door, there is a double belfry, but only one bell.

The interior seems untouched by time: there are seven box pews, six of them lined together on the south side, all of the seating made to face an extraordinary three decker pulpit which occupies the centre of the north wall. Boxed in between the clerk's desk and reading desk, the hexagon pulpit stands up on a four feet high block of stone, too high to be well lit from the window, and causing the sounding board to press up against the ceiling. On the flagstone floor beneath it is a huge coffin bier. All of the furniture is painted and panelled. The plain font is late twelfth century.

The altar is set back some distance, which has led to the suggestion that there may have been more seating here at one time. The railings are original and just beside them is a small wall monument, perhaps to the man who paid for the building, and

Pembrokeshire Georgian, intact and unspoilt

a curious coat of arms carved in stone on which crescent-shaped snakes intertwine.

The church was also used as a school and is thought to date from around 1812, making an interesting comparison with Burnett's Hill Chapel, built that year in the south of the county (although the chapel's surviving interior arrangement is later). They share the same atmosphere of plainness and simplicity, the same basic rectangular plan, an angled and boarded roof, a few square-headed windows, and an intense focus on pulpit rather than altar, although at Bayvil, church tradition is respected by giving the altar still its separate place.

To find these things at Bayvil suggests at least a local patron absorbed in and responding to the new winds of chapel culture, wanting to cast church worship into modern surroundings. But in 1812, the Church itself had still not got there: Bayvil's churchman numbered this and two other Pembrokeshire parishes in his pleasant personal income of tithes (one of them, curiously, the parish where Burnett's Hill Chapel was being built) – but he lived and worked in Hampshire. Even the curate lived over the mountain at Eglwyswrw. A glance at the interior confirms that, almost alone among Pembrokeshire churches, Victorian attentions never reached here either, keeping a Georgian inheritance intact and unspoilt.

Abbot, bishop, king and saint: Cynin's four-square holy power

202

Eglwys Gymyn*, St Margaret

SN 231 106

Carmarthenshire's little wayside churches and chapels are a rich seam of quiet pleasures, hidden in green lanes or hedged on hillsides, small gathering places for local communities, evocative, vernacular, perfect for their purpose. Among these unsung masterpieces are early chapels like Jerusalem at Capel Gwynfe, Bethel Cynwyl Elfed, Libanus Llansadwrn, Peniel at Pant-teg and a small stone building, not much more than 15 feet across, which may be the oldest church site in Wales still in use as such. Eglwys Gymyn is a breathing survival of the ancient Irish influence upon the south, as well as of the marcher lords and the eighteenth century Methodist revival, and, perhaps most unexpected of all, has a place at the heart of the Arts and Crafts movement.

The road skirts around a churchyard so raised, the path cuts a three foot deep trench to the door. At the west side in a screen of trees, where steps lead down to the field, the drop is six feet. The full embanking wall is still more or less standing, marked in places with initials of the farmers who looked after each part of it, and a couple of dates, 1771, 1791. The field curls around to the north like the moat or protective ditch it once was until it loses itself in undergrowth, and the view extends away for miles, revealing the grandly chosen site. This is only the central of three concentric ramparts. South of the road, there are traces of the other two. The pattern marks it out as an Irish rath, the residence of a king.

More keys to the past emerged in 1856: evidence of bronze age cremations gave the site a three thousand year religious heritage, and a memorial stone was unearthed by the chancel, inscribed in Latin and Irish script, to Avitoria, daughter of Cynin. Its debased Roman capitals, like those on the inscription to 'Velvoriges' at Llandysul, helped to date it to around the late fifth century. It is thought that Cynin, a grandson of the Irish chieftain Brychan from whom Brecon gets its name, must have buried his daughter here in a Chapel Royal within his manor – hence the name of Eglwys Cynin, a kind of church quite different and separate from the llan at Llanginning where Cynin's own saintly shrine would rise after his death, and whose miracle powers permeate the poems of the great fifteenth century Carmarthenshire *cywyddwyr* Lewis Glyn Cothi.

The walls do justice to the church's antiquity: the west wall thickens and splays to the north, and the north, which cuts into rising ground to the east, is a great screen of ancient masonry, broken only by the ruin of a thirteenth century hermit's cell. On the south, the low mark of an older doorway shows how far the ground has risen. There is a deep porch with stone seating, rising to an acutely angled roof which repeats inside on a grander scale. The nave's solid stone vault is made by building up the walls, without any structural framing, to close gradually in on each other as they rise until they meet at twenty feet. Plainly limewashed, it gives the church, as George Treherne remarked, "a simple dignity often lacking in more ambitious structures". This part of the building is thought to be owed to Guy de Brian, lord of Laugharne, a confidante of Edward III along with his church-building neighbour Bishop Gower. His niece Margaret led the life of a nun at nearby Llandawke, and the church's rededication to her and her name-saints must have been linked to this rebuilding.

The north wall has four faded layers of painting. Over an early geometric pattern, the ten commandments have been written first in ochre, then in Gothic black – both times in English – before being written over again in Welsh. The last could not have happened until the late sixteenth century, but the first version has been said to be fifteenth century. If so, it is an early sign of the coming Reformation, and may perhaps be linked to the internationally-minded John Donne, lord of the manor from 1462 to 1490, whose altarpiece portrait by Hans Memling is in the National Gallery in London.

When reformation came again, Eglwys Gymyn was one of the parishes at the centre of the charitable work of Rev. Griffith Jones of Llanddowror, whose launch in 1731 of the hugely successful 'circulating schools' both educated and evangelized the rural poor. He was funded chiefly by his emotional confidante, the pious and beautiful Bridget Bevan of Laugharne, whose company was said to be 'a taste of heaven' in itself, but ran into sharp opposition from John Evans, the absentee rector of Eglwys Gymyn, who attacked him in hostile pamphlets. "Should the traveller be disturbed", wrote Jones, "by the little animals that bark at him on his way?" Peter Williams from Pendine, curate here in the 1740s, built on Jones's work with the first Bible printed in Wales, containing the first full Welsh commentary. The church has a first edition, with an inscription in Bridget Bevan's handwriting. (Sadly this has not been on display in recent years). Williams is also thought to be the translator of 'Guide Me O Thou Great Jehovah', for the English-speaking people of the parish. He too was too much for John Evans, who dismissed him from his post.

In 1901, to help restore the church, an appeal was launched to all the Margarets in the country, and George Treherne called in the Society for the Protection of Ancient Buildings, a recent brainchild of William Morris. Thus Philip Webb, the revolutionary architect of Morris's Red House, came to Eglwys Gymyn. His characteristic work includes the oak cupboards, chests and beam at the west end. Some of the pews retain the sawn-off stumps of posts on which the oil lamps used to hang. They were removed when electricity arrived, but would have been very much part of the intended effect. The work was not completed – a new chancel was left with bare stone walls, intermittently decorated with old tombstones like Peter Chapman's of 1718, displaying a round-faced cherub with leaf-like wings.

Outside in the churchyard are fine nineteenth century gravestones by Tom Morris of Pendine, with scrolls and flowers, and beside the path, an inscription recording that the 'yew trees on either side of the approach were planted in honour of the coronation of Edward VII'. There is no sign of them now.

*The spelling of Eglwys Gymyn is a true flowering of the Welsh genius for varia-
tion. Alternatives of Cymyn, Cummin, Cynin, Cymin and Gummin are all in use
in the sources, and all seem equally acceptable – even sometimes in the same
account. An authentic Irish spelling, for the man himself, has been offered as
Chummein.

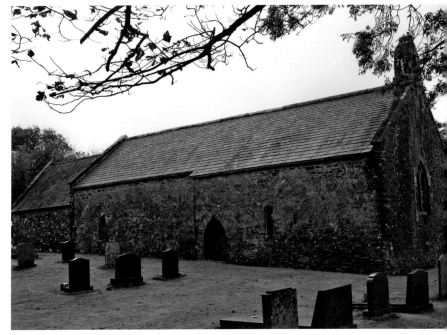

A great screen of ancient masonry

Haverfordwest/Hwlffordd, St Mary

SM 952 155

In Pembrokeshire all roads lead to Haverfordwest, the capital of Little England beyond Wales. As castle, estuary port and market – a conquest settlement of English and Flemings in a place from which the native Welsh were forcibly expelled – it thrived for centuries, turning over considerable wealth to the church. Through the medieval years, there were two of Wales's largest churches here, the Priory down at the river edge and St Mary's up on the hill, as well as others dedicated to St Martin and St Thomas.

Almost nothing remains of the Priory, but St Mary's still stands as the grandest of parish churches in this part of Wales. The creep of the town around it, and the loss of its tall spire in 1801, have closed in on the role it once had in commanding the prospect from the bustling riverside or the castle hill adjacent. Old Haverfordwest, approached by sail or steamer, passing into the Cleddau by Milford sound and Pembroke, needs to be reimagined.

In the steamer years the town filled with chapels. According to John Brown in a local history he wrote in the 1800s, the population took the divisions of dissenting less to heart than in Welsh Wales, going to church by day and chapel by night, even the gentry helping to fill the Wesleyan chapel, which was entered then from St Martin's churchyard as a kind of shared ground. Nearby Tabernacl sets the easy tone, its façade untypically colourful and curving and its interior full of swirling ironwork and a branching seven-light apse to symbolise its name – the confident, outward-looking product of a seafaring town so different from its weighty mining town contemporaries further east.

There were ministers like Mr Truscott, 'God Almighty's own preacher'; Mr Christian Gothelf Ike, Bohemian born and an artist, who could write the Lord's Prayer within the compass of a shilling; and Mr Evans of Albany, who would trounce his opponent in theological debate and then take his side, winning the argument the other way.

St Mary's stood in the midst of all this, even acting as the gaol for French troops in the last invasion of Britain in 1797. They whiled away the time by damaging the monuments. Another nineteenth century account suggests parishioners came here 'more from fashion than choice', and only as a pause in the weekly round of playing card games. Down in the front pews "it was but lately that a lady of the whist club, when roused from her nap by an apostrophe of the parson more than ordinarily vociferous, bawled out 'Spades are trumps'". This was the 'world maddening after pleasure, holding all its dazzling fashionable follies' evoked on the altar-side monument to 'lovely Hessy Jones'. Sir John Pryce, buried near her, used to sleep beside his late first and second wives, embalmed beside him on the bed, removing them only when urged to do so by the newly married third.

Inside, the church feels rather heavy with the monuments of worthies from those days, and the darkening glass which some of them commissioned. But the medieval structure, its stone arcading and ornamented roofs, are full of grace and splendour. The Decorated arcades and chancel arch of stone from Caen have been compared with work at Salisbury and Wells. Their cathedral quality is the visible expression of how close to royal patronage was this strategically important boom town in the early thirteenth century. The earldom of Pembroke was passing from royal hands to William Marshal, soon to be Regent of England, the champion fighter of his age whose challenges to single combat were usually enough to silence opposition. Builder also of the great keep of Pembroke Castle, he gave Haverfordwest a period of peace between its earlier burning by Lord Rhys and a second, almost as soon as he had died, by Llywelyn Fawr – but the mark of these events on the townsmen's state of mind is visible in the teeming life carved in the capitals of the nave, quite pointedly directed at the nearby foreign Welsh. An ape plays a Welsh harp, and a pig plays an old Welsh fiddle. The portrait heads in the chancel arch are said to be of Aymer de Valence, another Earl of Pembroke, and his wife Joan de Clare, a union

Caen stone, Welsh beer

of conquest families. The wooden roofs above them are intricate and complex, and can be dated by their Tudor roses to the reigns of Henry VII or Henry VIII, the former, of course, a locally-born boy. The wood and stones of St Mary's blazon its allegiances.

A bench end near the chancel arch depicts St Michael slaying the dragon, with the arms of England and France on the poppy head, which date it to the years of Agincourt. Originally carved abroad, it may be a survival from the Priory by the quay. From the same half-century is a rare pilgrim effigy recumbent at the west end of the nave, where rising ground results unusually in steps towards the western wall. Despite the damage, the pilgrim's long gown and the scallop shells of Compostela on his bag can still be clearly seen. There is a 1737 organ of 24 stops and its casing, a notable east window by Kempe and outside, a seventeenth century sundial, and thirteenth century gateway and bellcote.

Slaying the dragon at Haverfordwest

Llandeloi, St Teilaw

SM 856 268

Llandeloi is a bag of tricks for the explorer – a place where perceptions shift, expectations are set up and confounded, where no single perspective provides a full view. What is more, it was deliberately planned like that.

Only a bell turret is visible from the road. Once through the churchyard gate, the long north wall of the church comes into view, broken at intervals by slim roundheaded windows and a narrow doorway. The east end of the building cuts into the slope of the land – Llandeloi looks the essence of an ancient country llan, low-lying, undemonstrative, ingrained in its site.

The church door opens to a dark nave with the smallest possible west window. An octagonal font has been set on three great concentric stone steps, as though the base of the old churchyard cross has been brought inside. The space feels closed in by a huge weight of masonry, but there is light seeping through from the left, and a series of openings entice the visitor in, drawing him forward towards the light.

The nave is short, ending abruptly where a wooden screen butts up against a solid mass of stone with a kind of archway leading through it. The pulpit is set in more rock, and can only be reached by a separate passageway, as though entering

Hugging the land: Llandeloi's typically Welsh horizontal lines

from stage left. Off to the right another passageway, this time angled, leads to a short, unexpected transept, then angles sharply back to join the chancel. It is a nodding chancel, lit unevenly from three sides and rising in six steps, two blocks of three, to another massive rock of an altar. Behind this, a final unexpected passageway leads off to the right, but it ends anticlimactically, at a storage point. All through the church, above the heavy grounding of rough rubblestone, is a lighter, freer domain of wood. What is going on?

The answer is that from 1924 to 26, the Cardiff architect John Coates Carter took an old Welsh church, ruinous for eighty years, and used as much of its fabric and feeling as he could. He brought to it his deep sense of local vernacular, his long years of Arts and Crafts practice, and a touch of the new Expressionism. There is a whole tradition in the shifting interior spaces which looks back long beyond his early teacher Voysey to men such as John Soane, but among his Pembrokeshire inspirations must surely have been the old priory church on Caldey Island, still now functioning as a dark and shadowy prayer shrine beyond the island's ring of woods. Coates Carter had worked on Caldey earlier in the century, building the pinnacled and red roofed monastery ranges, and even the island post office, in one of the most distinctive sets of Arts and Crafts architecture in the country.

Llandeloi's holy well is still there, hidden deep in the undergrowth of the back half of the churchyard. To find it, stand at the south west corner of the church, walk straight towards the nettles – and keep going.

All innocence at the entrance

Llandovery/Llanymddyfri, Llanfair-ar-y-bryn

SN 770 353

Sometimes the line of Welsh history feels like an endless ebb tide. The Normans invade, pushing up the valleys even as far as this. The Edwardian conquest flows across the whole landscape. The laws and language, the power bases, slip back.

The great military tower of Llanfair-ar-y-bryn (St Mary on the hill) was built right in the wake of conquest by John Giffard, Edward I's man. Like the southern Pembrokeshire towers, drawn up to more than their full height, it looks the very essence of newly-won power.

But the tides in Wales are unpredictable things. This is the home of Vicar Prichard and William Williams Pantycelyn, resurgents of the culture, and an all Welsh

Imperium, c/o Llandovery

211

language church, one of the few among the country's most historic. Best seen in the summer evening, lit up by the sun across the fields from Cil-y-cwm, Llanfair-ar-y-bryn is a beacon of a tide that turned.

Why Llandovery is laid out as it is, a Norman castle among four rivers, an irregular town plan and both its major churches in the fields outside, takes some decoding. The church at Llandingat on the south side is certainly the original sixth century llan. In the conquest war it was burnt out by Payn de Chaworth's forces, which were already known for sacrilegious treatment of Welsh sacred places. Perhaps this fed the need for a new church to the north. But even more, it must have been linked to the swelling of the town with English settlers, and a new Anglo-Norman lord displaying piety and power. He chose the hill site, symbolically imperial, which had once been the Roman station of Loventium. There are signs in the walls of the reuse of Roman tile – one is prominent in the arch of a window on the south side.

In the patching of the centuries the church has been chopped about, a doorway blocked, a ceiling lost, a whole substantial side chapel disappeared. But it has been blessed more recently by sensitive handling: the high clean lines and large dimensions, and a fabric given room to age, have brought a certain stateliness to its vernacular atmosphere.

The frame of the tie-beam roof has all its pegs untrimmed, there are still indents in the walls where the rood loft once pressed, a medieval half face stares from its lodging in the stonework. The piscina and the Easter sepulchre are worn away. A door over the high inner arch of the tower suggests a priest's room. There is a Jacobean pulpit, and in the vestry, Pantycelyn's desk dated 1775. There is an admired eighteenth century organ, a good pulpit by Caroe. Two extraordinary column capitals, once in the south porch doorway and thought to depict Adam and Eve in their state of lost innocence, are now in the Carmarthen Museum. In the porch now is a French inscription on a tablet: 'Je remets mon âme en ta main car tu m'as racheté'. The church is full of clues to a past not all remembered. George Borrow came here, one evening in 1862, and heard a sermon on the 119th Psalm, "but owing to its being in South Welsh, I did not derive so much benefit from it as I might have done".

Vicar Prichard and William Williams have their memorials in stained glass, and outside in the churchyard an incongruous obelisk, not of their time. They were very different men, but their religious emphasis was strikingly shared. Faith for them both was an inward journey, of the heart more than the mind. What had force was goodly living, prayer, and Christ's redemptive power.

Vicar Prichard was a man of the establishment, educated at Jesus College, Oxford, chaplain to the Earl of Essex, chancellor of St David's. He moved among the local gentry, lived in a large house in town, building a reputation for his homilies and verses. In 1658, fourteen years after his death, the first edition of his works went to print. *Canwyll y Cymru*, Candle for a Welshman, went through 52 editions by 1820, expanding through the decades as more of the scribbled papers he had left behind were discovered and deciphered. "It was no sooner printed than in the hands and mouths of all… they soon made an almost entire change in the morals and behaviour of the whole country" reported an early translator. Its power and appeal were "scarce credible".

Pantycelyn lived in a farmhouse a few miles to the east. He was much more the man in a landscape, travelling 150,000 miles through Wales over fifty years, counting the stars of heaven in his hymns, imagining the hills burst open with Last Judgement brimstone, feeling the moment of conversion as the shiver of a breeze. He was an eighteenth century pilgrim, at work among the poor, his language of personal passion and mission defining the Welsh hymn, galvanizing Welsh Methodism towards independent life at the centre of a culture. But he started and ended in this old alien church on the hill, baptised in its font, and buried in its ground.

Manordeifi, St David's, Old Parish Church

SN 228 432

Across the long low bridge at Llechryd, a lane leads through often flooded fields to Manordeifi. The Teifi river dominates the landscape, sometimes widening, sometimes changing its course, making everything in the valley subject to it. The church was originally at the riverside, and sometimes, when the banks burst with floodwater, it can find itself back in the river's midst. This last happened in 1987. A coracle is kept in the porch, as if to row when needed over the fine churchyard wall of low flat stones. Above it, a fifteenth century bell still hangs in the craggy turret, inscribed in Latin 'St Lawrence pray for us'. The church leaflet has its own paean to this turret, mysterious to the uninitiated, to its drive gudgeons, stock hoops, and a clapper with no flight.

Over a hundred years ago, the parishioners of Manordeifi resolved to build themselves a new church somewhere less exposed, preserving in the old interior an early nineteenth century atmosphere made more mysterious by ancient walls and the disorienting crookedness of window leads, early font, flagstones and a chancel almost as long as the nave, and rather spare. It has a deep fourteenth century window on the south side, and painted altar rails with quatrefoil and candleflame patterning. The pulpit and the reading desk, which flank its entrance at the far end of the nave, are eighteenth century.

All the old box pews remain, their occupants intent on being comfortable. Those at the back have higher walls to keep out the drafts from the door, and are decorated with fluted columns. Those at the front have their own fireplaces with grate and chimney. All have wooden floors and one has a set of drawers underneath the seats with carefully inset brass handles. There are some open benches for the servants. The families can still be named from the stone memorials above their boxes: among them the Lewises of Clynfyw, Saunders Davieses of Pentre and the Colbys of Ffynone (a house by John Nash). Outside in the churchyard, their burial plots are privately partitioned off by sometimes brightly coloured iron railings – the box pews of the afterlife. Under low branching yews the Saunders family railings arch and curl over the rising pathway and climb up the steep bank, the ornamental urns cast to slope with the gradient. The Colbys marked out their part of the churchyard with distinctive coiling curls. A Lewis monument by the west door, with columns and entablature, occupies an arched recess in the churchfront, and is made of wood and slate.

Their preoccupation with enclosure in both life and death, so neatly symbolic of contemporary frictions in their rural society as they aggrandised their estates, makes Manordeifi church a visual expression of the stereotype Welsh gentry in the early modern years. They have had a poor press, accused of departing from the language and the culture in pursuit of capital, Anglicisation and conspicuous expenditure.

Here in Manordeifi they clung to their old church and its displays of social hierarchy, marginalizing themselves from the common folk around them, stranded on the muddy shore beside the flooding river of Welsh life. Through the nineteenth century their neighbours headed for the chapels, in a successive, rising scale still visible at Capel Newydd, Ramoth and Cilfowyr. It must have been difficult to know quite who had left whom. By the century's close, they must have been just talking to themselves, a movement taken to its logical conclusions by the Saunders' building of a private chapel at their house, and the raising, finally, of the new parish church close to where others lived, richly coated in mosaic, onyx, marble, serpentine and alabaster.

There is, of course, another side to the story: the church is silent on these families' sheer enterprise, in agriculture, metallurgy, even shipping tea from China, and they supplied too, in the role expected of them, rectors for the church and soldiers for the army. There is a Colby among the first October deaths on the Menin Gate at Ypres, and one remembered here on a memorial of palm leaves and weaponry, who died when 'seized on and torn by a tiger' at Rawalpindi on 27 March 1852, in the deceptive lull which followed on the second Sikh War. An engraving of it made the Illustrated London News the following year, alongside the transplanting of the Crystal Palace from Hyde Park, and the laying, not far off this coast, of the first submarine telegraph to Ireland.

The gentry make themselves at home

Martletwy, Burnett's Hill Chapel

SN 024 097

The recent loving restoration of Burnett's Hill Chapel, crumbling under ivy just a few years ago, by a trust of local Friends, is a real sign of hope that there is a new will to preserve important chapel heritage. Burnett's Hill is among the two or three dozen oldest chapel buildings in the country, a simple but harmonious example of the kind of building imagined and made by local nonconformists when, for the first time, they cut the bonds with the Church. The Methodist decision to split away came in 1811; the chapel was put up in 1812.

It was built in a field where open air services had been held, a plain stone cottage behind a wall. The left hand window was originally the doorway. The entrance moved to the gable end in the mid-nineteenth century when an early gallery was taken down, a fireplace removed, and the present interior made. A bank of raked seating slopes down towards the pulpit as at the contemporary Salem, Cefncymerau. The rear seven rows are just benches with slat-backs, probably from the first 1812 furniture; the four or five front rows are more substantial. Unusually for a chapel there is a central aisle, and the congregation retained right up until closure in the 1980s the habit of seating men on one side, women on the other, hence the different dimensions of the hat pegs on each side.

Four steep steps lead up to a raised and railed platform for the minister and elders, from which they could fulfil their role as overseers of the congregation's conduct. The pulpit is literally centre stage. The message 'God is Love' stands out in capitals behind it, below a small and undistracting window. From here the acoustic is remarkable – the Word reverberates around the room. The walls are thick and limewashed, and a single lamp hangs from the ceiling. There was no organ: the congregation sang without accompaniment. The first impression of simplicity belies a certain sophistication in the sense of proportions, the alignment of the windows and of the hat rails and panelled lower walls, the angled lines of which drive the gaze forward, even across the deep window spaces, to focus on the message and the stage.

For many years the chapel had no minister, and then shared one with the new Millin Chapel across the Cleddau: his Sunday schedule relied on the Picton rowing boat ferry. The chapel's first community was among the local docks and shipbuilding yards along the banks, and perhaps above all the miners at Landshipping. The disaster there in 1844, when the river burst into the tunnels killing forty men and boys, caused the remaking of the chapel interior for smaller numbers.

Chapelgoing colliers were a staple of Welsh life, perhaps associated most with the crowded valleys of Gwent and Glamorgan, but familiar also in more rural areas in the North East and in Pembrokeshire – and it is still hard to realise that that era has passed. Their tight sense of community, their hopes for better things to come and their heightened awareness of the suddenness of death shaped the religious atmosphere of many villages. At this period they came in great numbers to hear the quiet dialogues of William Williams Y Wern, perhaps the greatest of the early nineteenth century preachers, or such as Theophilus Jones, the man who opened Burnett's Hill, who had the *hwyl*, and the hellfire. This small Pembrokeshire building may be the oldest of the miners' chapels now surviving – and a would-be Pembrokeshire man, Richard Llewellyn, best translated their world to literature. His fictional chapel with a field by a river, built by the efforts of the congregation and too poor to have a minister of its own, bears more than passing resemblance to Burnett's Hill. His archetypal chapelgoing miner, Gwilym Morgan, dies in the rockfall when icy waters black with coal dust choke the tunnels, sweeping away the props as if they had been paper – and this honouring elegy, written back in 1939, has all the more resonance now: "How green was my valley, then, and the valley of them that are gone."

There is a cobwebbed chapel in the hills south west of Mynydd-llech above the Vale of Clwyd, also reminiscent of Burnett's Hill. It too is by a roadside on a field edge, cottage-like with plain sash windows, faces the congregation forward to the message on the gable end God is Love (*Duw CariadYw*), and is Calvinistic Methodist. But it has no local trust, is not in a national park, and is quietly fading.

Morriston/Treforys, Tabernacl

SS 669 978

The story of industrial society and the story of the chapels share the same centuries – an astonishing rise from early beginnings to dominate much of national life, and then the long slow falling away. At their peak the factories and chapels were built to accommodate thousands. An intelligent guess at when and where the largest chapel of them all would take shape would be Victorian Wales, round about mid-reign, and in the largest industrial conurbation of the time.

And that's exactly where it is. Morriston Tabernacl is built like a rock cliff on its hillside. Huge pillars rise in two pairs above a vast ground of rusticated stone. It was built under the direction of Daniel Edwards, the founder of the huge neighbouring Dyffryn Steel Works, now long gone. The chapel provided for the workers Sunday services and programmes of education by Sunday schools and weeknight gatherings in vast built-in community rooms, food for heart and mind after long shifts pouring out tinplate from the Works' three steam-driven mills. It was one more expansion of the industrial township of Wales's *Copperopolis*, the port and hinterland which produced and exported more than half the copper in the world. More than six centuries on from the time of the largest ever churches, this was a quite remarkable new tide.

Waves and waves of growth, and the confidence, people and money that came with them had put pressure on the old ideas of chapel simplicity. The minister, accompanied now by an architect, made a tour of the country to look for ideas to build in the new dispensation. Then, from their menu of options – temple porticoes, Corinthian capitals, roundheaded arches and windows, a towering steeple, a belfry, a series of great community rooms – they ordered the lot.

The architect was John Humphrey, a local miner's son who grew up to be a deacon in his childhood chapel of Mynydd-bach – and a carpenter. The quiet and devout demeanour his contemporaries described gave no hint of the towering conceptions in his mind. His chapel interior is virtually unaltered. Even on this scale, it still retains an old-style chapel's cool plain walls above dark pine seating, and tall clear windows. Ornament is limited, patterns being made by line in the circles and semi-circles in the window heads or the repetitions carved into the gallery facades. Painted acanthus leaves on the gallery columns, a pale blue compartmented ceiling, and two small stained glass windows decorated with vermilion roses, are among the few intrusions of colour. A painted scroll on the facing wall proclaims '*Addolwch yr Arglwydd mewn prydferthwch Sancteiddrwydd*': Worship the Lord in the beauty of Holiness.

An all-embracing gallery sweeps around the four walls and plunges down almost to touch the raised pulpit with its curved steps and twisted balusters, standing centrally within a grand *set fawr*. The pews of the lower congregation curl around it

From the menu of architectural features, they ordered the lot

as if to get closer to the words. But at Morriston the Word is supercharged with music. Above the pulpit is a wall of sound: choir and organist and three great blocks of organ pipes which reach up to the ceiling. At full tilt, with a singing congregation banked against the other walls and packing the lower floor, Tabernacl epitomises all the great late Victorian temple-chapels from Holyhead to Newport, the apotheosis of the communal, spiritual and choral traditions of Wales.

Its history encapsulates the whole chapel story. The first meetings in the district were in a farmhouse, then in an old thatched cottage, through the seventeenth and eighteenth centuries. The evangelists Howel Harris and Daniel Rowlands met at one in 1759, amazing the congregation by breaking out in fierce argument. Copper smelting began in Landore in 1719 and by the 1790s local landowner John Morris was building his planned town and works, named after him as Morriston. In 1782, he gave a plot of land for the congregation's first purpose-built chapel – under instruction not to hold a Sunday morning service, so as not to become a separate church. They named it Libanus, the Welsh for Lebanon.

All over again in 1796, 1831, and 1857 it had to be expanded or rebuilt to cope with larger numbers. Then came the 1859 Revival. Libanus decided to build again, this time a Tabernacle, a grander chapel than they had ever seen – to seat 3,000 people, at a cost of more than £15,000. It was an astonishing sum, almost double what their most ambitious contemporaries like the Baptists at Newtown were spending. And by the time it was ready late in 1872, they had to keep the old chapel open for services in English, while the new one stuck to Welsh. Its ministers were leaders of Welsh culture, and 'Blaenwern' was only the greatest of the music composed by its choirmasters. Tabernacl is still the home of famous choirs.

The creators of Tabernacl have other legacies: some say that Capel Seion Newydd down the road is John Humphrey's masterpiece; and the owner of the firm which made the organ was to plough his profits back into music, building an opera house on to his garden at Glyndebourne.

Nevern/Nanhyfer, St Brynach

SN 084 401

The Nyfer is an unsung river, streaming from Preseli into wooded valleys down to the sea at Parrog beach. Caman brook pours into it at Nevern, running along the churchyard wall, still a bubbling mountain stream, dividing secular garden from gravestone and yew. Many threads of medieval Wales are drawn together here at this meeting of water: an ancient llan, legends of a founder saint, Celtic crosses, pilgrim sites, an adjacent fortress hill, Norman conquest, and a church built like a rock.

This is a church surrounded by sacred signs and blessings – the traveller is drawn into its atmosphere by roads across the stark range of mountain, marked by the great cromlech of Pentre Ifan with its huge floating capstone, and down into the ancient sessile oakland of Ty Canol, a gnarled wildwood of mutely gesturing branches. The eye flies on to close in on the church's huge, immoveable, undatable tower and dark approaching avenue of yews, one of them famously bleeding with thick red resin running down its bark. Nevern's heartland is magical, resonant of being a nemeton, a sacred Druid grove at the almost-edge of the land where everything visible has a hinterland, as though the fragile light and shifting air are loaded with more weight than they can seem to bear. A fifth century memorial stone, casual witness to the site's long history, is ranged beside the great High Cross, a thirteen feet high sentinel

The dark approaching avenue of yews

of the past one thousand years. Each of the four sides has a row of interlacing patternwork, some like groundplans or mazes, with endless lines to represent eternity. On the east side, the largest pattern features two diagonal crosses with angled ends, and all consistent in direction but for the one at the top left. The lettering on this side is mysterious. On the west side, 'dns' is taken to be 'dominus' – 'Lord': Celtic sculptors were the text messagers of the first millenium.

The claims for Nevern, some of them first made more than a thousand years ago, continue to proliferate – that this was the valley where King Arthur and his knights pursued the wild boar *twrch trwyth*; the Caman llan which must be Camlan, his last battlefield and falling place; that this was the river which St Brynach turned hospitably to wine, and that on the crested mountain of Carn Ingli angels fed his dreams, and the rocks have taken up the shape of Rhiannon reclining, with her long stone limbs and swollen womb.

On to the stones memorialising unknown men have been projected the names of Vortigern and Maelgwn Gwynedd, the fiercest native warriors of this collapsing corner of the Roman world, and on to the cross-mark incised on the castle hill, the sign that it was here St Helena, the Celtic mother of Emperor Constantine, entombed the relic of the True Cross itself. Such claims are prospering in their new home on the web, as virtual and layered a place as Nevern llan itself, but all that can be safely said is that this cross, cut in the rock by the hairpin bend in the road and

The huge undatable tower

with a kneeling recess below it, was a pilgrim marker, a natural shrine on the route to St David's. The fifth century inscriptions on the stone just by the church porch are written in Latin and Ogham, the early Irish alphabet, and record the name Vitalianus. On the far side of the building, the outer north wall contains the vestiges of an inscription even older, in the corner of the middle chancel window, and on the nearby east wall of the transept an ancient consecration cross survives.

Inside this house of charms there is only a Victorian renewing of a medieval nave – when centuries of accumulated earth and burials which had raised the nave floor several feet were shovelled away – and anti-climactic memorials of poetry and gentry including that of George Owen, the Renaissance man of Cemais who wrote about the hills, the birds, the soil, the crops, the lives of sixteenth century Pembrokeshire with so much quirky, prescient curiosity, and whose inscription purposefully records him as the Father of English geologists, in puzzling defiance of these profoundly Welsh surroundings.

The south transept windows have become the relocated homes for two more ancient stones as sills. One has another dual inscription in Latin and Ogham: Magloclvni (miscut as Magloclvvi) Fili Clvtor – 'Maelgwn son of Clutorius', perhaps Clether, the chieftain said to have granted St Brynach the land. The other is a strange cross, a unique variant of Celtic knotwork taking its starting point from the pattern in the High Cross head outside but turning, like everything at Nevern, into something with another meaning: it conveys in abstract form and with startling imagination and economy not just a cross, but a man on a cross. The horizontal bar is an eternal line, interlaced and threaded just like the ones in the great cross circle. But the thread of the vertical bar has two ends, like two legs. Halfway up, at the 'pelvis', the thread divides on each side, but no single real thread – even divided in the middle – can be made to do what this design conveys.

Pontargothi, Holy Trinity

SN 510 227

Morriston Tabernacl and Pontargothi's Holy Trinity are two sides of the same Copperopolis coin, expressions of the surging new wealth of Victorian Swansea: one public and community-based, a temple for the workers; the other the dream of a copper millionaire, at the edge of his private estate. It says something for the spirit of that time and place that all the porticoed grandeur went into the building for the masses, while the rich man dreamed of a small, simple church with a plain exterior, on an old religious site in the curve of a stream. Its rounded doorways mix with pointed windows as though it had accumulated there over centuries like any ancient llan. This rapt tribute to medieval Welsh tradition intensifies inside, with a jewel box interior of coloured glass, muralled walls and dark embracing wood.

The patron was Henry Bath, who came down on Sundays from his house at Alltyferin, crossing the little bridge over the Cothi, on a path wide enough for master and mistress to walk arm in arm, while a narrow path beside it kept the servants respectable in single file. Bath's ships ran from Valparaiso to Swansea, bringing copper ore from Chile to smelt in Welsh furnaces. He named his ships after the Greek letters of the alphabet. In the 1860s and 70s his flagship was the Zeta: it is said one Swansea captain kept the name in the family until, over a century later, it crossed the Atlantic again to anchor in Hollywood.

Bath chose a Swansea-based architect, Benjamin Bucknall, who in his early twenties had conjured the great Gothick masterpiece of Woodchester Mansion into the hidden valley of the Inchbrook, where it still stands, roofless, haunted and bursting with bats. Bucknall's is the Seaman's Church on Swansea quayside, and the one-time chapel of Swansea Grammar School in its Mount Pleasant days, where Dylan Thomas "scribbled and smudged and yawned". He repeated there the partnership formed at Pontargothi, with the Somerset painter Alfred Stansell. His life made a strange arc from youthful inspiration by angular Gothic at Viollet-le-Duc's Notre Dame to the long last years in Algiers, pushing aside ill health to make Moorish villas.

Here he is already eclectic, mixing timber with stone, Gothic with Romanesque, adding the small playful gesture of a wooden spirelet and hexagon belfry. The exterior Bath stone dressings must be a punning tribute to his patron, and extend inside to the reredos inscribed with Alpha and Omega, which had, of course, another pun for him. Built between 1865 and 1878, it is early in the awakening of Arts & Crafts. The skill of the craftsman shapes everything in the interior, paintings, hangings, furniture, glass, from the decorated barrel vault to the climax of the chancel. Twenty-five wall paintings along the nave tell Biblical stories, each set in traceried Gothic arches as though viewed beyond a screen, the verses depicted inscribed at the base. Clayton & Bell glass fills the windows with prophets and evangelists, and in the large west window, portraits of Henry Bath (holding a model of the church), his nephew, and his wife, wearing pendulous earrings, who alone of the three lived to see the church completed.

St David's/Tyddewi, Cathedral

SM 752 255

For so many centuries pilgrims came here westward, crossing the land to its extremity, that distance and remoteness are in the fabric of the air at St David's. The inlets, bays, the towering cliffs, the force of the Atlantic, give Dewisland its charged sense of being at an edge of the world, where earth and air and water interchange.

But this was not quite how it was in the sea-borne century when Dewi (David) came here first, and ideas and people exchanged by boat with Ireland or across the Channel or the Severn Sea. St David's was the front door to western Wales. Perhaps

Dewi's house in the hollow

Angevin grandeur: the late twelfth century nave and aisle

in some renewed Wales it should be entered like Venice, motor boats scudding the modern tourist down the sea-lanes through the thousand rocks and little islands to Porth Clais or St Non's, to set foot at a grand and spiritual centre, and clamber up beside the chapel ruins, with the sea glowing out to the long horizon.

Dewi lived in the sixth century. His mother Non gave birth to him while holy water gushed up from the ground. He accumulated legends. The poet Waldo imagined him wandering the shoreline after the night's yearning, singing to the dawn as it broke over the mountain. The monastery he founded just inland was famously tough, its men living on bread and herbs and water, pulling the plough by the strength of their shoulders. The buildings sit hidden from view until close on arrival.

In one of the Welsh classics of description of place, Jones and Freeman's *History and Antiquities of St David's* which first appeared in 1856, a still partly ruined church shelters in a lost landscape "so little known, until of late so utterly inaccessible", the whole district beyond it exposed to the sea-winds, tree-less and barren. On a bad road, one slow omnibus made the journey out from Haverfordwest two days a week. Climbing uphill for six miles, the view opened out at Roch on the open heath and

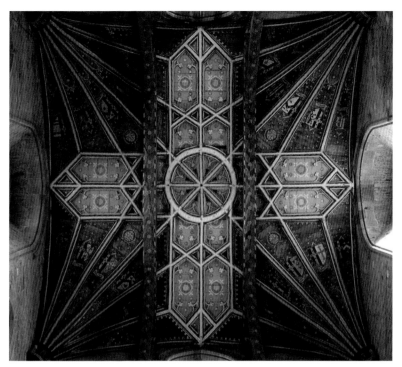

A medieval colour scheme revived in the crossing

rock and island-studded sea of Dewisland ahead, stark against the settled farmland that spread below back to the east. Arriving, the village was decayed, a few shambling streets of cottages thatched and whitewashed among pigsties. Beyond them, the awesome ranges of cathedral buildings veered up like a kind of 'life-in-death'.

On foot from the High Street, the top of the cathedral tower appears disconcertingly at eye level. A gateway called Porth y Twr is oddly conjoined by a tall belfry. Passing through into the walled close, the land falls away with sloping paths down below a row of 39 Steps. From Porth Clais or Castle Street, the first view is of the little river Alun splashing down the field among trees, with the ranges of buildings behind. The heart of St David's is rural. Taking the eastern path, skirting the back of the cathedral, a way leads alongside houses into the old farm and garden lands of the monastery, and the former homes of members of the church community. At the furthest reach, Pont-y-penyd, a little bridge with a seat beside it takes the winding lane across the Alun, heading to the outcrops of bare rock at Carn Llidi and the sweep of Whitesands Bay, where the ruins of chapels of other saints are scattered. Another lane leads back through the close on the western side of the Alun.

The cruciform cathedral church that rises from among these fields and scattered buildings has accumulated over centuries. The tower was built tentatively, reluctant to be seen beyond the valley, adding a second storey only in the safer fourteenth century, a third in the peace of the fifteenth. It was topped with an eight-pinnacled parapet quite different in character and stone. The mass of the cathedral, quarried from the western cliffs at Caerfai and Caerbwydy, has a rarity of colour which evades precise description; purple, ochre, plum and silver grey appear to mingle in haphazard sequence, setting up vibrations in the shifting light.

The porch's inner door has sad remains of what was once a Jesse tree, and Holy Trinity with angels. Inside, the cathedral, simply put, is a sequence of spaces in a line. The best route to take, if there were access, would be straight up the middle, nave giving way to pulpitum, choir, presbytery, and eastern chapels, each with a role in a series alternately confining and opening out, and always ascending – the floor level rises from west to east by the full height of the west door – to dramatise approaches to St David's shrine.

The nave is the greatest space, eccentrically leaning both outwards and upwards. A sixteenth century Welsh poem imagines it filled with herbs. It is robustly late twelfth century Norman, with solid piers and zigzag ornament, and early signs of Gothic in the upper windows. The wooden roof has a contrasting delicacy: pendants hang like Chinese lanterns, with an interweaving of Italianate and quatrefoil designs which date it to the early Renaissance.

At the east end of the nave the pulpitum begins with a screen in fourteenth century Decorated style. This is the first-seen of the works of Bishop Gower, who remade St David's in the mid-fourteenth century from all the wealth that pilgrimages brought. In his vast neighbouring palace, a hall nearly ninety feet long in a great complex of service buildings was required to provide for all arrivals. There is nothing quite like it in Britain: a shared space, more like the public palaces of Italy – the palazzi communali of Piacenza or Siena, the parapets, battlements and arcading of which are echoed here so strongly, and the Venetian Doge's Palace, exactly contemporary, with identical layout of courtyard and grand inner staircase. The palace had its own grand chapel. Its finely sculpted walls remain in part, and should be seen, wrote Jones and Freeman, "most of all by moonlight". As a prince of the Roman Church and a bulwark of Edward III's cross-Channel court, Bishop Gower reimagined St David's public spaces at the leading edge of European thought. He was not reticent: the great screen at the focus of the nave houses his tomb, and its weepers are not family, nor even angels, but the apostles themselves.

Gower also built St Thomas's chapel and its rich vault, just off the north transept. In the south transept is an early Welsh tombstone almost Egyptian in style, the head fully carved emerging in relief, and the 'Abraham stone' with a Celtic cross in a wheel – the nine hundred year old graveslab of the sons of Bishop Abraham, who had himself been killed by raiding Vikings.

An entry just beyond the transept leads to choir and presbytery. The choir fits unusually beneath the tower's lantern ceiling, with resounding consequences for acoustics. The stalls date from around 1500, one marked out for the monarch and one much more towering for the bishop, carved with spectacular show on the front, but pleasingly revealed from the back as just plain tall planks bound roughly together. The vernacular stamp shows through even here in the cathedral. St David's celebrated choir seat misericords are a gallery of medieval folk art, sea-faring and religion. A boatman strains with the oar against rough weather, while a passenger leans seasick over the side. A cargo boat is in for repair, one shipwright hammering a peg into the side, the other drinking, his axe at his side. In a third, two well-dressed men set about a meal of pig's head. Two more poke fun at the church: a fox in a friar's cowl, and a goose in a bishop's mitre taking food from the now-veiled fox. A fat owl sits on an ivy branch, and a drunken man sleeps off his drink.

The presbytery is the long-sought destination, the heart of the complex, the place of St David's shrine. Here medieval pilgrims would crowd in anticipation of blessings and cures, and feel some of the long years of their wait in Purgatory peeling back. Only its base, dated c. 1257, survives by the north wall. It has arched recesses where the pilgrims knelt, placing offerings through small holes in the central quatrefoils. The old stone flooring, now replaced, was worn into hollows by their knees.

More pilgrims jostled behind the east altar wall, and peered in through a recess at the relics. This area, once an outside yard within the complex, was roofed and elegantly screened and vaulted in the early sixteenth century. It has its own splendid though much damaged altar, with fourteenth century saints in a reconstructed reredos. The recess is still there, and still contains, one and a half thousand years on, the relics of St David.

Resurrection c. 1504, the latest High Renaissance style
on the tomb of Bishop Morgan

St Govan's Chapel / Capel Gofan Sant

SR 967 930

"*I'r cynfyd y camwn wrth groesi'r ffin i sir Benfro*" wrote Gwenallt: "I walked into the early world crossing the Pembrokeshire border." One hundred and seventy miles of coastline in one small county have kept westernmost Wales in the sway of sea and ancient rock, and the mark of the Celtic saints is still ingrained in its meshed and battered shores. The south is a fortress of great limestone cliffs swinging round from Linney Head, the piled up crush and bone of millennia of sea-life. Sailing east past Bullslaughter Bay and the gulping fissure of Huntsman's Leap, the towering line is barely broken until, just before its jutting southernmost headland, the sheer rock face appears suddenly to part, and a stairway rises up from sea to cliff top – a magical access between the sacred elements of earth and water.

The placing of St Govan's, a small chapel wedged in the rock, halfway up this entryway – and southernmost where St David's and its tributary chapels are westernmost – is another revelation of the honouring of landscape by our Celtic ancestors, a tribute to the intimacy of their knowledge of it, and their urge to show what they had recognised. A broken column of cliff butting into the water marks the entry like a shattered bell tower.

The chapel stands high above the spume and spray in a scree of seabirds, its thirteenth century walls a bare accumulation of stones over an earth floor, with a little

The bare interior of chapel and cell
Opposite: the splitting of the rock: Govan's house between earth and water

belfry and one small window facing out to sea. The altar is much earlier than the walls and is said to hold St Govan's bones. Beside it is a niche for holy water, and behind it through another doorway, a recess in the rocks. By tradition this was the saint's cell and hiding place, the grooves in the stone the imprint of his ribs. A holy well, now dried up, is still marked by a shelter of stones nearer down by the waterline.

St Govan is believed to be a fifth or sixth century saint, perhaps once the abbot of Dairinis near Wexford. Some time later his name was conflated with Gawain, the Arthurian knight whose Welsh original, Gwalchmai fab Gwyar, was said to be buried in Dyfed, and to whose Green Knight legend the Mabinogion tales of Pwyll, prince of Dyfed contributed so much. To the nineteenth century Arthurian revival, St Govan was no one but Gawain, of the brotherhood so linked to these Welsh and Cornish coasts.

Perhaps the link was sealed here in the surge and whitewater of a winter storm, to the New Year's Day climax of Gawain's legend, where through cold and driving rain Gawain climbs by cliffs and crags to the gate of the chapel where he must face the Green Knight, and hears the honing of a sword blade like the rush of a millwater race. In the story's merging of the ancient ritual war on death and winter with a fierce final moral of conscience and honour, the great medieval poem shows all its kinship, in fusing the Celtic and the Christian, with the little chapel on the Dyfed coast.

Come here on an early summer's day, and it is a different world: the guillemots nest and cluster on Eligug Stack, and the sea and sky are radiant blue.

> And one may wonder – and who can tell –
> If good Saint Govan likes Heaven as well
> As his cell by that sounding sea ?

> A.G. Prys-Jones

Tenby/Dinbych-y-pysgod, St Mary

SN 135 004

At Tenby on a warm blue day the Pembrokeshire coastline turns rococo. The edge of land and sea curls down from headland to beach, then up again to fortress mound and round curving bays. Offshore emerge the islands of St Catherine and Caldey where, in Peter Sager's wonderful phrase, you can buy perfume while looking at monks.

The view shifts from medieval castle to brightly coloured Georgian, seasonal residences for the better classes. What Tenby was before the castle is little known: just a passing mention of its oaken church in a ninth century document. The holiest Celtic sites on this coast lay elsewhere, at Penally, and in Gumfreston's trinity of bubbling springs and resonating atmosphere. But to know what Tenby was between the building of the castle and the spread of the resort, St Mary's is the place to go.

The tower is the oldest part, a watchtower from the castle age pushed forward from the west end to the east to command the hill brow more effectively. But the rest is largely a fifteenth century church, broad, spacious and filled with daylight, a prosperous peacetime church, a corporation church lined by the monuments of tradesmen mayors, and more at one in style with those on the West Country coast just over the water, with which its merchants and sea-captains must all have been familiar.

Christ with meditative angels on the ceiling of the nave

To the fifteenth century belong the arcades which separate the three broad aisles (one with West Country hood mouldings carved with oak leaves and acorns); the majestically raised chancel, made airy and open to the aisles by the removal of the chancel arch; and the central barrel roof arrayed with bosses. Over the chancel, the wall posts holding the roof are carved as standing figures. Above them is a medieval mix of beasts and bishops, grotesques and saints – Veronica with her veil, John the Baptist with his head on a charger – and whales and mermaids for a touch of the sea. There used to be a gallery chapel up here dedicated to St Anne. Above the nave Christ in Glory, holding his empty cross, is encircled by wiry-headed angels with eyes meditatively closed. Outside, the same century produced the beautiful double-ogee west doorway and a tapering spire for the tower, on top of which still sits an ancient weathercock, probably three hundred or more years old.

The new prosperity which gave the town the chance to remake its church also reveals in individual commissions a more personal, intensified religious life. By the north door a churchman chose to be displayed in a cadaver tomb, while the two tombs of the White family, in prime position on the south side of the chancel, show how wealthy merchants – dressed in their effigies so differently from armoured aristocrats – could pay to be memorialized in alabaster. They were happy, it seems, to depict their wallets, slung from their shoulders, but wanted most to show themselves at prayer, the whole family gathered on the side panels in the company of their chosen saints, among them Catherine with her wheel and John the Baptist with a lamb – a domestic and intimate portrayal of ordinary men and women with those to whom

The intensified religious life of fifteenth century Tenby

234

every day they spoke and prayed and through whose personal care they were given some protection, just as in paintings by the Flemish and Italian masters.

Thomas White may have also helped to fund the roof. His initials appear on the most intense of its images, the pierced hands and feet of Christ. His moment in history was to slip the then-beleaguered Tudors in his own ship across the sea to Brittany, where they would remain for fourteen years before sailing back to make their bid for the Crown, and the riches of his son may be due as much to the rewards this brought as to the success of their trade in wine: John White proudly wears the Tudor rose, hanging from a chain of beads around his neck.

The church has monuments of note from other times: a grey stone tomb to an unknown fourteenth century lady, her parted hair and ornamented hairband carved with touching delicacy; mayor William Risam (1633) with musket shot damage from Cromwell's time; Margaret Mercer and Thomas ap Rees, their almost lifesize figures raised on a grand Jacobean showpiece; a modern slab to Robert Recorde, the Renaissance Tenby astronomer, doctor, and algebraist who invented the equals sign '=' because, he said, two parallel lines were the most equal things he could think of; and a tablet for a certain Peggy Davies: 'To preserve from oblivion the Memory of Peggy Davies, bathing woman 42 years to Ladies who visited TENBY. Her good humour respectful attention & Gratitude made her employers Friends. On the 29th Septr 1809 In the Water She was seized with Apoplexy & expired. Aged 82.'

Thomas White, Tenby wine merchant: he shipped the beleaguered Tudors across to France

V

THE SOUTH EAST

BLAENAU GWENT, BRIDGEND, CAERPHILLY, CARDIFF, MERTHYR TYDFIL, MONMOUTHSHIRE, NEWPORT, RHONDDA CYNON TAFF, TORFAEN, VALE OF GLAMORGAN

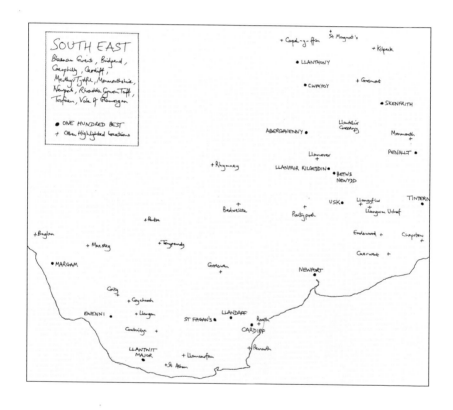

Abergavenny/Y Fenni, St Mary

SO 302 141

Abergavenny has the finest gathering of medieval sculptures in any parish church in Britain. Commissioned from artists right across the island, they are the single best insight into those who ruled the territory in the later Middle Ages, and they show the rise to great power, finally, of a native family, after the long exclusions of the conquest.

The Braose, Hastings and Herbert dynasties were successively lords of the castle, now just a ruin on a nearby mound, whose lives were locked into the battles of succeeding centuries: the fierce Marcher struggle, the Hundred Years War and then the Wars of the Roses. They needed all the prayers they could get from their local community of monks, whose single most important role was to sustain an endless round of supplication for their souls. The canopied choir stalls from which they did this in the fifteenth and early sixteenth centuries, with carved royal beasts and badges signifying Tudor patronage, are a major survival at the heart of the church: the monks gazed out at the wood, stone and alabaster images of those they worked to save, depicted still dressed for battle. The long choir and chancel open out on both sides to chantry chapels, a memorable sight on turning the corner from the transept, their lines of raised recumbent effigies like a harboured fleet embarking for the afterlife. As a local man, Octavius Morgan, wrote back in 1872 in the only book ever devoted to them, "they have not received that attention which they deserve".

Safe in their alabaster chambers: Agincourt glamour at Abergavenny

Jesse: the last and sole survivor of the giant oak icons

But the visitor's first encounter is with another extraordinary monument which faces down the nave, the last and sole survivor in Britain of the giant oak icons which took the honoured places in its medieval churches: a ten foot long, fifteenth century carved figure of a robed and bearded patriarch. It must once have been the base of a full tree of Jesse, and although not all the other figures would have been this large, its size and power must have been astonishing. It may have stood originally as the church's focal point behind the altar, like the stone tree at Christchurch in Dorset. Jesse lies back on a cushion held by an angel, wearing the expression of one who has looked on worldly things unimpressed. The carver has lingered over details – a thin buckled belt, clog-like shoes, the sweep of the folds in the clothes, the long fingers of a huge left hand, and a parted beard with a small unexplained cavity at the base.

By his side is another rare oak effigy, of John de Hastings (d. 1325), the rebuilder of the priory and one of those border lords who had to ride the sudden shifts and moods of power under Edward II. He took the surrender of Llywelyn Bren and was part of the force which laid waste to Glamorgan in the effort to destroy the base of Hugh Despenser. His success is shown by this fine courtly image of a knight at prayer on a stone tomb of a fashionable new type where the sides were lined by images of his kin. Lawrence de Hastings (d.1348) was an international figure, Earl of Pembroke and Lord of Wexford, who defeated the French at the sea battle of Sluys: it was said there were so many in the water that the fish began to speak their language. His feet rest on a bull and there is a lone weeper on one side. William (d. 1349, in the Black Death) lies in a traceried recess with his feet on a greyhound, a lithe, spare image with small, delicate quatrefoils on the sword-sheath and belt. "The features have a fat swollen appearance and the expression is not pleasing", thought Octavius.

The three alabaster Herbert tombs are almost in a row. They combine the insistent military imagery of the Hastings tombs with a greater emphasis on personal devotion – in this case to the Virgin – and a whole new presence and status for their remarkable wives. In the middle is the founder of the dynasty, William ap Thomas (d. 1445) and his wife Gwladys, who was known as the Star of Gavenny. Their fame came from Agincourt, where William fought alongside Gwladys's first husband and her father Dafydd Gam – Davy Gam of Shakespeare's *Henry V* – who died together there: this was the ancestry of which the poet George Herbert was later so proud. On one end of their sumptuous tomb is an Annunciation, Mary surprised in a canopied room with God looking on, as in a Memling or van der Weyden. William's allegiances are marked on the tomb in Yorkist sunbursts, but they did for his son Richard when the Lancastrians hit back at the battle of Banbury. He was captured and swiftly beheaded in the market place, but not before he had famously cut through the opposing ranks twice, with a poleaxe. By Richard's side on their tomb is his wife Margaret, sister of Rhys ap Thomas, with two of her lapdogs: their tomb-end image is of her name-saint with the Virgin and Child and St Catherine.

William's grandson, another Richard (d. 1510), has a tomb recessed in the wall with a pinnacled Gothic canopy. Small images of his family are arranged on either side of an elegantly elongated Virgin in an image which combines her Assumption into heaven attended by angels with her Coronation by the Holy Trinity. Both the Trinity and family have been badly smashed by an iconoclast who must have had his own compelling reasons not to touch the face or body of the Virgin. When this tomb was pulled out of the wall for restoration a small sculpted monk holding rosary beads – a 'sleeping beadsman' – was discovered beneath the sole of Richard's left foot, as on the near-contemporary Mathew tomb at Llandaff.

Back on top: an early Tudor Welsh dragon

239

Across the chancel is another memorial chapel, which has a fine 1580s tomb with images of ships and books and hearts of oak for David Lewis, first Principal of Jesus College Cambridge and a judge of the High Court of Admiralty. The church's oldest monument is kept nearby, a small funeral effigy – one of the first of its kind – for Eva de Braose (d. 1255), holding a heart in her hands. The adjacent tomb, although it dates from a hundred years later, has sometimes been proposed as belonging to her mother, another Eva de Braose and the daughter of William Marshal. Eva's husband had been hanged by Llywelyn Fawr in front of eight hundred men for adultery with his wife, an act which led on to his most curious surviving letter, in which he wondered aloud to Eva whether, having killed her husband, it would still be all right for his son to marry her daughter. The answer, it seems, was yes: even the far corners of Wales were meshed together by alliances of blood and calculation. Others suggest the tomb is for Margaret Plantagenet, daughter of Edward III who came here as wife to a later John de Hastings. It used to be a curiosity for an image of a pet squirrel hanging from a chain around her neck, but only the chain now remains. The lady, according to an old chronicler, "was killed with a fall following a squirrel from the top of the castle wall".

Betws Newydd (dedication unknown)

SO 362 058

This little stone-tiled church lies on the edge of its quiet Monmouthshire village, where the land falls away to the south to open out the view. There is a mounting block on the outside of the circling stone wall of the churchyard, and the path to the church is lined by two extraordinary yews, one of them among the largest in the country with a thirty-three foot girth. Betws Newydd thus takes its place among the county's rural churches, which are rich in the distinctive marks of rounded boundaries, ancient yews, and memorable riverside or hillside settings, long pre-dating in origin their counterparts in the castle settlements which so strongly bear the French stamp. It has the slightly lower, narrower chancel characteristic of this rural group, but its unusual west entrance plan is shared in the region only by a near-neighbour at Llangyfiw, similar enough in date and atmosphere to suggest the same builders or patron. The footings of the long lost churchyard cross are specked with quatrefoils and lichen, and the crosses of St Andrew and St George.

Stone seating lines the porch. The west door is encrusted with huge nails smashed through on the outside and bent in on the inner side, and iron hinges stretch across the breadth of it – a memory of vulnerable borderland which must predate the broad-windowed Perpendicular form in which the building now appears. Overhead a funeral bier rests in the old roof, dowels untrimmed in the beams.

Inside, the view ahead is filled by the rood loft, a great wall of timber which covers the whole width and height of the nave. One of the two most celebrated Monmouthshire lofts, Betws Newydd is by contrast with its famous Llangwm Uchaf neighbour bluffer, plainer, inexpert at dazzling honeycomb effects – but it has a completeness and a place in its original fabric and surroundings which make it unlike any other survival.

The rounding wagon roof frames a solid tympanum in which big structural beams preserve the echo of the Cross. To either side the watchers in the loft could look down through traceried windows to the altar's secret ceremonies. The south wall still contains the steps they took to climb there and the doorway through which they passed. The west face has a curious pattern, repeated fourteen times across the breadth of the nave, of quatrefoils topped with crocketed heads that seem from a distance to resemble pine cones: close up, each one is irresistibly varied and complex. The supporting beam is packed unusually tightly with carved leaves and fruit, a band of oak leaves strangely elongated into almost-vine leaves and the row of vine leaves having oddly squared-off edges.

In the chancel there is a small side chapel, and the roof remains boarded and unplastered. The back of the screen has miniature gothic spires, and viewed from here the cross beams are the raw plain cut of a tree trunk. On a sunlit day, light floods in to these separate and half disclosed chambers of the church, in a reassuring blending of timber and stone. Leaving, there is the bowl of the font, ancient – not much less than a thousand years old – with some rudimentary carving on the underside. And down the road is Llangwm Uchaf, the most grandly conceived of all the Welsh lofts, yet as delicate and various as any, an astonishing creation of local medieval craftsmanship with so many multiple bands of leaf-trail that some have wondered whether parts have been integrated to it from a second screen. It is also, like its church, much reconstructed, and its dragons are wingless, and half gone.

500 year old loft, screen and ceiling at Betws Newydd

Cardiff/Caerdydd, St John the Baptist
ST 183 763

St John's is where an urban church should be – right next to the market, in amongst the shops and the pubs and the people. In the days when the river flowed along the castle wall and next to the Westgate, the tower would have faced out to the docking boats down the narrow connecting streets. This was the heart of the tightly packed old castle quarter which for seven centuries was the whole of Cardiff, until the great industrial expansion kicked in from the 1820s, and the church and castle are its only medieval survivals. But St John's was not the main medieval church: it took on a greater role from around the 1460s when St Mary's, a street away, was caught up in a swinging oxbow of the river, which finally destroyed it in the flood of 1607.

A circuit around the outside and through the pleasantly green churchyard reveals a rather spreading building, almost a series of buildings, but inside it feels wonderfully integrated. St John's is a combination of the two most expansive periods of Welsh parish church building – the later fifteenth and nineteenth centuries. A hundred years or so ago the chancel was raised and outer aisles added, giving height and articulation to a newly broad interior.

The tower is pure Perpendicular, built in the late 1400s and much celebrated for the soft grey stone, high windows, and almost oriental lines of the base arches and

Pure Somerset transposed across the Severn Sea

243

fretwork complexities on the parapet. Topped by a profusion of pinnacles, it is a piece of pure Somerset transposed across the Severn Sea, an expression of the maritime, south-facing cultural focus of late medieval Cardiff, and perhaps also something else: when Jasper Tudor became Lord of Glamorgan and Gwynllwg he oversaw the rise of tall, sea-watching towers at Newport, here and at Llandaff, which this one most resembles. He came to power through his own sea-fleet invasion further west along the coast, with his nephew Henry and their army, and it is possible to read a certain nervousness as well as celebration in his main remembered contribution to the churches in his territory. Access is sometimes open for the 130 feet climb up to the top.

At the end of the north aisle, an entry leads into the Lady Chapel through a late Gothic screen with winding lines of wheat and vine carved in the doors. Its curiosities are best seen from within, especially the small wooden panels in which there are medallions of rude onlookers of the Passion scene, tongues protruding as if from a contemporary painting by Bosch. Two Herbert brothers, William and John, share the fine early seventeenth century marble and stone memorial on the north wall of the chapel. One a soldier, one a diplomat and lawyer, their effigies are dressed accordingly. The feet say it all. They were closely connected to the 'incomparable pair' of Herbert brothers who were the dedicatees of Shakespeare's First Folio, and William ran gangs of armed men through the streets of Cardiff like any Capulet or Montague: his instigation of their violent riots in the 1590s is a part of the directly contemporary backdrop to the writing of *Romeo and Juliet*. John was by contrast a negotiator, Secretary of State to both Elizabeth and James, a solid man to count on in the era of the Essex rebellion and the Gunpowder Plot. The black restraint and cool sophistication of the monument suggest the guiding hand of patronage belonged to John.

The church has plenty of good Victorian glass. A Morris window at the west end of the north aisle features his own images of Peter, James and Paul, Ford Madox Brown's Abraham and Isaac, and Burne Jones's Melchizedek, Noah and his ark. Some of these same subjects are reimagined in distinctly post-Raphaelite Michelangelo style in Goscombe John's animated figures on the raised main altar, part of the High Anglican art east end with a reredos by John Prichard and glass by Ninian Comper. Comper also designed the reredos in the south chapel dedicated to Kitchener, which has a 1930s screen complete with daffodils and rugby ball.

These expensive commissions from leading artists of the day are part of Cardiff's astonishing expansion, which sprang from the new docks built to export the coal and iron pouring out from the valleys upriver, their vast all-night furnaces making glowing red moonlight in the northern sky. A spirit of demonstrative boomtown affluence, along with High Church beauty of holiness, lies behind many of the churches for the new populations but, as Cardiff was never Chicago, contained within the modest and community-minded frame of a local place of worship. St

German's and St Margaret's Roath, the latter full of Bute tombs and money, may be the best of them. The chapels here aspired more to look like churches than in any other part of Wales – more Gothic and more Anglicised – and most of these new buildings shared the multi-coloured brick and stone exuberance launched by Butterfield's St Augustine's at Penarth. But the grandest of the chapels is the most traditionally classical, with a columned façade but no pediment, and a Welsh language preaching heritage built up by the work of Christmas Evans: the 1865 Tabernacle in The Hayes, just down the road from St John's.

A Renaissance woodcut from the Herbert chapel

Cwmyoy / Cwmiau, St Martin

SO 299 233

Cwmyoy church stands in the rolling green landscape just to the west of the strikingly-shaped valley which gave it its name – the vale of the yoke – and in the shadow of a massive, cliff-like mound of old red sandstone, from which it has been built. Its heavy walls, punctured with a few small doors and windows, articulate a chancel, nave, porch, and squat barely battlemented tower. But this is not what first catches the eye.

At Cwmyoy, nothing is quite vertical. The chancel leans down the hill, pressing its weight against the largest of the buttresses. The tower has swung in the other direction, nodding towards the north so much that only two of its six bells can now be rung. Centuries ago, landslide or subsidence must have made all its walls awry. Inside, beyond a steadied nave, the raised east end seems to have lurched backwards and sideways. As Nick Jenkins says in his book of local walks, go to Cwmyoy if you feel inclined.

The half-light, the plainness and age of the interior add to the atmosphere – great grey flagstones, a pre-Tudor medieval wholeness to the structure, a roof which thrusts out of the walls in a single frame, at seven hundred years old one of the most ancient in the country. A low doorway and steep stone steps lead from the back of the nave to the bells. The tub font is Norman. There is a small pre-Gothic window in the north wall, and narrow slanting lancets in the chancel. They outline a fine Jacobean altar rail, at which the old parishioners of Cwmyoy must have taken communion queasily.

Stones and wall inscriptions record their brief memorials, and the appropriately wayward aspirations of their rhymes and design over a couple of hundred years from the Restoration. In the chancel, in clear continuous lines from 1682: 'Thomas Price he takes his nap in our common mother's lap waiting to heare the bridegroome say awake my dear & come a way'. Others, such as James Prosser's from 1775, are from the distinctive local workshop of the Brute family. Joan Williams has an elegant oval in the splay of the one Tudor window, and another, her namesake nearby, died at the age of three. The porch has a finely scripted memorial to a churchwarden's daughter and some unusual plaster panels, one bearing a cross, which are seventeenth century.

The church's most extraordinary possession is a stone cross carved with the image of the crucified Christ, thought to date from the 1200s. The figure, wearing an old-fashioned crown resembling a bishop's mitre, combines a ribbed but abstract torso with more natural limbs and twisted feet, and has a straight and outward gaze. It may have been a marker on the pilgrim road which passed this way, heading west to Saint David's. In the 1960s it was stolen from the church, but turned up in an

The old red sandstone church beneath the mountain's shadow at Cwmyoy

antique shop in London, where it was spotted by a Keeper from the British Museum.

Outside, there are the steps and base of the medieval churchyard cross, many old gravestones, and an inscribed memorial pathway leading through them.

The Cwmyoy Christ

Drefach Felindre, Capel Penrhiw
(now at St. Fagans: National History Museum)
ST 115 773)

Drefach Felindre lies deep in the rural lands above the Teifi valley, in the shadow of
Moelfre mountain and some twenty miles from the sea. These days it is home to the
museum of the Welsh woollen industry, which built its early factories straggling
down into Cwmpencraig. Dyes were made from local plants, heather and gorse for
yellows, madder for pink and red. Dolmion, one of the oldest mills, was run by the
Adams family which produced two early American Presidents. This part of Wales,
south Cardiganshire and north Carmarthenshire, became the stronghold of
Unitarian worship, or *Y Spotyn Du* – the Black Spot, as the orthodox called it.

Among their gathering places was Penrhiw, a small barn chapel of 1777. The
chapel ground remains, up a steep lane between stone walls and hedges, a bull
bellowing in the neighbouring field. The minister would have looked out through the
low window opposite the pulpit to the graveyard and ring of low hills beyond.

Penrhiw is Wales's most intimate chapel. It is perhaps no more than thirty feet
long, twelve to fifteen feet wide. Light enters from all sides, falling across the deep
sills on posts and panelling, arcades and balustrades, below the rafters with their
cargo of funeral biers. Box pews press up against one another, the paleness of their
colour set against the darkness of the benches. The congregation was jumbled
together on seats at different heights, facing in different directions but facing each
other too, everyone known and eye to eye, the minister and elders in amongst them
and not peering down a long chancel to an orderly row of pews. The whole plan
evokes a close and shared experience, a small group bound together in unorthodoxy,
deeply aware of their difference from their neighbours. Here they shared the
nervous excitement of new and dangerous ideas, and of believing they were right.
The singing must have been loud against the ear, the boards creaking as feet shuffled
or weight shifted, the readings and sermon at the pitch of conversation, like listen-
ing, gathered round, to a storyteller. At Penrhiw, the mystery was all in the words.

The building began as a barn, its front wall then adapted to chapel style with a
central pulpit window and a door to either side, and stone seats outside for use at
open air preaching. It would originally have been thatched but is now tiled with
stone. Inside it has an earth floor, except at its heart in front of the pulpit, where
communion was given. In the early nineteenth century, the hayloft was converted to
a gallery ranged around three sides and filled with benches, with a staircase leading
up from by the door.

The congregation was always too small to afford a minister of its own – their
preachers came several miles downriver from Llwynrhydowen, the indomitable
Ceredigion chapel which was such a powerhouse of free thinking in late eighteenth
century Wales. So the list of Penrhiw's early ministers, men like Dafydd Dafis

Castellhywel and David Lloyd, is resonant with names of those who first aired the new spirit of the rights of man, libertarianism and religious questioning, and – through a wider Unitarian circle of Tomos Glyn Cothi and Iolo Morgannwg – yielded also a literary flowering and the relaunch of the Gorsedd of Bards. One of Llwynrhydowen's founding families, the Lloyd Joneses of Blaenralltddu, were the ancestors of Frank Lloyd Wright who, immersed in Welsh Unitarian moral and literary culture from childhood, was to take on Iolo's motto 'Truth Against the World' and produce an architecture which, in its absorption in the natural landscape, its horizontal lines, asymmetry, integrated interiors and human scale, placed all these ancient Welsh wisdoms about built spaces for one astounding twentieth century moment at the forefront of world design.

One more name jumps out from the list, the minister here for half a dozen years in the 1860s and 70s: Gwilym Marles, the spirited preacher-poet remembered for his battling against the stubborn customary oppression of the rural poor, and as one of the "towering dead" in the mind of his great-nephew Dylan Marlais Thomas. "The enemy can only take the candlestick," Gwilym told his congregation, but "the flame and the light are God's." Dylan saw behind the brave outer face of the Teifi valley radical to the Carmarthenshire man with more than a touch of softer Tywi valley, *Grongar Hill* innocence in his poetry, and paid his tribute to him in the peerless and affectionate humanity of *Under Milk Wood*'s Rev. Eli Jenkins, into whose thoughts and cadences Gwilym Marles's work, even in translation, seems effortlessly to melt:

> Our chiefest duty here to work and strive
> To His great glory while we are alive
> (For whether we last the night or no
> I'm sure is always touch and go.).

Ewenni, St Michael

SS 913 778

A country lane, winding aimlessly along a riverbank, ends at the walls of an ancient priory, a working farm, and glimpses of a grand old house set back behind. Redolent of spiritual and rural community, and of the timeless round of seasons, these first impressions are wholly misleading of its origins. Inside the great gateway in the outer wall there are traces of violent defence – shafts for a series of portcullises, roofholes for pouring down boiling tar. There are battlements and arrowshot piercings on the priory tower, and all original windows are placed high above attacking reach. The traces of 600 yards of wall around the settlement enclose no less than five acres, suggesting the size of garrison required and the perceived degree of threat. Ewenni is the church as conquest fortress.

The weight of masonry dominates the interior spaces of the nave and its columned arches are primitive and plain, as castle builders rather than church builders make them. It ends abruptly at a solid stone screen, more than eight feet high, fronted by a wooden screen of oak, with fourteenth century details and some Tudor linen pattern restoration. Its wooden doors push open to a high presbytery, the former monks' domain of barrelling stone vaults and wall arcades, with disconcertingly-placed outbreaks of windows, carved heads of trailing beasts and a resonating choir acoustic. Still the most atmospheric Romanesque space in Wales, it had altars only visible to others through deep splayed squints like the one which survives in the north wall. The high arcade with alternating columns of squares and cylinders led to the dormitory, and also to the watchtower.

The floor is casually lined with ancient fragments – a crudely cut Celtic cross, a curious twelfth century figure of a human head riding on a donkey, thought to be an image of Christ entering Jerusalem, and the miscellaneous tombs of generations of

An early image of the entry into Jerusalem

patrons. One sculpted lid, rich in floriate patterns and fine Lombardic letters, begins its inscription 'Ici Gist [Here Lies] Morice de Lundres, le Fun Dur [the founder]'. It is like finding in a hallowed place of honour the unmentionable name of MacBeth.

William and Maurice de Londres were among the hard men of the Norman invasion, taking the bruising gain of pushing the front line westwards, locking up the west end of the Vale with their castle at Ogmore then breaking through to Gower and beyond, turning first footholds into tougher stone bastions, trapping the Welsh behind their estuary outlets, and getting damned as high and far away as Rome for robbery and murder. They and their cohorts took the fight to Deheubarth, killing the native ruler Rhys and his son Goronwy, drowning Cynan in a lake, taking on the next son Gruffydd and Gwenllian his Gwynedd princess wife. At a famous battle outside Kidwelly, in a field still called Maes Gwenllian, the men of Maurice de Londres killed Gruffydd's son Morgan, wounded and captured Gwenllian, then summarily, shockingly beheaded her.

More than the blank and conscienceless ruins of their castles, Ewenni Priory lights up the time and mind of a William or Maurice de Londres, the brute fighter making his show of faith while building up another beacon tower, the colonist as overlord yet prisoner behind his own protecting walls, and prisoner perhaps also to his beliefs and his remorse – like MacBeth "cabined, cribbed, confined, bound in" by spiritual doubts and fears. In 1141 Maurice, sensing the reckoning ahead, turned over the stolen estates and revenues of six southern churches to the Benedictine order. The move lays bare the conqueror as supplicant, fighting now to build his bridgehead to the next world, paying at Ewenni for endless walled-in Benedictine prayers to edge his soul forward through the torment of Purgatory, just as in his lifetime he hacked on through the fracturing landscape of Wales. Turner, painting here in 1797 in his moody, burnished Petworth style, caught the purgatorial half-darkness of the presbytery, made earthy by the grunting of pigs and the wing-brush of farmyard fowl. This strange interior darkness persisted here for two hundred more years until only months ago, and still surely lurks beneath its new superficial skin of limewash.

Originally a cross-shaped church (there is the ghostmark of the lost north transept on the outside wall), each transept had a small chapel projecting to the east: the floor of the north one, now in open ground, has tiles with the symbols of Gloucester Abbey, to which Ewenni had been given. There was always a nave and north aisle but no south aisle, as a cloister ran in its place. The current north aisle is nineteenth century reconstruction, hence the larger windows alien to the first design, but has some of the Priory's original floor tiles at the east end. The older windows are in the nave, small, high, deep and roundheaded. The gap between screen and roof has been filled with a vast new span of glass by the Swansea-based artist Alex Beleschenko, in which, just as at Llandaff fifty years ago, visionary Resurrection imagery has been floated over the nave. This warring masterpiece of a church was largely complete by the mid 1120s – almost two hundred years before the Edwardian castles – but Maurice's tomb suggests the whole walled complex and the long term oratory funding took both generations, as did the castles. The font is older than any part of the building.

A floriate cross slab for Maurice de Londres, made decades after his death

Llandaff, Sts Peter, Paul, Teilo, Dyfrig and Euddogwy

ST 156 781

Llandaff may look these days the epitome of the traditional cathedral, quietly sited at the foot of wooded slopes beside the green watermeadows of the Taff. The steep secluded Dean's steps leading down to it among old lampposts give it almost an air of old Montmartre. But this is a building which has been repeatedly smashed down – and always reconstructed in the cutting edge of modernism.

Bishop Urban's towering construction of c.1120 was in the first wave of Romanesque in Wales. In the then near one thousand year history of Christianity in Wales, no church on anything like this scale had ever been seen – and by raising such buildings here and simultaneously at Chepstow, Ewenni and St David's, the Normans were branding their first enclaves of the Welsh landscape with their mark of possession. Demolishing a predecessor just 28 feet long, the new Llandaff was toweringly high, and in a powerful new church building material: stone. The shock of the new can rarely have carried such a punch.

c.1120, the first great stone church rises, with Romanesque pattern on the chancel arch, and the face perhaps of its builder, Bishop Urban, over the north door

254

Six hundred years later, the overgrown ruin of the nave was in-filled by John Wood, the architect of Bath, with a new church resembling a temple. It was the forerunner, by many decades, of the temple-style chapels which were to rise across the country, and oddly enough just when they were rising, it was demolished. Llandaff was recast again, this time in new Gothic. Interior commissions were handed to a controversial band of young artists, whose vivid colour and earthy realism were already making waves. Their names were Dante Gabriel Rossetti, William Morris and Ford Madox Brown.

Another century on, on a bitterly cold, moonbright night, 2nd January 1941, a parachute came drifting slowly down in a shower of incendiary bombs. It was carrying a large naval mine. The parachute caught in Llandaff spire and flung down its cargo into the snowy churchyard, setting off a huge explosion which propelled shattered tombstones like missiles at the walls and tore the roof off nave and aisle. Among the shellshocked was the Dean who, having failed to find his helmet, was said to have been wearing a colander.

The rebuilding caused new shock in the 1950s, with an architect inspired by Le Corbusier and a sculptor whose work routinely generated public vitriol: the American Jacob Epstein. Their signature piece for Llandaff is a great, 16 feet high aluminium sculpture of Christ, suspended over a concrete arch across the nave, with a cylindrical concrete organ case at his back, as though in mid-ascent by jet pack. It is the most audacious siting of a modern masterpiece in any ancient British cathedral, a figure whose grandeur and compassion seem both to challenge and reach out to the entrant at the door.

Yet what is most striking now about all this determined modernity is how nostalgic, how retrospective in intention it all was – the Normans evoking ancient Rome; Pre-Raphaelites escaping to their idealised Middle Ages (though their altarpiece, with its nod to a firmly post-Raphael Veronese, fell slightly short of the distance); and Epstein, pre-Renaissance, even Byzantine, in inspiration, yet unmistakably honouring another later icon of Venice, Bellini's 'St Francis in the Desert', with whom his Christ shares the long robes, the gently raised and vulnerable hands, and the transcendant gaze.

This Christ extends a long tradition nurtured at Llandaff: there is no church in the country where the imagery over a millennium has been so centred on the resurrected Christ. For most of these years, the central figure at the entrance was the superb thirteenth century Christ in Majesty, now so weathered it has come inside. A Llandaff bishop absorbed in this tradition like Edmund Bromfield, buried in St Dyfrig's chapel at the east end of the north aisle, chose to have Christ enthroned carved on the face of his tomb, and in an even more personal touch, an image of the newly resurrected Christ directly meeting the gaze of his own effigy, as though the first thing he would see on Resurrection Day. *The Book of Llandaff*, an amazing survival from the mid-twelfth century (now in the National Library of Wales), has

c.1220, the completion of the west front, with a blessing at the entrance and Llandaff's first great image of the risen Christ (opposite page)

on its cover a gilded Christ suspended on a rainbow, an image from the Revelation of St John renewed in the twentieth century by the nave's high and slender curve of concrete.

The original plan had been to cover this concrete rainbow with mosaics of the Last Judgement by Stanley Spencer: he and Epstein travelled down to Llandaff together by train, Spencer talking without pause until Epstein at last told him to shut up. The project did not materialise. But the present arch did help to realise the architect George Pace's intention to integrate the whole length of the cathedral, stripped of screens and other blockages to give a through view from the west end, up the Gothic arcades to the great decorated Norman arch at the entry to the Lady Chapel, and to the eastern light beyond.

One of these blockages was Rossetti's high altar triptych, which was moved to the west end of the north aisle. The adoration of the newborn Jesus is flanked with depictions of David in each wing, as sling-wielding shepherd and crowned king

seated on a very aesthete peacock throne. Along with this high-toned message of Jesus's relationship to high-born and low comes the high spirited exuberance of the Brotherhood as young men, depicting none other but themselves in costume. The holy child is adored by Burne Jones (a shepherd) and Swinburne (a king), while resting in the arms of Janey Morris. Red-haired angels not unlike Fanny Cornforth look on, while her husband models the young David, and William Morris the harp-playing king. The painting dates from the years around 1860.

There are five surviving Pre-Raphaelite windows. Among the best are Madox Brown's 'Miraculous draught of fishes', and 'Christ walking on the water' in the north aisle, unusually animated work for this group of artists. St Dyfrig's chapel has six Burne Jones terracotta panels of the Days of Creation, in which every day a new angel arrives with the latest works.

The cathedral's remaining gathering of art and sculpture forms a major collection, still too little known. The tradition honouring Christ is almost matched by the honouring of Mary: her motherhood in a painting attributed to Murillo, her death

c.1393. Edmund Bromfield contemplates the Resurrection

in a fifteenth century Flemish carving in the south aisle. In the north aisle a painting from the same period shows Bishop Marshall watching her Assumption into heaven as angels fly about her, which was once part of the throne on which he sat in the choir. She is crowned amid the foliage of a brass chandelier (of a type also found at two small parish churches in Denbighshire) currently in the cathedral archive. In the Lady Chapel dedicated to her, which retains its late thirteenth century proportions and vaulting, the niches of a medieval reredos have been filled with small modern bronzes depicting some of the flowers which, in the Welsh language, have Mary's name.

The sanctuary has the remains of the tomb of a third figure honoured here since medieval times, the sixth century Welsh saint Teilo, still marked by a thirteenth century effigy. A powerful local dynasty, the Mathew family, was especially engaged in protecting Teilo's bones. Long after the Reformation they continued to preserve his skull near the remote and atmospheric well-shrine of Llandeilo Llwydiarth at the edge of the Preseli hills. There are three remarkable alabaster Mathew tombs. One of two from the early Tudor years has a sleeping beadsman at the knight's foot, like the Herbert tomb at Abergavenny. The older effigy is of Sir David Mathew. He was the Standard Bearer to Edward IV at the vicious decisive battle of Towton in 1461, a man whose size, strength and terrifying capacity with a longsword is still conveyed by the huge head and girth of his effigy.

Among other treasures are a tenth century standing cross which is the one remnant of the pre-Norman Celtic church, a 'Trinity corbel' near the south door with three faces but only four eyes, the deeply carved Norman doorways in both aisles (best seen from their outer sides), the elegant alabasters of Lady Audley and Bishop Marshall with a shield of Passion emblems, and the fine late Victorian effigies of Dean Vaughan and Bishop Olivant.

For much of its life an Anglo-French outpost in an alien Wales, wrecked by Glyndwr, left to fall down by its bishops who came to prefer to live in Mathern within reassuring sight of the east bank of the Severn, blown down by storms and bombs, here still stands Llandaff, its curious pair of towers reaching upward to the green on the high ground above where, so many centuries ago, bells used to ring in the Norman belfry, and crusades were once preached, 'the English standing on one side, and the Welsh on the other'.

Llanfair Kilgeddin, St Mary the Virgin

SO 357 087

St Mary's is set back in a large tree-shaded and grassy churchyard in a rural bend of the river. There is nothing in the approach to mark it out from so many others clustered along the banks of this fertile and sheltered stretch of the Usk – comfortable llans for less ascetic saints. The gravestones dotted round are surprisingly unweathered by the centuries, like Robert Ridley's table tomb of 1677, 'Foreknow that my redeemer liveth', or that for Polly Ann Agg of Pontypool, 'a child of much intellectual promise and…amiability of disposition – her death is not deeply regretted by her relatives but much so by neighbouring friends'. She was three. The church has a typically simple plan of wide nave leading on to slightly narrower chancel – no aisles or tower, with just a bellcote at the western end, and a few squareheaded windows in the walls.

But the interior is a great surprise. It is packed with huge pictorial murals cut deep into the plaster. They have vibrant lines and a sheer delight in nature, like a shout of joy at the created world, an echo of the old saints in their landscapes. There is an evocation of weather in all its freshness: ice hanging from branches and snow falling; summer's golden corn; seagulls wheeling in the wind; brilliant depictions of sky, the blustering cumulus clouds casting slanting rain over the familiar outlines of neighbouring hills, Skirrid and Sugarloaf, and Blorenge rising underneath a rainbow. The inscription beneath is 'O Ye Mountains and Hills Bless Ye the Lord Praise Him & Magnify Him For Ever'. This ancient prayer is the Benedicite, reborn here in the spirit of Pre-Raphaelite manifesto, that Art is Praise and Art is Truth to Nature.

But the cycle has the same dark undertow as so much Victorian art: this celebration of life is founded on a death. It is a widowed rector's memorial to his lost wife Rosamund, who died in 1885. In the most dislocated and thoughtful of the pictures, above the words 'I Heard a Voice from Heaven saying blessed are the dead which die in the Lord', a shrouded figure of mourning takes its place among a child with a butterfly and a spinning hoop, a mother, and workers out in the fields.

The artist was Heywood Sumner, a striking bearded presence on the London Arts and Crafts scene, who could turn his hand to textiles, paper, glass or furniture. Within months of placing his initials – and the date 1888 – under the panel depicting 'All Ye Beasts', he was a founding participant in the first exhibition of the Arts and Crafts Society, and five years later his designs were chosen for the walls of Victor Horta's Tassel House in Brussels, the first complete flowering of Art Nouveau. He pioneered the rediscovery of sgraffito, the technique by which individual layers of coloured plaster are applied to a wall then scraped back at differing depths to make the picture. He worked on other churches, such as All Saints on the edge of Hyde Park, spiritual home to the mysterious Irene in Alice Thomas Ellis's novel *The 27th Kingdom*. But Llanfair Kilgeddin's deeply felt and vivid panels may well be his

Blorenge, Skirrid and Sugarloaf on the wall at Llanfair Kilgeddin

masterpiece. They tapped in, too, to an old family connection with the place – his grandfather had lived in the parish when Bishop of Llandaff, and was remembered as the first for centuries to live within reach of his cathedral. Sumner's father also was a bishop, and his mother the founder of the Mothers' Union.

He came here through his friend John Dando Sedding who had restored the church a decade earlier – adding characteristic touches to the altar, roof and screen – and who had learned his architectural trade at the offices of G.E. Street, along with Philip Webb, Norman Shaw and William Morris. Sedding was in many ways another Morris: the same bounding enthusiasms for all the branches of the arts, the same commitment to making as well as managing, and the same gift, when contemplating nature, to be as awestruck as a child. He is remembered scatting across scaffoldings or hopping like a bird between his many drawings, to communicate some new idea. He spent his early career in Cornwall, immersing himself in the genius of its country churches – so similar in origin to those of Wales – and the ties he made then with local stonemasons stayed with him: he brought men from Liskeard to rework the failing walls of this Monmouthshire church. They also put a new head, to Sedding's design, on the old churchyard cross. In a curious pendant, Sedding may have passed on Sumner's image of the surfacing whale with seagulls spreeing in its wake to his partner Henry Wilson, who made a variation on it for his bronze cathedral doors on Morningside Heights in Manhattan.

At the entry to the chancel, a more conventional iconography begins: Jesus with gold wounds in his feet, apostles with their fishing nets, an east end Annunciation with an art nouveau true vine – but there is no doubting where the artist had caught fire. Instead, the chancel has the best of the old church fabric: bosses in the panelled roof, a dragon among them; fragments of medieval glass in the north east window, saints' heads, pinnacles, roses, a lily; a cross-slab tomb by the altar, and other stones delicately inscribed, like the one for Jane William dated 1701.

Llanthony – deep in Nant Honddu's cloister of mountains

Llanthony/Llanddewi Nant Honddu, Abbey

SO 288 278

In the Age of Saints, the age of great monasteries, and again in late Victorian Wales, the call of Llanthony renewed itself. Its gaunt ruins seem little to show for fifteen hundred years of spiritual responses to the grandeur and remoteness of the place.

The llan in Nant Honddu – the name which elided into 'Llanthony' – has associations with St David himself. The site of his original cell is now marked by a single-naved church, the east window of which is said to be precisely aligned with the sunrise on St David's Day. By the late eleventh century, the llan was just a ruin when William de Lacy came riding up the valley, and decided to renounce the world and stay. The result was the first Augustinian monastery in Wales. It lasted some decades until, during the collapse of Norman power in the reign of Stephen, Llanthony's Norman monks retreated to the safety of Gloucestershire, where they founded Llanthony Secunda. Fifty years later they returned, and began some serious building.

At this time the first recorded impressions of the place were written – as evocative as any since – by the incorrigible Gerald of Wales. His depictions of the deer on the high ridges, the deep valley "no broader than an arrowshot", and the monks enjoying their contemplative surroundings in their cloister of mountains, are an airy idyll he floats before us, only to puncture with a list of their early deaths and vices. The high and narrow landscape still dominates the atmosphere, but the human contribution is a curious assemblage of farmhouse, gatehouse, church and church ruin, and even, in the west range of the monastery buildings, a small and unexpected hotel and bar. The church's great west front, intended to impress and greet all new arrivals, now butts onto a small enclosed domestic garden, in which sometimes the washing is hung out.

Gothic was emerging out of Romanesque as Llanthony went up, making for a fine seven-bay nave of pointed arches, nostalgically mixed with some roundheaded windows in the towers. The transition dates the building precisely. There are substantial remains of a huge crossing tower, on which the steep diagonals of the lost nave roof are clearly marked. At the crossing and in the transepts, there is at last some decoration, and foliage on the bosses and corbels. But as elsewhere in Wales, the spirit of the building is simplicity, austerity, a reduction of the scope of Gothic to its functional essence – and in this it is united with the native Welsh aesthetic, a fusion which might claim to owe something to spiritual humility, something to a recognition of the inability of buildings to outcompete such settings, and something to a plain and simple shortage of money. Llanthony's gaunt stones raise thoughts of other absences. On a day with the cloud set in, Hilary Llewelyn Williams saw the heathen rain "falling in smoke-drift down the long nave like a shaken benediction", shambled around with camera in hand, shivered at the cold, went off to the pub.

Gothic emerging out of Romanesque: Llanthony c.1200

The domestication of the church seems to have started early: around 1350 the north transept became the monks' kitchen. By 1799, the abbey long left to ruin, there are descriptions of a private home, and the church's south west tower has become a shooting box for the hunting season. The estate was bought by the poet Walter Savage Landor, who found in the solitude "the audience chamber of God". His irascible, pedagogic, sentimental writing, studded with allegories, showy displays of the ancient classics and penetrating moments of wisdom make him seem like no-one so much as Gerald of Wales, back again in Romantic guise, after six hundred years. His best legacy may be the hundreds of fine trees he planted here in damp seclusion, before he sold up and made for Italy.

Then in the late nineteenth century, a singular priest called Father Ignatius launched the building of Llanthony Tertia, a few miles north at Capel-y-ffin. As a monastery it lasted a couple of decades or so. It was intended as a replica of the original, and in a curious way has become so – its own hotch-potch of lodgings and ruins, and a church complex which became a house.

In the 1920s the residents were an unlikely group of artists escaping the world of industrial capital, including the half-Welsh poet-artist David Jones, and the sculptor and typographer Eric Gill, to whose daughter Petra Jones was engaged. Both men were the sons of evangelicals, attracted to the aura and tradition of Catholicism, Gill the idealist, angular and volatile in the Llanthony pattern. Jones found his style here, painting the hills and streams in long and sensitive lines, letting the Black Mountains seep into his memories of the Western Front in first drafts of his poem *In Parenthesis*, some dozen years before he unleashed to the world his Modernist masterpiece, *The Anathemata*. His fading Crucifixion mural is still in what used to be the monks' refectory, before its first redeployment as Gill's studio. Gill's sculptures, exported down the old rough road in a pony cart, arrived at the valley mouth already chipped and troubled. They are a rare spiritual spur in the shiny era of Art Deco. The isolation, and the rain, eventually drove them out too, leaving Capel-y-ffin to the pony trekkers, and its own two small religious houses on either side of the little river – the early chapel to the east and the church on the west in a tight ring of yews, its white interior filled with bench pews and an ancient font.

Llantwit Major/Llanilltud Fawr, St Illtud

SS 966 687

The Vale of Glamorgan is rich with churches in fine settings. Sometimes, as at first sight of Llanmihangel or St Lythan's, they can feel as far away as Normandy. A deeper Celtic twilight seems to be at work down in St Donat's in the hollow underneath the fortress rock, or at crumbling Llancarfan, or Llangan churchyard propping up an ancient Crucifixion stone, a weatherbeaten Pietà.

But the mother of them all is Llanilltud. Its medieval survivals are exceptional, both from the High Middle Ages and the earlier centuries when this great monastic centre seems also to have functioned as a royal mausoleum for the kings of Glywysing, whose heartland fortress was at nearby Dinas Powys. Their court was culturally connected to the Mediterranean south in direct succession to the days of Roman empire: this area of south east Wales, astonishingly, was the only place in the entire empire not to be seized by external invasion, making it a crucial conduit to carry forward to the new and pagan surroundings of north west Europe the scholarly and classical tradition of Roman Christianity. Few churches in Britain can make greater claims. In the late fifth century Illtud taught here some of the new leaders in the shared culture that spread across Wales and the West country, Brittany and Ireland – Samson, Gildas and Paul Aurelian – and unsubstantiated claims have been made for David and the founders of Irish monasticism. From this ground soil the Christian religion was spread from the Celtic heartland into Scotland, northern

Fourteenth century royalty: crowned Virgin and child

266

Mary Magdalene and the alabaster box of precious ointment: one of the oldest surviving murals in Wales

England and many parts of northern Europe. There are fifteen churches dedicated to Illtud in Wales — one as far north as Meirionydd — and seven in Brittany, like the resonant parish of Lanildut, Aber-ildut, Leon. He may also be the mysterious St Aldate, to whom churches are dedicated in Oxford and Gloucester.

The best place to make sense of the layout of the surviving church building is from the south side of the churchyard, by the small ruin that was once the chantry priest's house: it survived until 1940 when a bomb, astray from a raid on Cardiff or Swansea, made a direct hit. The far left range of the church — a ruin too — was a

Ninth century royalty: the Houelt Cross

chantry chapel, a fifteenth century extension devoted to prayers for the Raglan family dead. To the far right, the thirteenth century east range with the tower was the part reserved for the men of the monastery. In the middle is a high stone porch, also thirteenth century, and behind it the fifteenth century 'west church', which still retains its first oak-raftered roof with bosses carrying the arms of its patrons. This functioned as the parish church, and marks the exact site of St Illtud's original 'quadrangular church of stone' to which, according to a bracing account of his life, he would go every night at midnight, after prayer in a cold bath.

Three Celtic monuments in the west church, all from the century around 900, convey Llanilltud's status in the southern Welsh kingdom of Glywysing. Large standing stone crosses with a head like a wheel were a distinctive regional style, combining sophisticated geometric patterning with lettering so childlike they suggest that the stonemasons' usual skill could not counter their illiteracy. The Houelt cross inscribed 'pro anima Res' (for the soul of Rhys) was raised by King Hywel ap Rhys of Glywysing for his father. It is carved out of one piece of stone which tapers as it rises in beautiful fretwork before broadening out into a wheel in which a fretwork cross is set in a ropework frame. The later and taller St Illtud or

Samson Cross has more obsessive ropework and a hit and miss deployment of the patterns on the sides. It is damaged and has lost its wheel top, which was probably a narrower, separate piece of stone on the model of the crosses at Nevern and Carew. The third, known as the Pillar of Abbot Samson 'Samsoni Abati', was raised for his own soul and those of "Iuthahelo Rex et Artmali et Tecan", the first perhaps Ithel, a king of Gwent who died in 846.

Near these stones is a massive tomb figure of a lady in Elizabethan dress, a small child at her shoulder, and a stunningly designed and executed early twelfth century grave slab of incised swirls, circles and diamonds leading up to a tonsured head in a niche – the earliest surviving commemorative image of a face on a Welsh tomb, although the Latin inscription, intriguingly, is for a woman.

A Jesse tree which forms a small wall niche in the east church is even finer, an intricate survival of the early 1200s. In this part of the church there are a number of wall paintings: a remarkable thirteenth century Mary Magdalen, statuesque with one hand raised in blessing, the other carrying her jar of precious ointment; a fifteenth century St Christopher made with some knowledge of perspective; and over the chancel arch a painted chequerboard background for the lost Crucifixion scene, with symbols of the Passion at the top. At the far east end the huge stone screen with twenty two niches dates from 1430, all its saints long lost except for a tender Virgin and Child now kept by a window in the south aisle, and which probably predates it. In the Lady Chapel is a rare pre-Reformation stone altar.

Margam, St Mary

SS 802 863

Margam is an unexpected assembly: an ancient Celtic site full of pre-Conquest relics; an early Cistercian abbey church still roofed and in use; and the finest gathering of post-medieval sculpture in Wales. Where Celtic remains are concentrated, the landscape is always telling. Margam is the single place on the whole south coast where the high mountains come closest to the sea, sweeping down over a thousand feet in less than two miles to the sand dunes and the breaking waves. There is a glut of earthworks up on the commanding heights. The spirit of place may still be breathing beneath the grey haze of the steelworks and the roar of the M4.

This narrow lowland, always a through route, is not the customary sheltered valley of Cistercian choice. Something else put them here in 1147. The Normans had seized power on Gower and in the Vale, and Henry I's son Robert built castles at Kenfig and Neath to guard the narrow route between them. But the Welsh controlled the mountains above it, and when Norman power was beaten back in the west and civil war raged in England, Robert must have pondered how best to

Twelfth century Cistercian – with accumulations

safeguard this most vulnerable point. In a synthesis of spiritual and military acumen, he gave it up to God. By doing so he brought in to this corner of Wales directly from St Bernard's Clairvaux the leading cultural movement of his time, a new force of faith, and some of the best land managers of the Middle Ages.

A good deal of the twelfth century nave remains: the west front's late Romanesque doorway and three windows above (now filled with Morris glass), and the straight-from-Clairvaux austerity of the arcade columns. But the length of the surviving church is well under half of the original, and the site of the old altar is marked in the grass well to the east. Among the ruins around it are those of an elegant dodecagon chapter house, its fragile vaults as eloquent of lost strength as the great floored branches of the tree which spreads across the cloister garden. It spins nine tall windows round a central clustered column, and was entered from a clever three-way vestibule. It dates from 1200: the age of austerity was over.

In the south aisle of the church are the marble and alabaster tombs of the Mansels, a family who came with the Conqueror and set up shortly afterwards in Gower. Four hundred years on, Sir Rice Mansel got the job of closing down the monastery at Margam. He bought it for himself, rearranging many of the stones into a family home even grander than the one he left behind at Oxwich. His tomb begins a series in the family line which culminates in contrasting Jacobean monuments: long-bearded Sir Thomas lies between two duplicate wives while Sir Lewis and his wife are sober, distinctive and exceptional, in stonework worthy of any grand Renaissance church in Lombardy. It is attributed to Maximilian Colt, the tomb-sculptor of Elizabeth I herself.

The Mansels went on to intermarry with the Talbots, owners of the adjacent Port and pioneers of photography who made grainy early images on Margam estate. The north aisle tomb portrait of Theodore Mansel Talbot, a face straight out of Pontormo, is a masterpiece of Henry Armstead, a kindred pioneer of nineteenth century naturalism, and the chief sculptor of the Albert Memorial. His rendering of the commanding, lived-in face of Bishop Olivant can be seen across the Vale at Llandaff. In catching in Talbot all the inner strength of a gentle man, Armstead achieved as moving an expression of faith as Victorian Wales was to possess.

The rest of Margam's heritage of sculpture is assembled in the small former schoolhouse north of the churchyard. Among its treasures are two of the best surviving wheel-crosses from the ninth or tenth centuries. The Conbelin cross appears to mark a phase of transition in Celtic art, when the representation of Christ was to move from that of a blank cross within a haloing circle to the familiar later image of the crucified figure with Mary and St John looking on. Here Mary and John have taken up their places, but the cross they gaze at is still traditionally blank. The inscription in the right hand panels of this cross appears to be to a man named Conbelin (the original, perhaps, of Shakespeare's Cymbeline), and another inscription on the outer rim edge above it reads 'Sodna crucem X fecit' – 'the cross of

Christ made by Sodna'. There is a hunting scene on the back. The other cross is six feet high with interlacing patterns and a panel at the base inscribed 'this cross of Christ, Enniaun made for the soul of Guorgoret'. Even older stones include a mid sixth century Maltese cross to 'Bodvoc, son of Catotigirnus, great grandson of Eternalis Vedomavus', found at Twmpath Diwlith on the mountain, and one 'set up in the reign of the Emperor Caesar Flavius Valerius Maximinus, the Unconquerable, Augustus'. The headless effigy of an armoured knight dates from the time of the abbey: at the tip of his elongated shield is Margam's only dragon, sinking in its teeth.

The Conbelin Cross, a first millennium Celtic pietà

Newport/Casnewydd, St Woolo/Gwynllyw

ST 308 876

Newport's cathedral is one of the best of Wales's urban churches, but there was no city anywhere near when St Woolo's was founded on a lonely hill one and a half millennia ago. Only in the nineteenth century did Newport make it up the slopes to surround it, planting the fine chapel at Victoria Place along the way. Its hill spur site with the land falling steeply away on three sides is reminiscent of Llanbister while its closeness to the coast makes it one more link in the maritime chain of early Christian South Wales, sharing some similarities of groundplan with Llanilltud Fawr.

The exterior view is of a sequence of building behind a solid tower, mostly something early Tudor or restored, among its clues a damaged badge of the royal rose, a headless statue of King Henry's uncle Jasper, and Perpendicular windows which run along the side aisle walls. But within this outer frame a classic twelfth century church fits, in the church's own phrase, like a Norman jewel within a Tudor casket. It has five bays of rounded columns, arches and high windows in a Romanesque design surprising for its lightness.

The way in leads through the great tower arch into an atmospheric corridor-like chapel sloping gradually downwards, lined with battered recumbent figures on their tombs. There is a heavily restored font which nevertheless follows closely the original twelfth century design still surviving on a section of the bowl. It has emblems of the cross and a wide-eyed creature swallowing ribbons which re-emerge through its ears.

At the far end of the chapel is the most remarkable interior doorway in the country. Medieval Newport was just a few miles downriver from Roman Caerleon, the Empire's fortress outpost known as Isca. The suggestion that the doorway's column shafts must have come from some tumbling Caerleon ruin has always been hard to resist. But the exuberant Corinthian capitals on top of them, and the curious creatures that gape out from their leaves, belong to no one but the medieval masons who made this church, and surrounded these columns with their signature zigzag. They must have been among the first displays in Wales of the new French art which came in with the Normans. The image of a man with upraised arms is matched in Burgundy at St-Benigne de Dijon, a Carolingian, Holy Roman church. The strange, floating, vertical bird would not be out of place in a painting by Paul Klee or Joan Miro. From here, the view takes in the splendid Norman nave and its wood-framed waggon roof.

Experts suggest dates of the 1140s for the main interior, a little earlier for the font, and sometime near 1100 for the capitals. In the 1140s, St Woolo's Church was in the hands of Gloucester Abbey, and Robert of Gloucester was Lord of Glamorgan and Gwynllwg. What made them build something important here, at a time of civil war, on the eastern estuary border of Robert's Welsh estates?

If the *Brut y Tywysogion* is to be believed, Robert of Gloucester was of the first generation of the mixing of the Welsh and Norman races – the illegitimate son of Henry I and Nest ferch Rhys (the 'Helen of Wales' from whose subsequent marriage all the Fitzgeralds of Ireland are descended – all the way to John Fitzgerald Kennedy). His grandfathers were William the Conqueror and Rhys ap Tewdwr, ruler of Deheubarth. His literary and artistic patronage was remarked upon in an age of illiterate warrior barons and in 1136 he was the dedicatee of Geoffrey of Monmouth's fantastical and hugely influential *History of the Kings of Britain*, a book which proclaimed the ancient Roman heritage of the Welsh royal lines and people against their parvenu and lately pagan neighbours. It restated the prophecies of Merlin that the Welsh would one day win their island back, and fired the Welsh tales of Arthur into the English and the French imaginations.

Robert's mixed blood must have given him a different, more multi-layered view of the Rome-evoking style of Norman church-planting. If it was the conquered who had the true Roman lineage, which side, in Wales, did such buildings most honour? The question had irritant power enough to make some Norman contemporaries attack the Roman wonders of Caerleon, as images of Welsh tradition which had to be smashed down. Then in 1141 Robert and his sister Matilda, who was, with striking significance, the widowed Empress of the Holy Roman Empire, seized and deposed King Stephen and took power in England. It was a high water mark to do full justice to St Woolo's Romanesque arcades, and their authentically Roman threshold.

These passionately held ideas of Welsh identity, nurtured through the subsequent centuries, were the ones which drove forward the Welsh armies of the Tudors in 1485, and it seems entirely fitting that their victorious wrapping of the English crown in the dragon of Cadwaladr was echoed here at Newport in the wrapping of the Norman church in Tudor walls.

In 1949 the building was raised to cathedral status and a modern chancel built to let the light flood in. The high reredos designed by John Piper and Patrick Reyntiens belongs to the 1960s. Rowan Williams, bishop here in the 1990s, left St Woolo's to become the first Welsh Archbishop of Canterbury in one and a half thousand years – another strand, perhaps, in Merlin's long design.

The new French art arrives in Wales: carvings at the threshold of Newport nave, c.1100

Penallt, Old Church (dedication unknown)

SO 523 106

The valley of the Wye is steep-banked and wooded in the miles above Tintern. The border wanders eastward from the river up beyond Lord's Grove, and to the west the road winds past Whitebrook's old mills and shaded ponds into a maze of lanes that reach the edge of the escarpment at the magnificently-sited church of Penallt. "The God who made this country," wrote a visiting George Bernard Shaw to Ellen Terry, "was an artist".

The land falls away steeply through the churchyard to the river six hundred feet below, and everything speaks of an ancient site – the water, the opening out of the view, a high site on a lee, a small well just above the church and a great spreading yew below. The buildings tumble down the hill towards it, tower, nave and chancel in a terraced line of gables like crests on the waves of landscape in which they are so totally immersed. Travellers who came to call here, diverting from the old road to Trelleck or climbing the hill from their boats or the old ferry crossing, included Compostella pilgrims on their way to the sea-route down the Severn. Their uphill road is marked by a round socket stone incised with crosses, some distance south of the church under a chestnut tree.

The old churchyard has a lychgate with a pitched roof, and the massive stepped base of a lost preaching cross near the pathway of pollarded limes. The church door is dated 1539, giving a first clue to the building's history – all the south windows with their squareheaded frames belong to near that time, when the whole south aisle must have been added, opening out the old nave wall with arches and columns. A new slanting passage was hacked through from the aisle to the chancel – in effect both a squint and a walk-through to open up access between different altars in the church. The feature is unique in the region and associated more with the southwest, in churches such as Castlemartin. The chancel was given a new unusually carved waggon roof. Such openhandedness at such a time gives this country church a place among the last expansive gestures of the medieval parishes, the harvest perhaps of a last trawl of the revenues of passing pilgrimage, and the end of a long road, a position which Penallt in its wooded retreats seems still to occupy another five hundred years on.

The nave, out of line with the chancel, approaches it through a great arch which was once the backdrop for the rood loft. The lower loft steps remain, and a small window above which would have lit the lost figures at the Crucifixion. Below is a Jacobean pulpit, carved and ornamented. There is a Queen Anne royal arms panel of 1709 on the west wall, and bosses are still being enterprisingly added to the barrelled ceiling. The north wall has been standing nearly eight hundred years, probably the first stone version of the church – which dates it to the time and power of William Marshal, a country companion to his sophisticated Haverfordwest – but its deep and filtering windows were not cut until the 1880s.

In the chancel, the altar rail is dated 1753. Beyond it, one old stone is the tombslab of 'Dorety', whose husband is described mysteriously as the 'vance'. Another, now covered up, says 'I am not ded but sliping here', an inscription which seems to suit the tilt of the floor. The altar was made in the First World War by a Belgian refugee who had worked as a carver at the cathedral of Mechelen. The ancient trunk of oak that used to be the parish chest is even older than the building.

Skenfrith/Ynysgynwraidd, St Bridget

SO 455 203

The three castles of Skenfrith, Grosmont and White Castle, which soon became one lordship, have their origins in the earliest Norman excursions into Wales. White Castle, the largest and most commanding, intrudes more deeply into Monmouthshire, while Skenfrith and Grosmont sit just across the border, on the west bank of the Monnow. What survives of them now can be dated mainly to the time of Hubert de Burgh, King John's powerful Chief Justiciar in the first years of the thirteenth century. In the end, de Burgh was to lose his status and his castles, leaving his huge unfinished effigy still beached in a dusty recess off Grosmont's cavernous nave. But in his pomp he toughened the castles, and transformed the churches alongside them.

At White Castle, the church is quite apart, an old Welsh llan in its own ancient – probably bronze age – fortification. At Grosmont the grand and spired edifice, much restored more than a century ago, is set slightly down the hill so as not to obstruct the sweeping views from the castle walls – a sign of how, more than a hundred years on from the seizure of this part of the country, its builders still thought and planned as an occupying power. The final battle here would not be for another two hundred years, when Monmouth-born Prince Hal put in some early practice for Agincourt, destroying an army led by Owain Glyndwr's son Gruffydd.

But at Skenfrith, the old castle and church sit right alongside each other, in a curve of the river crossing they both helped to defend. The church tower walls are five feet thick and topped by a timbered dovecote with the useful function of attracting fresh food to shelterers within. Long shafts of sunlight cast through the fine large windows into the arcades and wide aisles of the interior, spreading over the floor of heavy flagstones. Among the old vaultstones one near the door, marked with a cross, has lines made cryptic by damage, invoking 'Gren Fase Death'. St Bridget's feels ancient. Its fabric, even the ribs of the windows, has survived the many centuries largely untouched.

In the north aisle is the family pew and tomb of John Morgan, the last Governor of the Three Castles in the 1550s. He and his wife Ann, a Cecil, have their images incised on the roof of the tomb, with their four sons and four daughters on each side, the sons shown kneeling dutifully bareheaded yet keen to display their fashionable hats beside them. The sixteenth century presence of these Morgans and Cecils is another marker, as at other Anglo-Norman churches in the region, of the rise of Welsh families with the coming of the Tudors, a rise foreshadowed and to some extent prepared for by that of the Herberts. The trace of the Herberts at Skenfrith, kept here behind a curtain, is a rare survival of early Tudor silk and velvet church dress, probably a royal gift to them at Raglan. It depicts the Virgin and Child, and the Virgin ascending to heaven with angels, surrounded by saints under canopies and heraldic emblems of fleurs de lys, thistles and double-headed eagles. St Andrew holds his diagonal cross. The aisle has two tall Ten Commandments boards, careful modern copies of sixteenth century originals.

The chancel retains its rare stone altar table from 1207, a semi-circular piscina, Jacobean altar rails, fragments of medieval glass in the east window, and a reading desk which has recycled something of the church's long lost rood screen. Only the mortises to hold it remain in the plain carving of the chancel arch, which has just the slightest band of ornament on the south side. From here there is a fine view back down the nave to the open tower arch, the old timber roofs and door, and from the door another, through the south porch with stone benches and deep unglazed windows, to the yew tree and the old houses spreading down the village street.

Walls five feet thick, and topped by a timbered dovecote

Green to the very door: Tintern pastoral

Tintern Abbey / Abaty Tyndyrn

SO 535 000

The Cistercians chose the locations for their churches with something of the same eye as the early Welsh saints. They shared the passion for places of natural beauty, but focused more intently on the low-lying courses of fast flowing rivers, their winding valleys and their mouths into the sea. Tintern was the first of their chosen locations in Wales and only their second in all of Britain, after Waverley. They found a place a few miles upstream from the river mouth, under the protection of Chepstow castle whose lord Walter de Clare provided the land in 1131. The valley, typically steep-sided down to the water's edge, opens out on a gentler west bank at a broad bend in the river, a natural site for such an abbey. Beyond it on both sides the slopes are thickly wooded and sheltering.

These high ridges allowed for changes in the usual disposition of buildings, in which an abbey church was placed on the north side to shelter all the communal quarters from the coldest winds. Here the church could be built back from the river, on the slightly higher, safer ground which was south of much of the complex. The gain would be for better drainage, but there would also be a loss of sun-warmth and light from the cloisters for a large part of the day. Perhaps this was what most influenced the signature feature of the church: the sheer scale of its windows, which surge up to their airy heights almost out of the ground. On the simplest Cistercian plan, cruciform and square-ended, the four outer faces of the church form great cliffs of glass (now lost) held in reddish purple sandstone quarried two miles north. They respond to the local setting yet their spirit of heaven-pointed height is so French that a still-close allegiance to Citeaux and the cross-channel culture is evident even in this rebuilding of the later thirteenth century, 150 years after the founding monks came from L'Aumone.

One of the grandest churches ever built in Wales, it stretches 228 feet along an aisled, once stone-vaulted nave and through the crossing arches to the chancel. Its cruciform austerity was energised by vigorous tracery balancing trinities of circles on steeply intersecting arches, lines of closely packed and clustering columns intensifying in the chancel, and some carved leaf decoration still evident at the foot of vault ribs and in the six forlorn roof bosses now lying on the grass. Despite its ruined state for close on five hundred years, Tintern's impressive spaces still frame the wooded hills of Wales and England, opposed across the border river of the Wye.

Beside the grandeur of the church are some pleasingly domestic ranges for the monks and their lay brothers. The layout has a logic and design-for-living aptness that brings home the human touch of its community. To understand this best it is worth seeking out the small porch just to the side of the great west front. The medieval visitor would pay his respects to an image of Mary, once the occupant of the pointed oval niche on the west front of the church, and enter the small parlour intended for all social exchange with the community. Lay brothers would pass through on their way from their quarters, to the left, to their part of the church (the nave), on the right. They occupied the middle layer of the abbey complex, separating the guest houses, now in ruins across the modern road, from the inner layer belonging to the monks.

Beyond the parlour lay the cloister, the heart of the monks' domain, with kitchen, pantry, dining room, warming house and day room grouped together on the left, the kitchen carefully placed to serve the lay brothers' rooms on one side, and the monks on the other. Its serving hatch through to the monks' dining room remains. Next door the warming house retains part of its fireplace, sensibly central and open arched to gather around for warmth. The prior, equally sensible, had his lodgings above it. In the daytimes the prior could take his seat on the south side of the cloister, in the once-canopied recess from which he could survey his monks at study, read at his lectern, or contemplate his garden. The books were originally kept in the two roundheaded recesses on the far side of the cloister, and later in a purpose-built library alongside. Its moulded door shows the pride felt in possession – almost as grand as the nearby rather oriental processional entry to the church, which dates from the fourteenth century. Beyond the library is a still-vaulted vestry, which until quite recently housed a twelfth century effigy of a knight. Next door in the footings of the rectangular chapter house, some of its red-orange floor tiles remain. The monks slept in a vast room above, of which nothing remains but the line of its roof on the outer wall of the church. From here, they would file silently down the steep circuit of the night stair, to enter the church for first prayers.

A passageway at the far left led through to a second cloister, intended for those in the infirmary beyond, which was one of the largest buildings in the monastery. The stones which remain show a central common ward, with individual private rooms off to the side, some with their own fireplaces. A diagonal covered short cut was made to connect the door of the infirmary to the church. Set back a little, between this cloister and the river, the abbots of later less ascetic days had their private landing stage, hall and chambers, where the great church could not block them out from the warmth of the sun.

All of this lay in a wider walled estate, with gateways at the river edge (an arch survives by the inn), and on the hillside (the old gatehouse chapel is now a private house). Some of the line of the old walls can still be traced, on both sides of the road. The valley road, built within the last two centuries, changed everything in the prospect of Tintern. Romantics like Wordsworth had come to it by river, or by diverting through the deep woodland from the old hill road, looking down on its secluded ruins. Samuel Palmer, coming to sketch in 1835, found it in deep twilight, "rising from a wilderness of orchards". He would give all the Welsh mountains for it, he wrote, grand as they are. To recapture something of this now, best to take the climbing path on the far bank, early or late in the day, towards the Devil's Pulpit, where the Wye is still sylvan, and the inland murmur soft.

Usk/Brynbuga, St Mary

SO 379 008

St Mary's, like so many of the grander churches of the south east, owes its origins to conquest. It began life as a slim, spare, cross-shaped Benedictine nunnery of the 1170s, a thanksgiving by the Anglo-Norman Clare family for the recovery of Usk, which had been lost to them for some forty years during a time of Welsh resurgence. A nunnery was a rarity for Wales: there were never in any generation more than a few dozen nuns in the country – although the Lord Rhys founded a Cistercian counterpart in the same years at Llanllyr, so there was something in the air at the time. Usk provides us with the best remaining glimpse of this small sideline in Welsh history: its gabled gatehouse still stands by the entrance to the churchyard; the edges of its lost east end form scarlines on the outside of the tower, and the body of its nave still leads forward to the pure interior of the crossing.

The founder was Richard de Clare, known as Strongbow, son of Henry I's last mistress, whose deal with Dermont King of Leinster brought him storming into Waterford and Dublin with a millennium of consequences. He was, said his contemporary Geraldus, a tall man with red hair and freckles and a weak voice, who stood in battle "as firm as an immoveable standard". He went on to hold hostage the great Irish princes, to govern Leinster through his royal Irish wife, and, it was said, to kill his own son for cowardice. He was just the kind of man to found a nunnery.

Sir William Herbert, constable of Usk and lord of Raglan, the castle home where he brought up the future Henry VII as his ward, was something of a late medieval successor to Strongbow, but proudly Welsh in blood and culture. By the end of the 1460s he controlled most of the country, and he enriched St Mary's with two elegant late Gothic porches. His badge is on the parapet of the north porch, which has a finely carved and moulded entrance arch and a two-bay interior with decorative vaulting and bursts of stone foliage. The west porch is very similar: small variations include a parapet of quatrefoils in circles, and a stoup, and it is tellingly built not on the nuns' nave, but on the single (north) aisle which was the townspeople's domain, setting the seal on a recent substantial widening which showed the economic shift towards a new social – and racial – class, and serving for Herbert as both an affirmation of his power and a demagogic gesture. The shift was complete when in the 1540s, the town took the whole building over.

The resulting integration of nave and aisle, and the atrophying of the east end through disuse, changed the nature of the whole interior space – the building metamorphosing to match its changing congregation from the old Norman cross plan to the much more Welsh almost-square, and its pews, stretched out in long dark lines, suggest something of the plainness of a chapel. Yet the furnishings are rich in history and detail: late medieval traceried screens extending right across the church; a font that dates from the foundation; the draped urns, weeping palms and fallen columns of Georgian funerary wall tablets; an eccentric verse tribute to the soldier Walter Jones; a fine large 1862 organ intended for Llandaff; and pulpit and altar rails from the eighteenth century – a period illuminated by the painted board in the porch which shows the seating plan for 1726. On the back of the screen is a small inscribed brass, the oldest in Welsh to survive. It marks the death in 1430 of Adam of Usk, the idiosyncratic chronicler of the last days of the aesthete court of Richard II, and of the rising in the subsequent disorder of Owain Glyndwr, with whom Adam was at one time a fugitive, and to whose cause the fighting at Usk was to be so fatal.

Late Gothic elegance at Usk

Notes for a Glossary

A brief guide to elements of a church

Llan: A circular, holy enclosure, typically the base and subsequently the burial ground for a holy man or woman, and his or her adherents and followers in the faith. Llan place names frequently identify the name of this founder (such as Idloes at Llanidloes) but may alternatively honour an internationally recognised saint such as Mary or Michael, or describe features in the immediate landscape. Llan has no equivalent word in English and so is often translated for convenience as 'church', because a llan always (or originally) contains a church. The church building, however, has its own separate word – **eglwys** – to identify it, a distinction brought out clearly in a place name such as Lanteglos-by-Fowey (in Cornwall). Lanteglos is the Cornish variant of Llanteglwys – or more fully Llan-nant-eglwys – a church building in a llan in a dip.

The llan is the distinctive signature of a people who lived – and live – across Wales, Cornwall and Brittany, and who marked their presence and their beliefs into the landscape in this way around fifteen hundred years ago. The clustering of so many Llan- or Lan- place names in their three territories reveals in some sense the north, mid- and south of a country, even though, through the force of history, each part became differently oriented and some of their descendants now describe themselves as Welsh, some English, and some French. One day, perhaps, someone will write the book which shows how their common cultural outlook and heritage repeatedly asserted itself – not least in religious choices – through all the later centuries.

Before the arrival in Great Britain of the English and the Scots (as well as Danes, Norwegians and others), this people was also spread across what are now England and Scotland, and very many were absorbed into the subsequent populations. This means that the llan is a part of the heritage of the modern English and Scots as well as the Welsh. That there were some llans in these places too is certain: trying to recognise their sites and traces is one of the more intriguing aspects of visiting churches there. In a few places the memory of the original llan place name, predating its English renaming, survives. There is also an Irish share in this heritage. Although the Irish were recognised at the time as a different people, belonging to a different Celtic language group from Welsh/Cornish/Breton, the interplay of people and culture across the Irish Sea at the time when the llans were being established was substantial, and numerous llans appear to be foundations of Irish saints.

Tower: Usually at the west end of the church, offering a range of possible functions as lookout, refuge, landmark and bell chamber. Presents something of a contradiction to the old native Welsh instinct for low-lying and low profile church buildings, and was only built in Wales in significant numbers following the arrival, and under the influence, of the Normans. Most Welsh churches today still remain without them. While there are ancient towers built under Welsh rule at places such as Penmon and Llaneilian, the history of St David's is more illustrative of how long they took to make real headway, the tower there being slightly raised in each succeeding century, and only reached high above the nave at the very end of the Middle Ages. The Tudor era (1485-1603) was the west tower's golden age, and Wrexham steeple its masterpiece.

An alternative to the west tower is the central tower, which belongs almost entirely to cathedrals, abbeys and other Anglo-French-influenced churches – and to Victorian revivals of such designs. It is associated mainly with churches planned in the shape of a cross, the north- and south-facing arms of which are known as **transepts**, and the space beneath the tower the **crossing**. Spires on towers are even more exotic: there are very few and almost all were built in Victorian times by architects under the influence of an idealised vision of an English Gothic church.

Chancel: The east end of a church and originally the domain only of the clergy. It can be divided into two main parts: sanctuary (always present) and choir (present usually in larger churches). The sanctuary has a number of distinctive features, being above all the place of the altar, a stone or wooden table which is usually against the east wall and backed by panelling or a screen often richly carved or decorated, known as the **reredos**. There may be a cupboard on the north wall, called an **aumbry**, to hold the vessels used in communion, and on the south wall a recess in the stone with a hole for drainage, in which these vessels were washed: this is the **piscina**. Some chancels also have priests' seats set into the south wall: these are called the **sedilia**, and sometimes have elaborately carved canopies.

In the grander medieval churches these canopies can be outdone by those over the seats – or stalls - in the choir, which also have a unique feature owing its origin to the days when they were occupied by monks, required to sing for long hours through day and night, and standing up, with the seats lifted back. The underside of these seats provides a small ledge to provide some mild support for their tired bodies to lean against, and was thus known as a **misericord**, an abbreviation of the Latin word for mercy. The supporting woodwork for these ledges often attracted some of the most ribald, mischievous and original carving in the church interior. An important stall, or a row of stalls, may have high carved end-boards known as **poppyheads**. As well as being particularly associated with medieval monastic churches, choirs returned to favour with the revival in High Church Anglicanism in the 1830s and 1840s, and most Victorian churches make provision for them in their design. The chancel may also have a more ornate roof or ceiling than the rest of the church – sometimes they bear painted images or saints and are known as a **canopy of honour**.

Chancels appear to have been an addition to many Welsh churches, perhaps soon after 1200, in response to new winds blowing from Rome. In the churches around Snowdonia there is evidence that they disrupted the traditional dimensions of a double-square interior, to which they were tacked on the end as an extension. The Welsh instinct has been to underplay in the architecture the distinction between chancel and nave, tending to integrate them in one continuous rectangular space. By contrast the Anglo-French churches in Wales gave them greater separateness and higher status by making them narrower than the nave, and placing a grand arch at the entrance. However the Welsh were as enthusiastic as the Anglo-French in creating ambitious and celebratory wooden **rood screens** to front them. The screen supported a loft which was used by singers and other musicians, and which held the **rood** or cross on which was an image of the crucified Christ. Images of Mary and John stood at the foot of the cross. Where there was a wall behind these, it was often painted with a scene of the Last Judgement, sometimes known as the **Doom**. These screens and images were almost all destroyed with the coming of Protestantism.

Nave: The main body of the church, to the west of the chancel: the place for the congregation to sit or stand during worship, and for the priest to preach to them from the pulpit. Some surviving seventeenth and eighteenth century pulpits are **triple-deckers** which have below the pulpit itself a reading desk and a clerk's desk. They may also have a wooden canopy above, intended to redirect the sound of the preacher's words back down towards the congregation instead of rising into the rafters. This canopy is known as a **sounding board** or **tester**.

Some of the more grandly-built churches have arcades of columns and arches along the north and south sides of the nave, which support windowed higher walls in a space known as the **clerestory**. Beyond the arcades on either side are the **aisles**. A typically Welsh variant of this design is to have a **double-nave** – two naves separated by an arcade and without a clerestory, which feel more equal, inclusive and less segregated than aisles: more like one grand room. At Llangwnnadl there is a **triple-nave**, and numerous churches in Cornwall achieve a similar effect to this by having two aisles as wide as the nave and running almost the full length of the church. Many naves were also used as schoolrooms.

Porch: Frames and protects from the weather the entrance to the church, which is usually in the south wall of the nave. They multiplied in the fifteenth century, from which there are many fine examples both in wood and stone: there may have been very few before then. They played a religious role in providing on their east wall a **stoup** containing holy water, and also in sometimes having carved images with Biblical themes on the rafters or on the stone known as the **tympanum**, which stands above the doorway but within its arch. They also quickly acquired a secular role as public meeting rooms for business and conversation, and may be badged with the arms of their provider, as at Usk.

The French connection: the adulterous Siwan of history and theatre

A Brief Welsh Vocabulary

Mutations: One of the distinctive characteristics of the Welsh language is that certain first letters of words can change depending on the context in which the word is used. The map of Wales is studded with examples of mutations, because they can apply to the name of a saint when it follows after llan in a place name. So, for example, llans devoted to Padarn are Llanbadarn, those to Mary (Mair in Welsh) are Llanfair, and those to Michael (Mihangel) are Llanfihangel.

allt – hillside (often, or originally, wooded)

abaty – abbey

aber – rivermouth

afon – river

annibynnwr – Independent

bach – little

bedd – grave

bedyddiwr – Baptist

bryn – hill

cae – field

caer – castle

capel – chapel

carn – mountain, cairn

clas – a Welsh medieval mother church, a community of monks and their families

coed   wood

cromlech – a prehistoric tomb or *dolmen*, made of standing stones supporting a horizontal or capstone, and covered with earth. The earth may over the centuries have been washed away, leaving only the stones.

crynwr – quaker

cwm – mountain valley

cymanfa ganu – singing festival

cynefin – local patch, heartland

cynghanedd – a form of verbal dexterity which combines internal rhymes with alliteration in a number of strict sequences, and which can be used to enrich the lines of a cywydd.

cywydd (plural *cywyddau*) – a form of poem or song made up of couplets following certain metrical rules: its most famous and accomplished exponent is probably the fourteenth century poet Dafydd ap Gwilym

du – black

eisteddfod – arts festival and competition

englyn – a brief poem of distilled thoughts and metrical rules, close in spirit to a Japanese haiku

er cof am – in memory of

glas – green grey or blue (or, quite separately, can be a mutation of clas)

glyn – valley

Gwalia deserta – a Welsh desert, the name of a collection of poems by Idris Davies and applied by him to the industrial valleys of Glamorgan in the 1920s

Gwenallt – a twentieth century poet of Welsh community, landscape and religion

gwerin (y werin) – people, commonfolk

hafod – upland (summer pasture) farm

hen – old

hendref – lowland (winter) farm

hir – long

hwyl – passion; a spiritually – and emotionally – charged manner characteristic of much Welsh preaching especially in the eighteenth and nineteenth centuries, and described early last century by Rev. E. Ebrard Rees as involving "a rhythmic flow of niagaras of nouns and avalanches of adjectives".

isaf – lower

llatai – a love poem using the device of a messenger of love, which may be a bird, an animal, or an element such as the wind.

llyn – lake

Llywelyn Fawr (or Llywelyn ap Iorwerth) – a powerful prince of Gwynedd, a state which under him came to cover much of north Wales and had influence further south, in the first half of the thirteenth century. Married Joan (or Siwan in Welsh), a daughter of King John: their relationship became the subject of a twentieth century play by Saunders Lewis.

Llywelyn Olaf (or Llywelyn ap Gruffydd) – the last Llywelyn, a grandson of Llywelyn Fawr: his death in a skirmish at Cilmeri in 1282 marked the effective end of Welsh independence, and was mourned by Gruffudd ab Yr Ynad Coch in one of the most powerful poems in the language.

lon coed – a lane winding beneath a canopy of branches made by the trees along its banks

maen – stone or rock

maes – meadow

mawr (fawr) – great

merthyr – martyr

meudwy – hermit

moel – hill or mountain

nant – valley or dip in the hills, or the stream running through it.

newydd – new

niwl – mist; sometimes, on the coast or in the mountains, sodden, clinging and opaque.

Owain Glyndwr – the leader of a sustained and armed bid for Welsh independence in the early fifteenth century.

pen – top or head (of)

perllan (berllan) – orchard

pont – bridge

porth – port or gate

pwll – pool

sain or *sant* – saint

set fawr (or *sedd fawr*) – long shared seat for the elders in a chapel, usually just below the pulpit

uchaf – higher or upper

Waldo – Waldo Williams, a twentieth century Pembrokeshire poet of mystical nature and landscape

ynys – island

ACKNOWLEDGEMENTS

This book could not have been made without the vision and the backing of the Welsh Books Council and of Seren's publisher Mick Felton. We have had the enormously good fortune of being able to involve some of the best photographers in Wales – Patricia and Charles Aithie, Marian Delyth, Nick Jenkins, Robert Jones, Mick Frost, Greta Hughes and Patricia and Alan Barker. Seren's Simon Hicks, Jen Campbell and Clancy Pegg have taken excellent care of the many things involved in bringing a book to launch.

The book owes an immense debt of gratitude to all those who give their time and devotion to keeping old churches open for visiting. Among so many encountered over the years who have shown especial kindness are Alwyn Batley of Capel Caebach, Andrew Mathieson of Pentre Llifior, Elvet Richards of Trelystan, Ruth and Emrys James of Caerfarchell, Aled Lloyd Davies of Bethesda Mold, Griff Roberts of The Plough at Brecon, Edward Bond of Worthenbury and the memorable lady who greeted us on arrival at Pontargothi with the words "I don't know about you, but I can never say no to a *pikelet*", as she thrust a large and buttery plateful of them towards us. As well as their evident love for the heritage they hold, they are in some cases also *the* experts on their church's history. Others have generously shared their family memories, such as Lord Oaksey recollecting earlier days at Alltmawr. Because of all such individual people, it remains true even in the twenty-first century that the way to knowledge of this heritage is by visiting – encountering the setting *and* the oral tradition, and sometimes also a booklet into which a little of it has been poured.

Perhaps the richness of local information on these places removed the need for the curious to go looking in books, a point brought home to me at the British Library in 2001 when on asking for Gruffydd Evans's *The Story of the Ancient Churches of Llandovery* of 1913, I found that in almost a hundred years its pages had never been cut. There are treasures in the archives: I am hugely grateful to both the British Library and the National Library of Wales for their help and their astonishing resources. Among these are books such as *The Old Churches of Snowdonia* of 1924 by Harold Hughes, a model of how to evoke and document the particularities of a region, and some remarkable books on particular churches: Jones and Freeman's *History and Antiquities of St David's* of 1856 and Laws and Edwards's *The Church Book of St Mary the Virgin Tenby* of 1907 both set the bar at a height which has been difficult to match in the subsequent century, but newer books such as Tal Williams's *Salem: y llun a'r llan* of 1991 do so triumphantly. The contribution of these and numerous other such individual studies to my own work will be readily apparent to those familiar with them. Among the best background histories are those on the Welsh church by Glanmor Williams, and R. Tudur Davies's *Congregationalism in Wales*. I have drawn on the ideas as well as the information in many more specialist books, among them Oliver Davies's *Celtic Christianity in Early Medieval Wales*, Colin Gresham's *Medieval Stone Carving in*

North Wales, and Crossley and Ridgway's work on Rood Lofts and Screens.

By comparison the information in readily available books is thin on the ground. The long and remarkable project of *The Buildings of Wales*, now published rather appropriately by Yale, continues to emerge by region and has been a valuable source particularly of dates: I have relied on its authority in almost all cases. The arrival of the Pembrokeshire volume, when this book was taking final shape, introduced me to Burnett's Hill Chapel. The University of Wales's superb *Medieval Vision* by Peter Lord arrived just in time to save me from numerous errors, and much more than that it became the source of our connection with the Aithies, who had evidently been travelling a similar path across the country in the preceding years. Anthony Jones's book on Welsh chapels is a marvellous and definitive history of their changing designs, and its first edition broke new ground in giving a list of chapel buildings too important to lose (despite which, some have already been lost). Before all these came Jan Morris's *Wales: The First Place*, as perfect a brief evocation of the country as has been written, and its spirit was carried into the much fuller *Wales*, which covers much broader cultural territory. Although not, fortunately for me, about Wales, Simon Jenkins's book on English parish churches acted both as an inspiration to the final format – and the title – of this book, and as an enabler, in making it seem possible through its own huge success that there could be a readership large enough for us too to venture hopefully forth.

My thanks also go to Dewi Hughes, Christopher Potter and my family for their valuable suggestions and encouragement on the manuscript. I owe the greatest debt to my wife Vanessa who has travelled with me every step of the way, and to my parents and wider family who introduced me to the world of Welsh chapel life from the beginning. The fabric of every Welsh family's heritage is made up of many strands from the churches and the chapels, and not only the obvious, as my own may serve to illustrate. My great-grandfather, a young stonemason, lost his sight in the dust of building Bersham steeple. My father's father drove the country roads of Denbighshire, Flintshire and Montgomeryshire in a borrowed coal lorry, putting heating systems into churches which had never before known winter warmth, and *his* father helped to open a new chapel for those coming across the border to seek work in the mines of Rhosllanerchrugog. My mother's father, a collier and lay preacher, was one of those who, in Gwenallt's words, came up the mineshaft to heaven on Sundays. We have also carried the memory of an ancestor, Bardd Nantglyn, who wrote a poem in which he called on the king – George III – to send '*Beibl i bawb o bobl y byd*' – a Bible for everyone in the world. He is buried in a church-yard with a yew tree for a pulpit, a last image to offer of the telescoping and displacement of time in the Welsh landscape. Out of so many impressions, memories and stories, imbued from childhood, this book has slowly emerged. With these presences in my mind, I have tried to reflect that this is a story of people as well as buildings and locations, and that to walk in these places is to touch – and in some way to acknowledge – the memory of all our ancestors' lives.

Photography Acknowledgements

We are pleased to acknowledge the work of the following photographers and agencies:

Patricia and Alan Barker: 35, 200, 201, 202, 205, 208, 209, 210, 215; Wayne Boucher, Cambridge 2000: 127; CADW: 24, 56, 57, 82, 106, 107, 115, 116, 121, 175, 182, 183, 185, 186, 196, 262, 270, 272, 280; Marian Delyth: 101, 119, 124, 127, 143, 147, 157, 166, 167, 188, 198, 304; Ray Edgar Photography: 261; Ffotograff: 16, 18, 21, 28, 31, 45, 46, 53, 60, 68, 69, 80, 87, 88, 90, 93, 94, 97, 99, 109, 110, 111, 117, 125, 126, 132, 133, 134, 161, 168, 169, 171, 180, 207, 219, 221, 222, 225, 226, 227, 229, 230, 231, 233, 234, 235, 237, 238, 239, 242, 243, 245, 246, 248, 251, 253, 254, 256, 257, 258, 264, 266, 267, 268, 275, 279, 288; Friends of Cascob Church: 137; Friends of Friendless Churches: 48; Maddy Gray, the Cistercian Way Project: 277; Greta Hughes: 6, 37, 50, 62, 66, 67, 71, 75, 76, 83, 145; T.J. Hughes: 13, 26, 52, 72, 73, 77, 148, 159, 176, 178, 190, 192; Nick Jenkins: 64, 141; Robert Jones: 284; National Museum and Galleries of Wales: 250; Mick Sharp: 103; all other images: Seren.

Readers may be interested in the various websites associated with the photographers:
http://www.cambridge2000.com
www.cadw.wales.gov.uk
www.rayedgar.com
www.ffotograff.com
www.friendsofcascob.co.uk
www.friendsoffriendlesschurches.org.uk
http://cistercian-way.newport.ac.uk
www.cimwch.com (Greta Hughes)
www.freespiritimages.com (Nick Jenkins)
www.gwlad.co.uk (Robert Jones)
www.windowsonlosttimes.co.uk (Mick Sharp)

List of Churches Included

INDEX